BUILDING THINKING SKILLS®
Book 2

SERIES TITLES
BUILDING THINKING SKILLS®—PRIMARY
BUILDING THINKING SKILLS®—BOOK 1
BUILDING THINKING SKILLS®—BOOK 2
BUILDING THINKING SKILLS®—BOOK 3 FIGURAL
BUILDING THINKING SKILLS®—BOOK 3 VERBAL

SANDRA PARKS AND HOWARD BLACK

© 1984, 1998
CRITICAL THINKING BOOKS & SOFTWARE
www.criticalthinking.com
P.O. Box 448 • Pacific Grove • CA 93950-0448
Phone 800-458-4849 • FAX 831-393-3277
ISBN 0-89455-252-X
Printed in the United States of America

Table of Contents

CHAPTER NINE—VERBAL CLASSIFICATIONS

CHAPTER TEN—VERBAL ANALOGIES

CHAPTER ONE

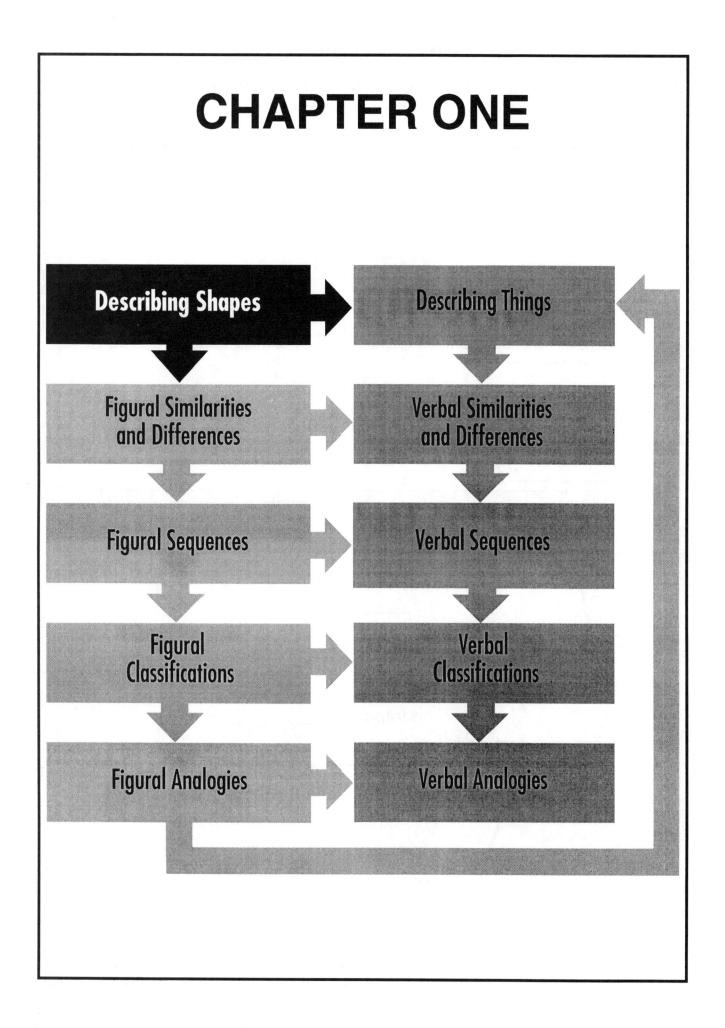

DESCRIBING SHAPES—SELECT

DIRECTIONS: Look at each shape. Read the words in the choice box. Complete each sentence with the correct words from the choice box.

CHOICE BOX: narrow, short, tall, wide

EXAMPLE: This shape is _____*short*_____ and _____*wide*_____.

A-1

This parallelogram is _____ and _____.

A-2

This parallelogram is _____ and _____.

A-3

This trapezoid is _____ and _____.

A-4

This trapezoid is _____ and _____.

DESCRIBING SHAPES—SELECT

DIRECTIONS: Look at each shape. Read the words in the choice box. Complete each sentence with the correct words from the choice box.

CHOICE BOX: no, one, two, three, four, five, six

EXAMPLE

This parallelogram has ___*four*___ sides and ___*four*___ angles.

A-5

This quadrilateral has _____ sides and _____ angles.

A-6

This triangle has _____ sides and _____ angles.

A-7

This pentagon has _____ sides and _____ angles.

A-8

This hexagon has _____ sides and _____ angles.

DESCRIBING SHAPES—SELECT

DIRECTIONS: Look at each shape. Read the words in the choice box. Complete each sentence with the correct words from the choice box.

CHOICE BOX: all, none, one, two, three, four, five, six

EXAMPLE

This triangle has ___*three*___ sides and ___*three*___ angles.
___*One*___ of the angles is square.

A-9

This rectangle has _____ sides and _____ angles.
_____ of the angles are square.

A-10

This square has _____ sides and _____ angles.
_____ of the angles are square.

A-11

This irregular pentagon has _____ sides and _____ angles.
_____ of the angles are square.

A-12

This hexagon has _____ sides and _____ angles.
_____ of the angles are square.

DESCRIBING SHAPES—SELECT

DIRECTIONS: Look at each shape. Read the words in the choice box. Complete each sentence with the correct words from the choice box.

CHOICE BOX: all, none, two, three, four, five, six, hexagon, pentagon, rectangle, square, trapezoid, triangle

A-13

This _____ has _____
        shape name

sides and _____ are the same length.

A-14

This _____ has _____
        shape name

sides and _____ are the same length.

A-15

This _____ has _____
        shape name

sides and _____ are the same length.

A-16

This _____ has _____
        shape name

sides and _____ are the same length.

A-17

This _____ has _____
        shape name

sides and _____ are the same length.

DESCRIBING SHAPES—SELECT

DIRECTIONS: Look at each shape. Read the words in the choice box. Complete each sentence with the correct words from the choice box.

CHOICE BOX: all, none, two, three, four, five, six, hexagon, parallelogram, pentagon, quadrilateral rectangle, square, trapezoid, triangle

A-18

This _____ has _____
              shape name

sides and _____ are the same length.

A-19

This _____ has _____
              shape name

sides and _____ are the same length.

A-20

This _____ has _____
              shape name

sides and _____ are the same length.

A-21

This _____ has _____
              shape name

sides and _____ are the same length.

A-22

This _____ has _____
              shape name

sides and _____ are the same length.

DESCRIBING SHAPES—EXPLAIN

DIRECTIONS: In each description box, describe the shape in the picture at the left. Use complete sentences in your descriptions.

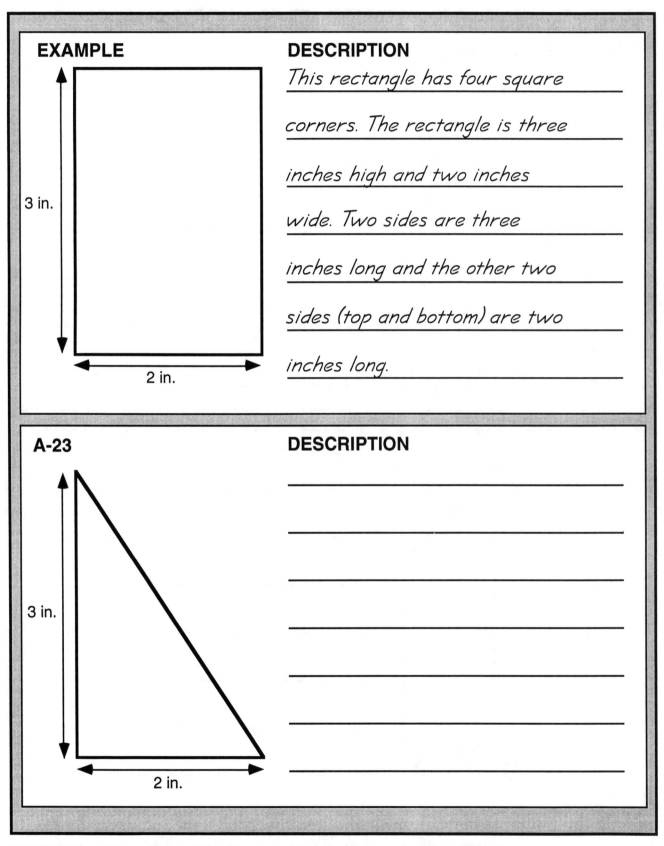

EXAMPLE

DESCRIPTION

3 in.

2 in.

This rectangle has four square corners. The rectangle is three inches high and two inches wide. Two sides are three inches long and the other two sides (top and bottom) are two inches long.

A-23

DESCRIPTION

3 in.

2 in.

DESCRIBING SHAPES—EXPLAIN

DIRECTIONS: In each description box, describe the shape in the picture on the left. Use complete sentences in your descriptions.

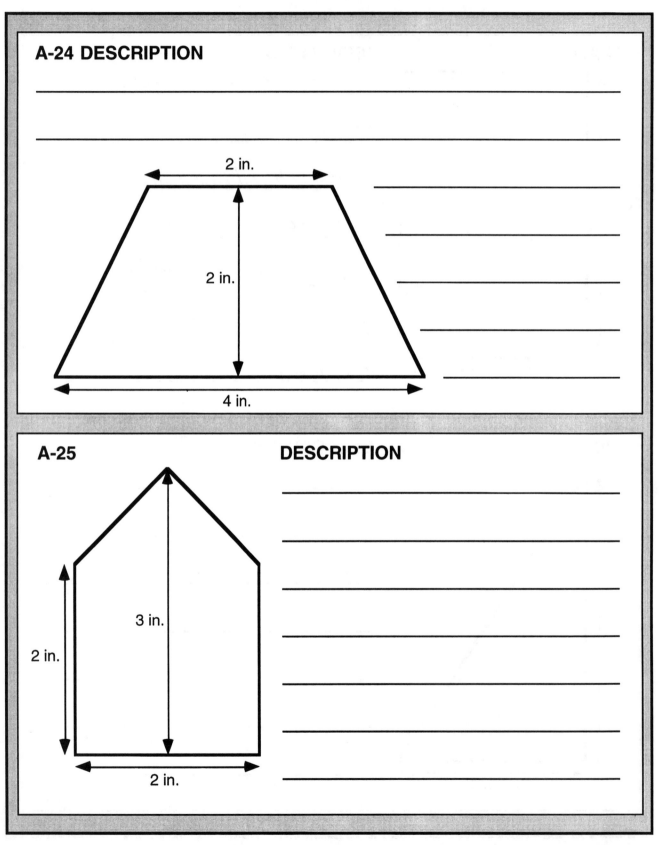

A-24 DESCRIPTION

2 in.

2 in.

4 in.

A-25   **DESCRIPTION**

3 in.

2 in.

2 in.

DESCRIBING POSITION—SELECT

DIRECTIONS: Write the words from the choice box that correctly complete the sentences. Draw a figure as directed.

CHOICE BOX

above, below, center, circle, left, right, square, triangle

A-26

The square is _____ the circle. The circle is _____ the square.

Draw a triangle below the circle.

A-27

The triangle is _____ the square. The circle is on the _____ side of the square.

Draw a black triangle to the right of the square.

DESCRIBING POSITION—SELECT

DIRECTIONS: Write the words from the choice box that correctly complete the sentences. Draw a figure as directed.

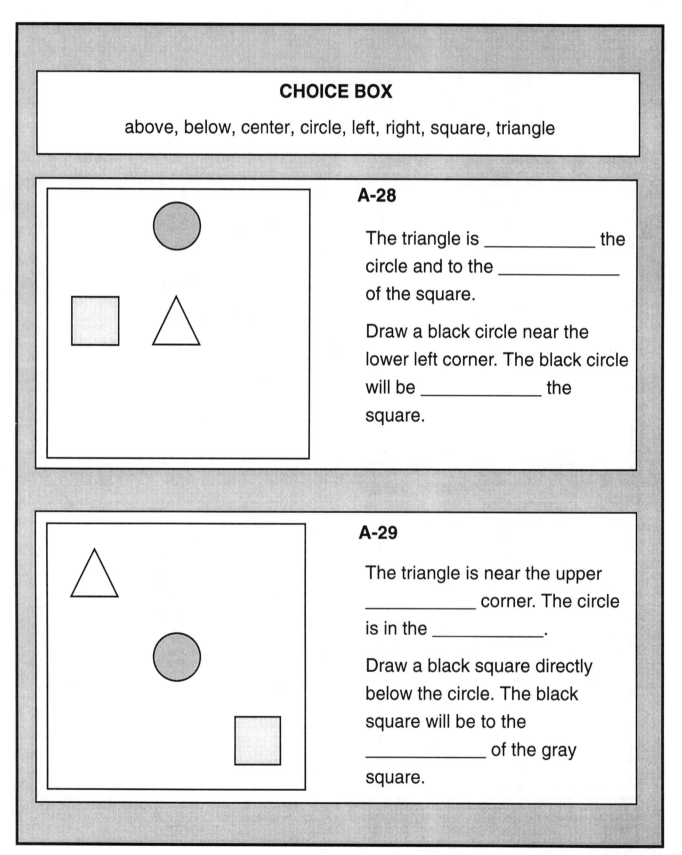

CHOICE BOX

above, below, center, circle, left, right, square, triangle

A-28

The triangle is _____ the circle and to the _____ of the square.

Draw a black circle near the lower left corner. The black circle will be _____ the square.

A-29

The triangle is near the upper _____ corner. The circle is in the _____.

Draw a black square directly below the circle. The black square will be to the _____ of the gray square.

DESCRIBING POSITION—SELECT

DIRECTIONS: Write the words from the choice box that correctly complete the sentences in the directions. Draw a figure as directed.

CHOICE BOX

above, below, larger, left, right, smaller

A-30

The _____ square is in the center. The _____ square is near the upper left corner. The large circle is near the lower _____ corner.

Draw a small circle near the upper right corner.

A-31

The circle in the center is _____ than the circle directly above it. The large square is to the _____ of the small circle.

Draw a small square directly to the right of the large circle. The small square will be _____ the large square.

DESCRIBING POSITION—EXPLAIN

DIRECTIONS: Describe the color, shape, and position of the figures in each drawing.

EXAMPLE

DESCRIPTION

The gray square is above the

white circle.

OR

The white circle is below the

gray square.

A-32

DESCRIPTION

DESCRIBING POSITION—EXPLAIN

DIRECTIONS: Describe the color, shape, and position of the figures in each drawing.

A-33

DESCRIPTION

_____

_____

_____

_____

_____

A-34

DESCRIPTION

_____

_____

_____

_____

_____

_____

DESCRIBING POSITION—EXPLAIN

DIRECTIONS: Describe the color, shape, and position of the shapes in each drawing.

A-35   **DESCRIPTION**

_____

_____

_____

_____

_____

A-36   **DESCRIPTION**

_____

_____

_____

_____

_____

_____

CHARACTERISTICS OF A SHAPE

DIRECTIONS: Look at the pentagon in the center of the diagram. Write a characteristic of the pentagon in each of the four boxes. Use these characteristics to write a description of the pentagon in the description box.

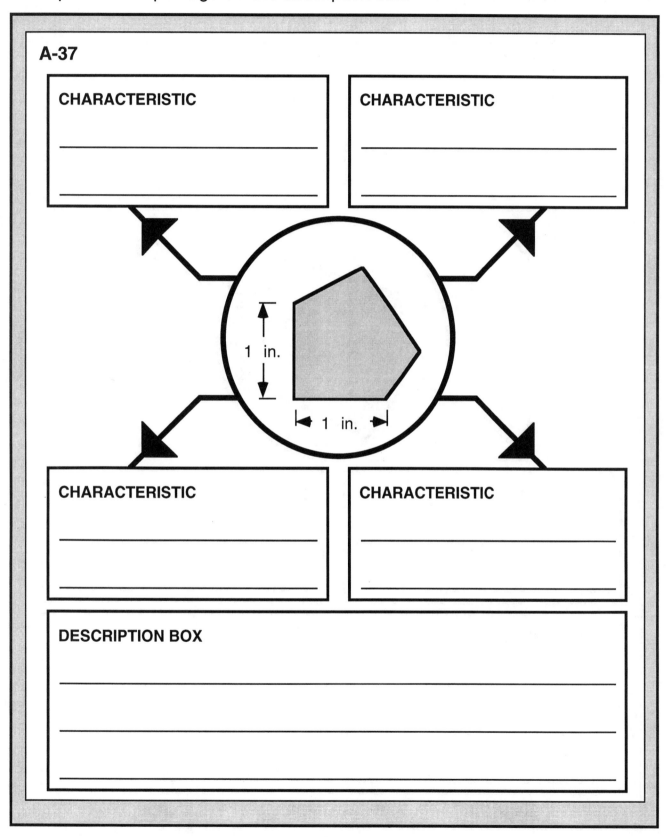

A-37

CHARACTERISTIC
_____
_____

CHARACTERISTIC
_____
_____

1 in.

1 in.

CHARACTERISTIC
_____
_____

CHARACTERISTIC
_____
_____

DESCRIPTION BOX
_____
_____
_____

CHARACTERISTICS OF A SHAPE

DIRECTIONS: Look at the hexagon in the center of the diagram. Write a characteristic of the hexagon in each of the four boxes. Use these characteristics to write a description of the hexagon in the description box.

CHAPTER TWO

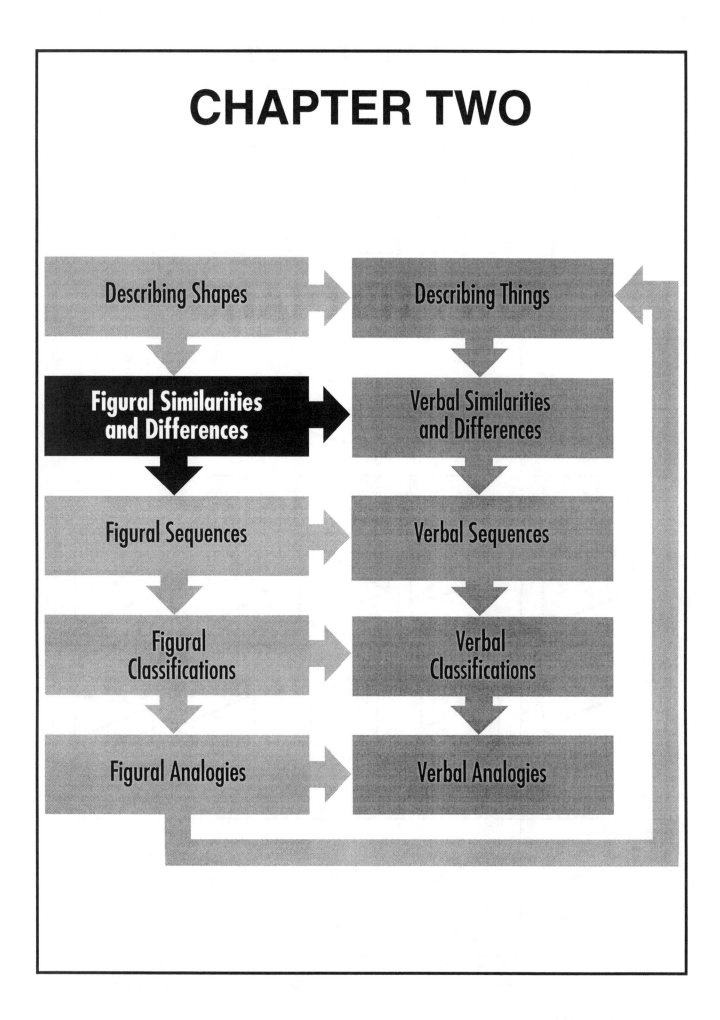

Describing Shapes → Describing Things

Figural Similarities and Differences → Verbal Similarities and Differences

Figural Sequences → Verbal Sequences

Figural Classifications → Verbal Classifications

Figural Analogies → Verbal Analogies

MATCHING FIGURES

DIRECTIONS: In each row, circle the figure that matches the one in the box on the left.

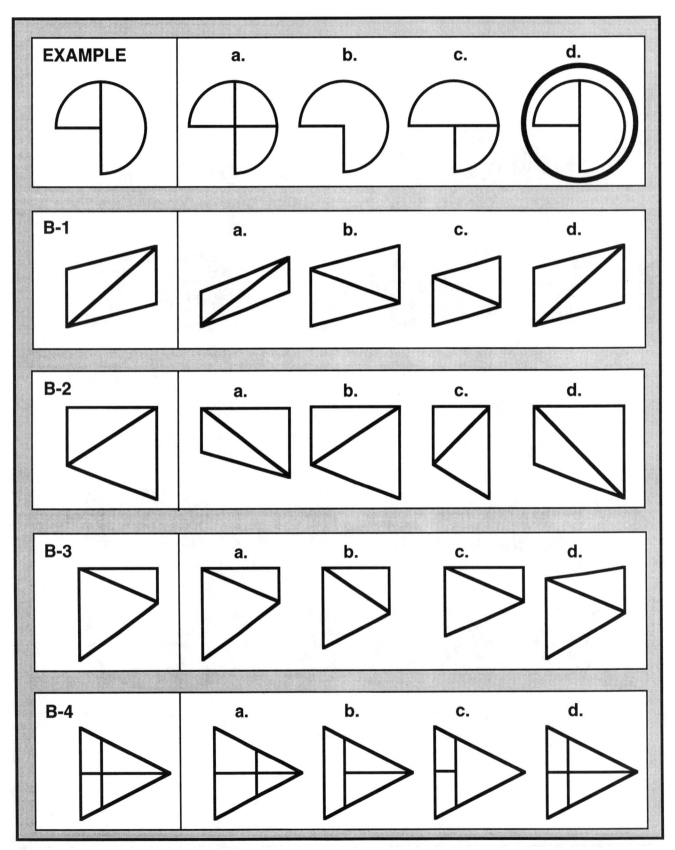

MATCHING FIGURES

DIRECTIONS: In each row, circle the figure that matches the one in the box on the left.

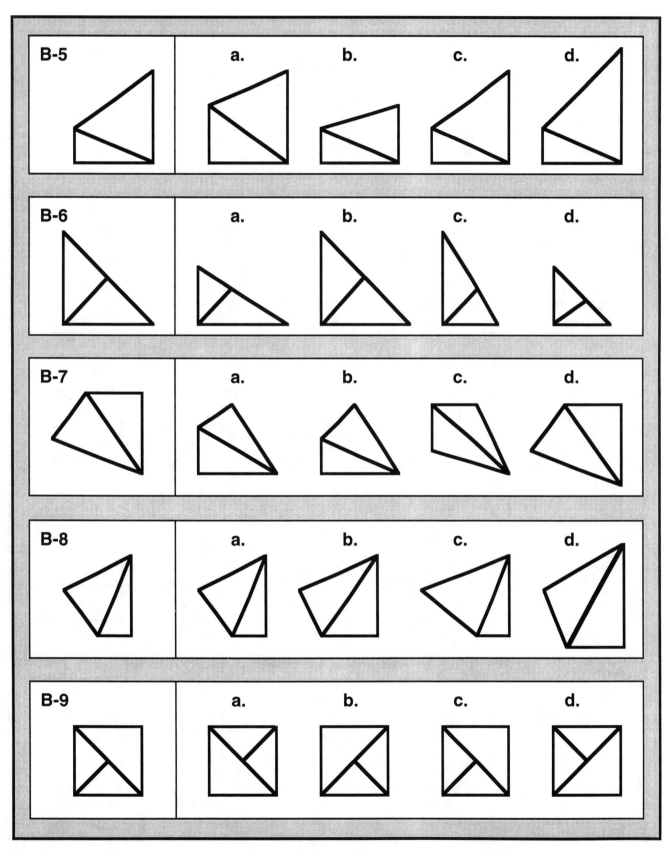

MATCHING FIGURES

DIRECTIONS: In each row, circle the figure that matches the one in the box on the left.

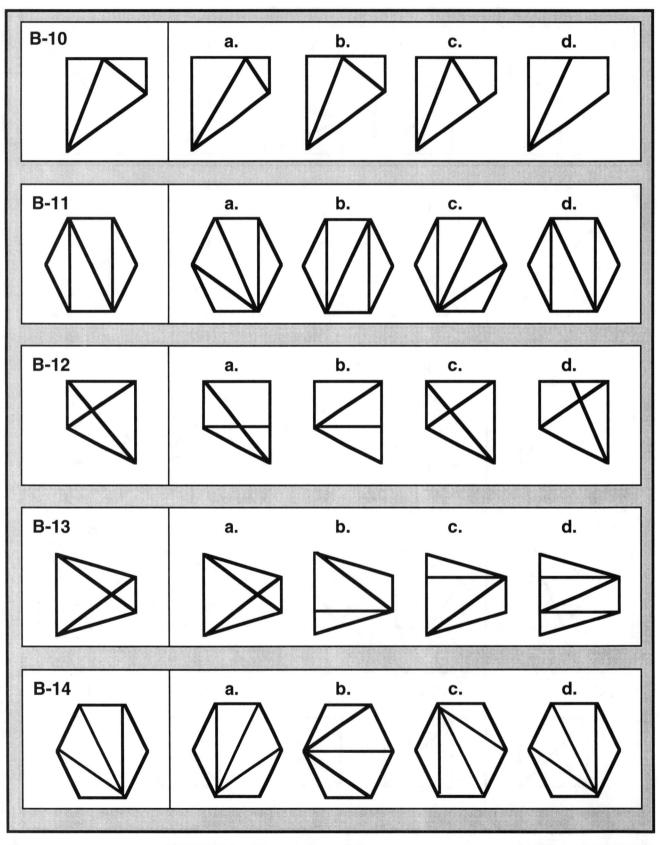

MATCHING SHAPES

DIRECTIONS: Circle the shapes that match the one on the left. The matching shapes must face the same direction as the shape on the left.

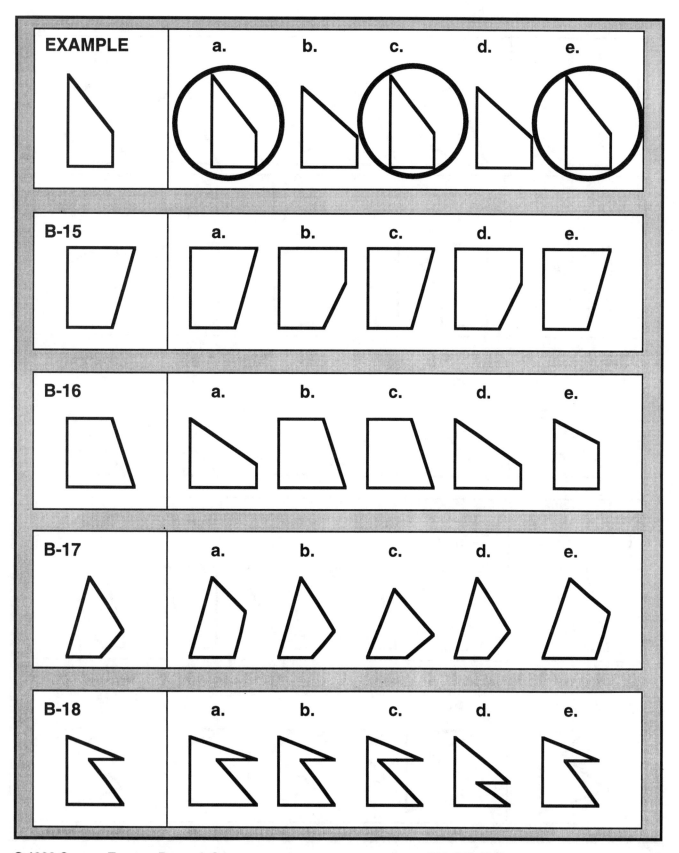

MATCHING SHAPES

DIRECTIONS: Circle the shapes that match the one on the left. The matching shapes must face the same direction as the shape in the box.

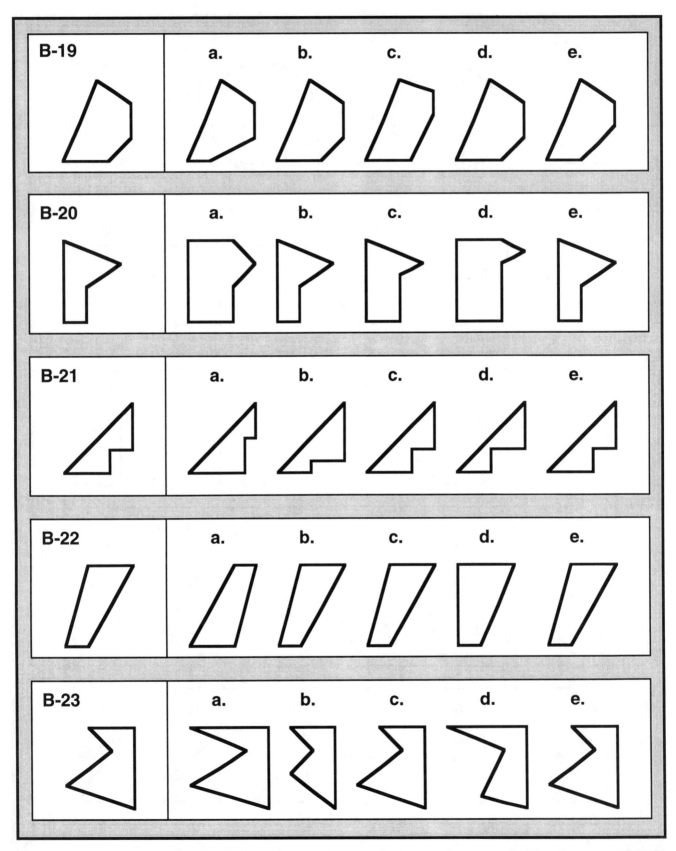

MATCHING FIGURES

DIRECTIONS: Circle the figures that are the same in each row.

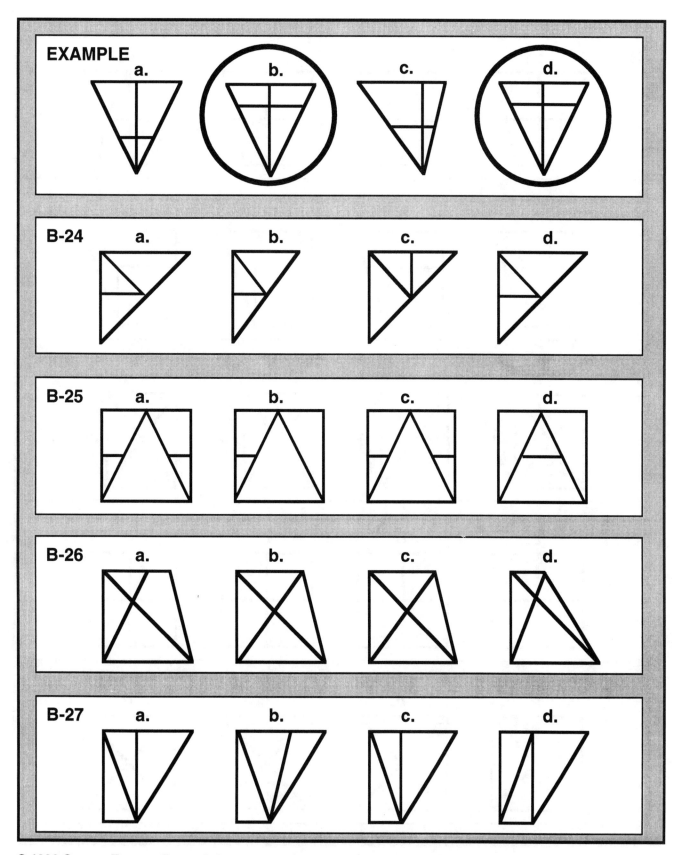

MATCHING FIGURES

DIRECTIONS: Circle the figures that are the same in each row.

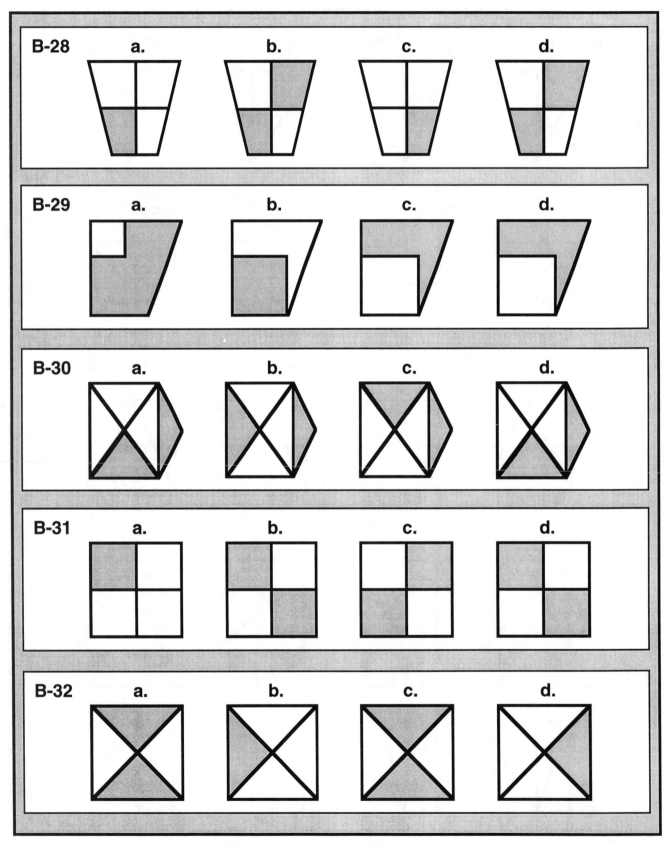

WHICH SHAPES DO NOT MATCH?

DIRECTONS: Cross out the shapes that DO NOT match the shape on the left. The matching shapes must all face in the same direction.

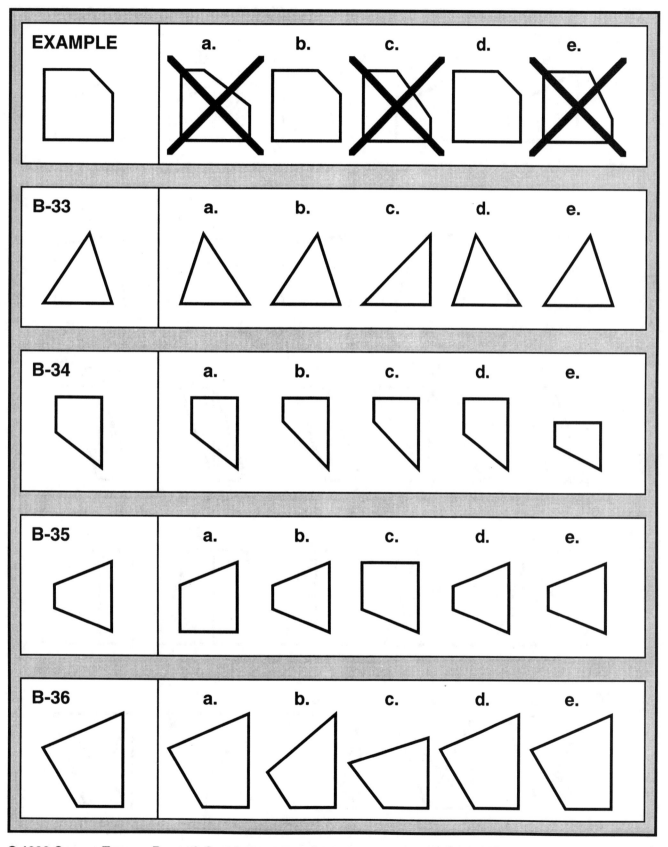

WHICH SHAPE DOES NOT MATCH?

DIRECTIONS: In each row, cross out the shape or figure that does not match the other four figures.

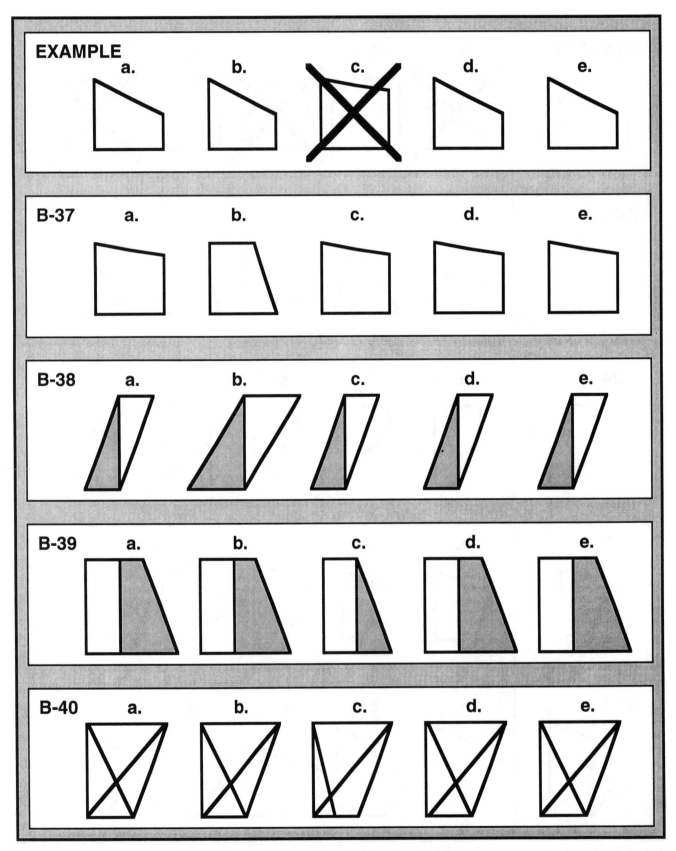

WHICH FIGURE DOES NOT MATCH?

DIRECTIONS: In each row, cross out the figure that does not match the other four figures.

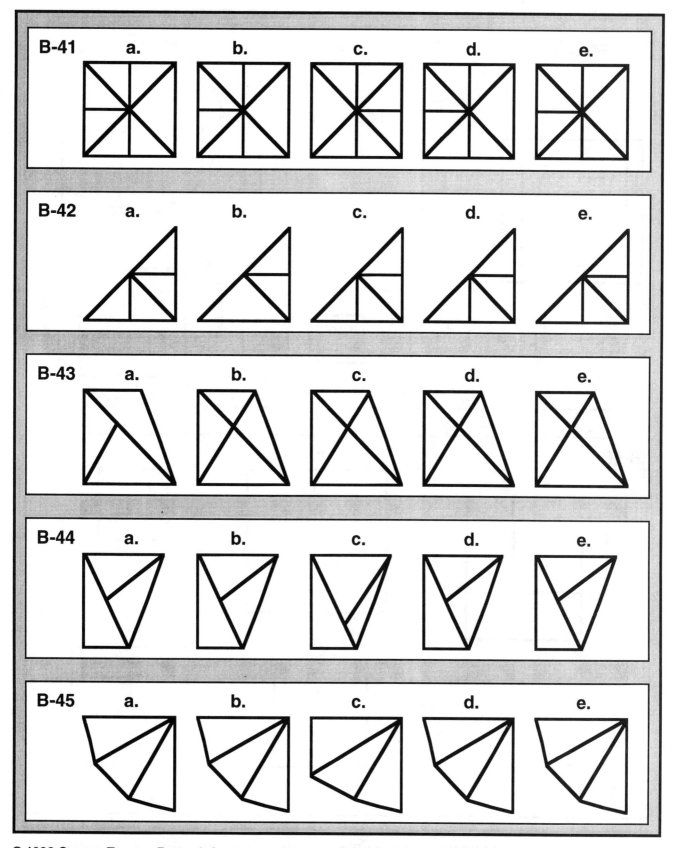

FINDING SHAPES

DIRECTIONS: Circle any shape that exactly matches one of the shapes in the figure on the left.

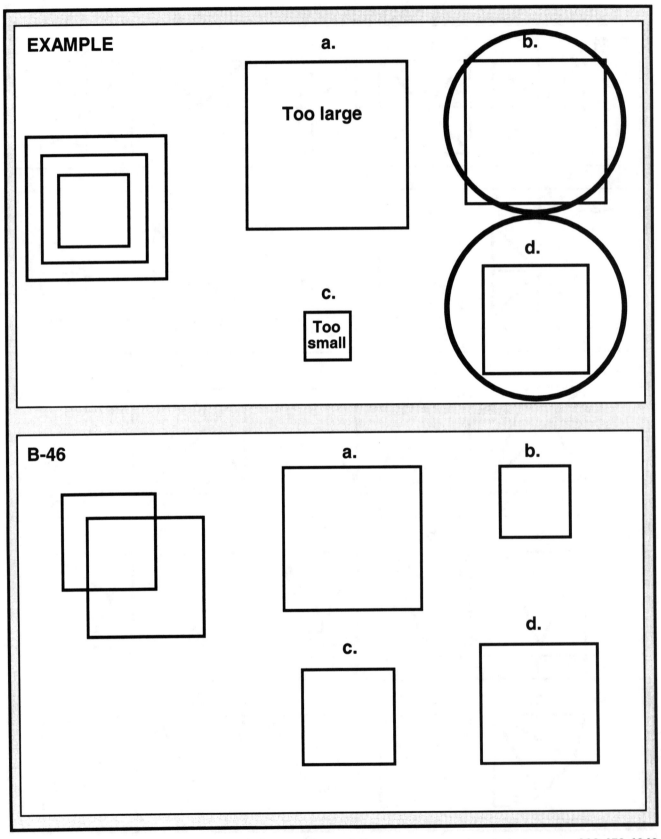

FINDING SHAPES

DIRECTIONS: Circle any shape that exactly matches one of the overlapping shapes in the figure on the left.

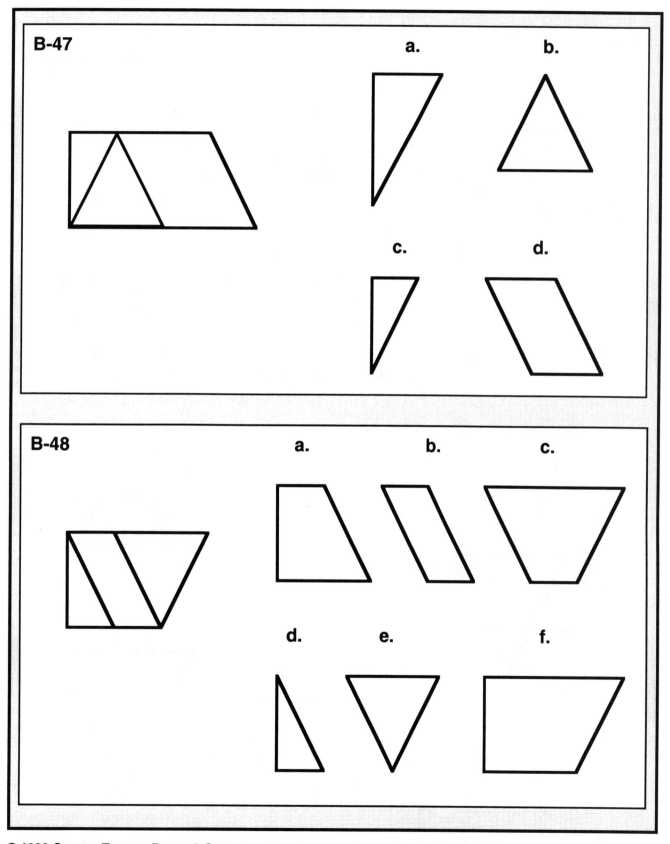

FINDING SHAPES

DIRECTIONS: Circle any shape that exactly matches one of the overlapping shapes in the figure on the left.

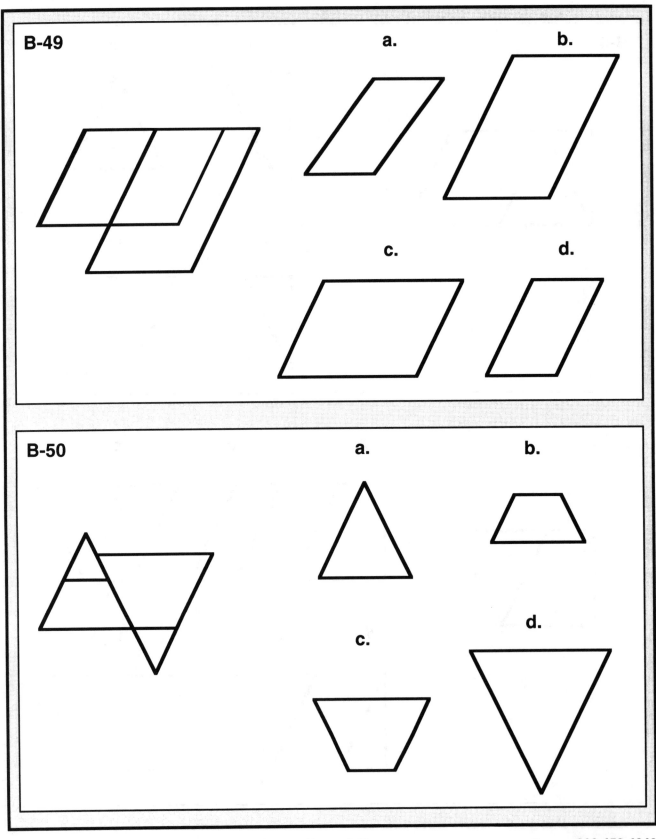

FINDING AND TRACING PATTERNS

DIRECTIONS: Circle any figure that contains the figure on the left. The figure must be in the same position but may have extra lines. Trace over the matching figure to make sure you are right.

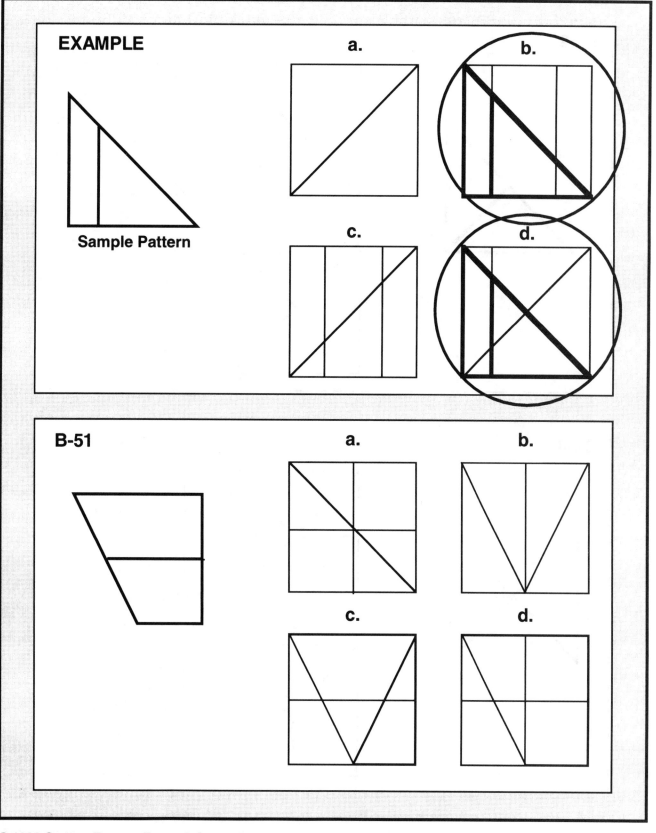

FINDING AND TRACING PATTERNS

DIRECTIONS: Circle any figure that contains the shape on the left. The shape must be in the same position but may have extra lines. Trace over the matching figure to make sure you are right.

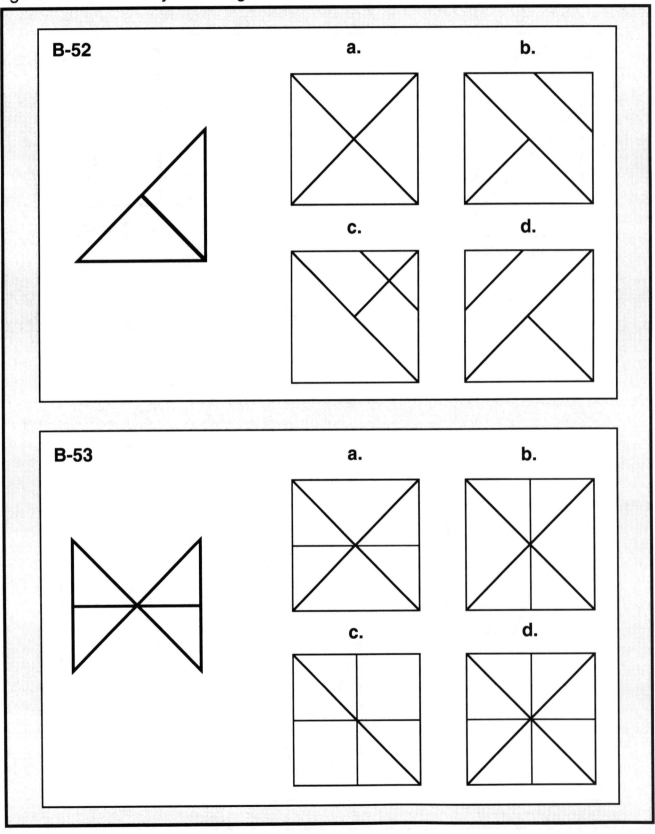

FINDING AND TRACING PATTERNS

DIRECTIONS: Circle any figure that contains the figure on the left. The figure must be in the same position but may have extra lines. Trace over the matching figure to make sure you are right.

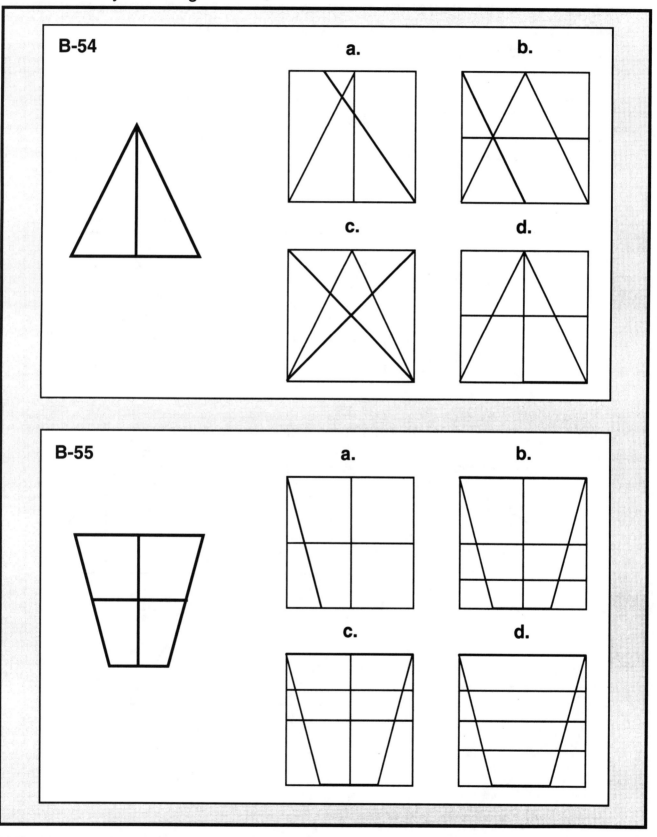

COMBINING SHAPES

DIRECTIONS: Check the figures that can be formed by joining the three shapes in the box. Shapes may be turned or flipped.

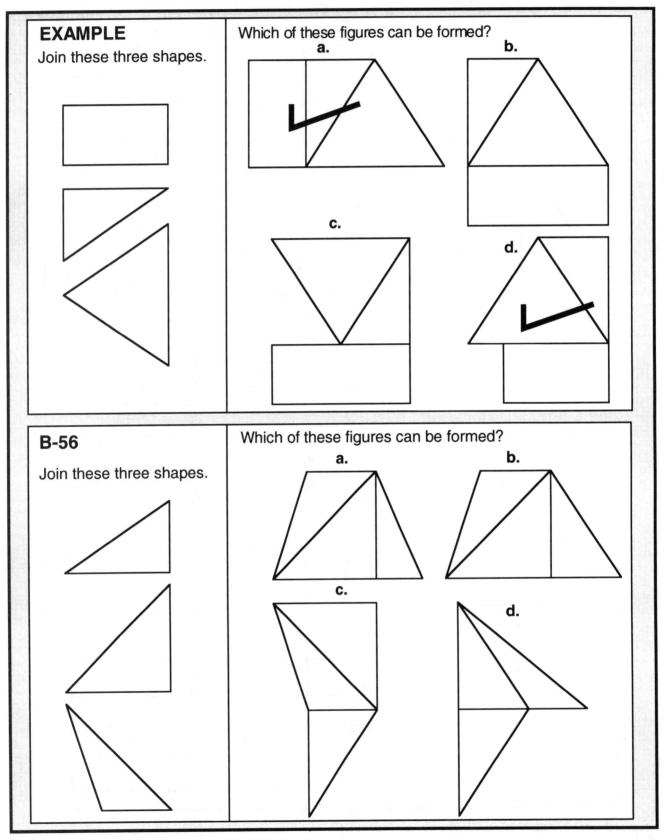

COMBINING SHAPES

DIRECTIONS: Check the figures that can be formed by joining the three shapes in the box. Shapes may be turned or flipped.

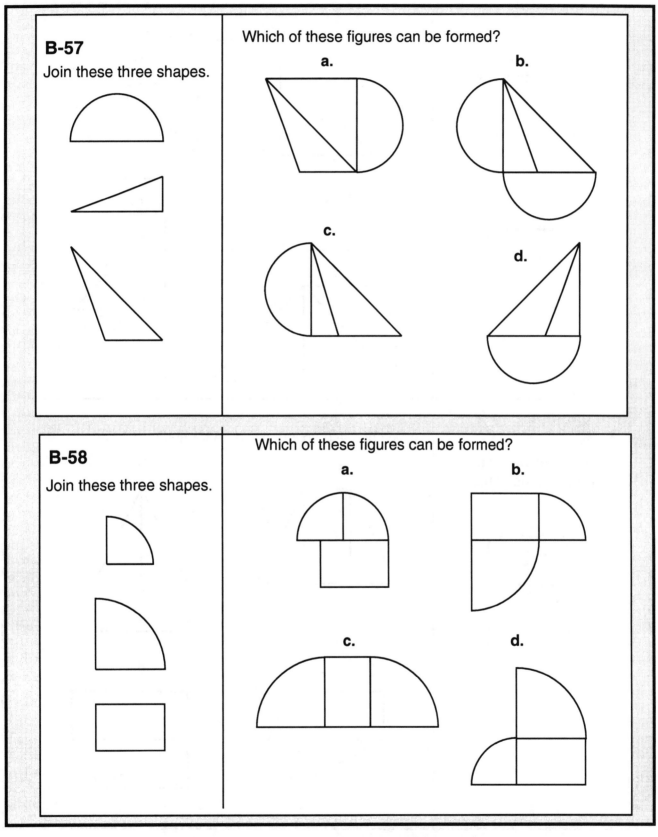

B-57

Join these three shapes.

Which of these figures can be formed?

a.

b.

c.

d.

B-58

Join these three shapes.

Which of these figures can be formed?

a.

b.

c.

d.

COMBINING SHAPES

DIRECTIONS: If a square were cut into three parts, check the figures that could be formed by joining those parts.

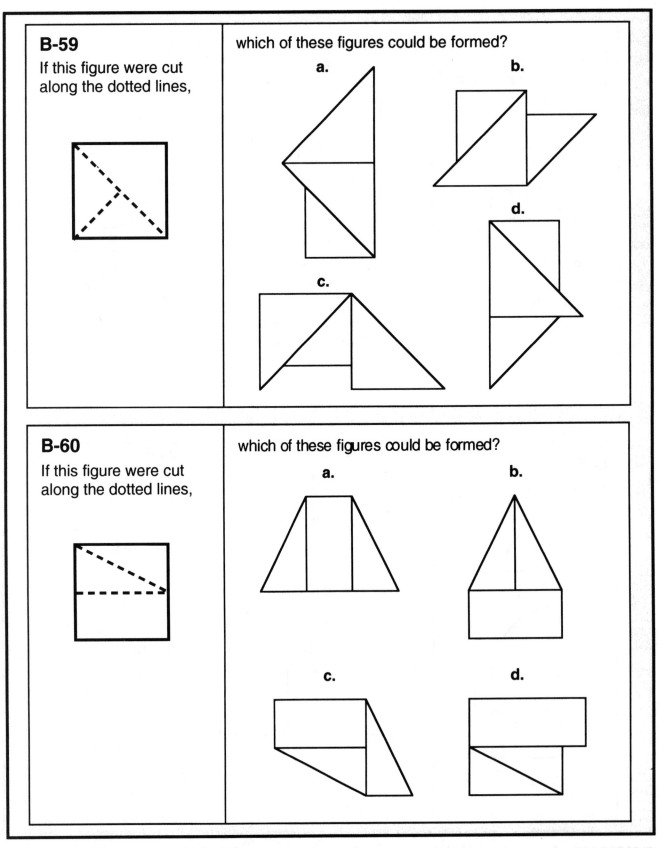

B-59

If this figure were cut along the dotted lines,

which of these figures could be formed?

a.

b.

c.

d.

B-60

If this figure were cut along the dotted lines,

which of these figures could be formed?

a.

b.

c.

d.

DIVIDING SHAPES INTO EQUAL PARTS—A

DIRECTIONS: Look at the two parts of the square. Answer the question, "Are the parts exactly alike?" Write *yes* or *no* in the blank below each question.

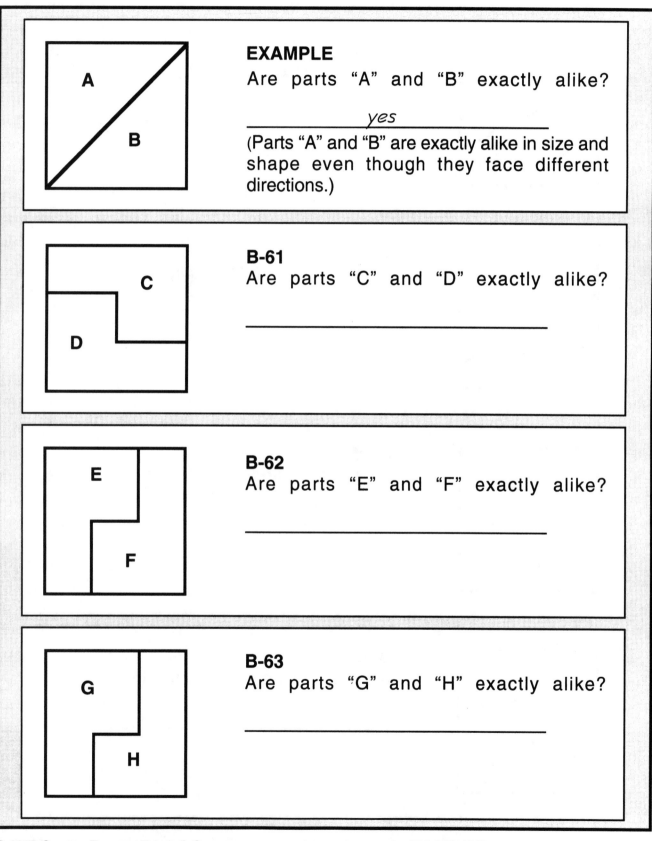

EXAMPLE
Are parts "A" and "B" exactly alike?

_____*yes*_____

(Parts "A" and "B" are exactly alike in size and shape even though they face different directions.)

B-61
Are parts "C" and "D" exactly alike?

_____

B-62
Are parts "E" and "F" exactly alike?

_____

B-63
Are parts "G" and "H" exactly alike?

_____

DIVIDING SHAPES INTO EQUAL PARTS—A

DIRECTIONS: Look at the two parts of the square. Answer the question, "Are the parts exactly alike?" Write *yes* or *no* in the blank below each question.

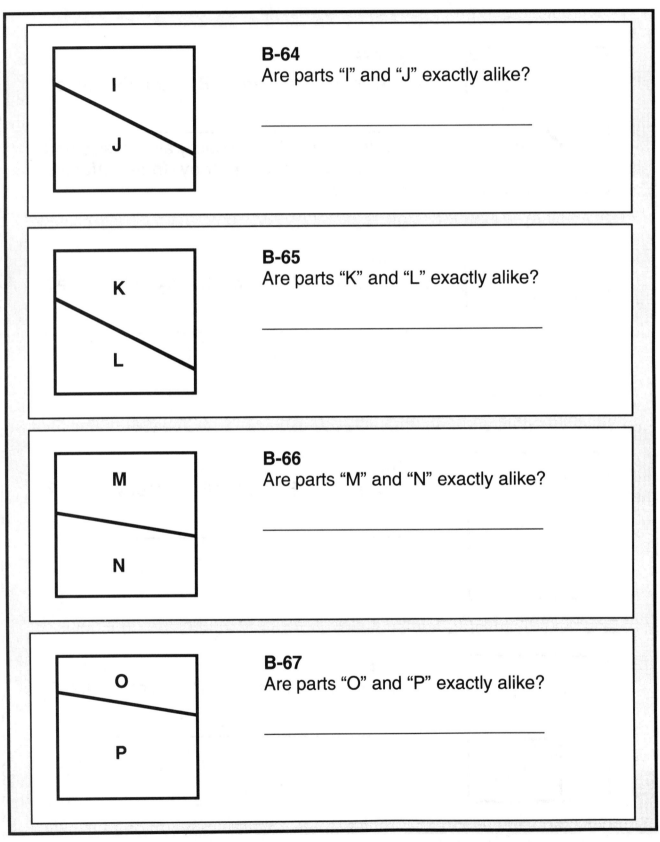

B-64
Are parts "I" and "J" exactly alike?

_____

B-65
Are parts "K" and "L" exactly alike?

_____

B-66
Are parts "M" and "N" exactly alike?

_____

B-67
Are parts "O" and "P" exactly alike?

_____

DIVIDING SHAPES INTO EQUAL PARTS—A

DIRECTIONS: Look at the two parts of the square. Answer the question, "Are the parts exactly alike?" Write *yes* or *no* in the blank below each question.

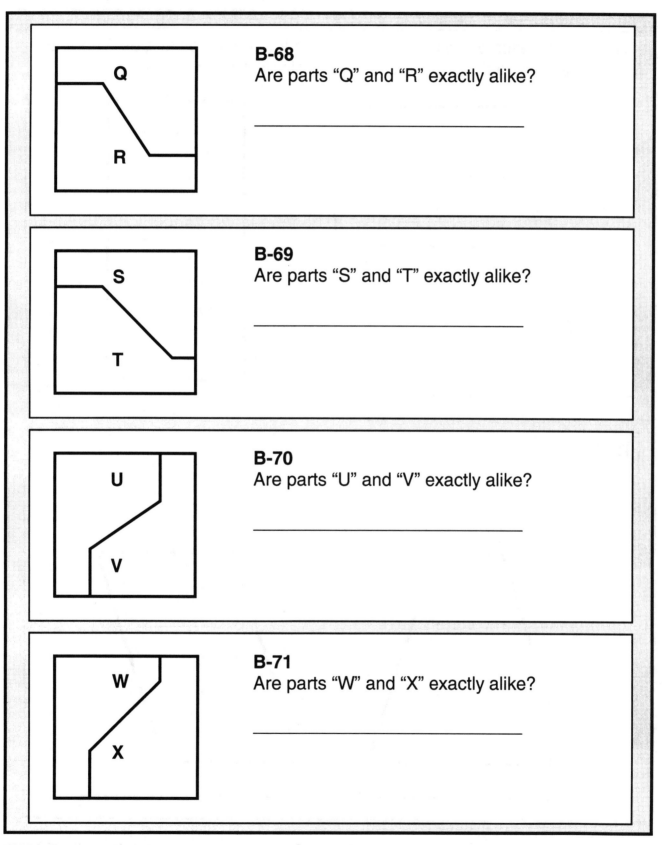

B-68
Are parts "Q" and "R" exactly alike?

_____

B-69
Are parts "S" and "T" exactly alike?

_____

B-70
Are parts "U" and "V" exactly alike?

_____

B-71
Are parts "W" and "X" exactly alike?

_____

DIVIDING SHAPES INTO EQUAL PARTS—B

DIRECTIONS: Divide each shape into equal parts as directed below.

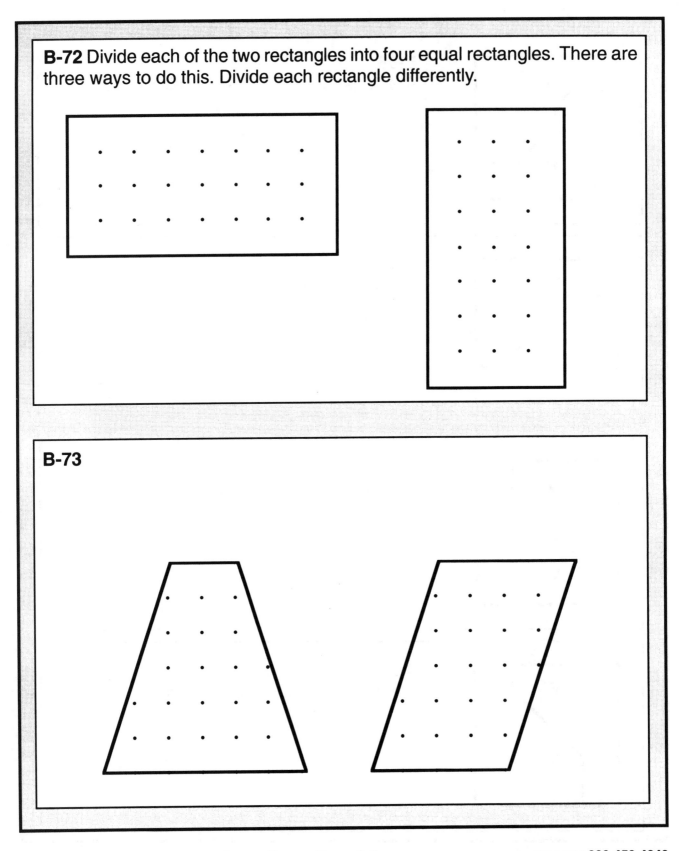

B-72 Divide each of the two rectangles into four equal rectangles. There are three ways to do this. Divide each rectangle differently.

B-73

DIVIDING SHAPES INTO EQUAL PARTS—B

DIRECTIONS: Divide each of the rectangles into two equal parts. Do not draw squares or rectangles. Divide each rectangle differently.

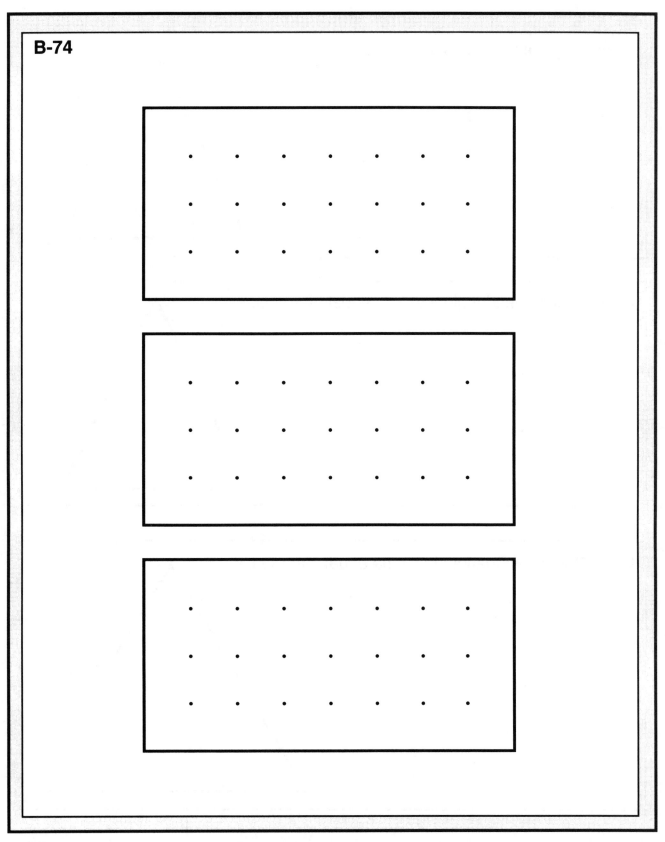

B-74

DIVIDING SHAPES INTO EQUAL PARTS—B

DIRECTIONS: Divide each of the triangles into equal parts as directed below.

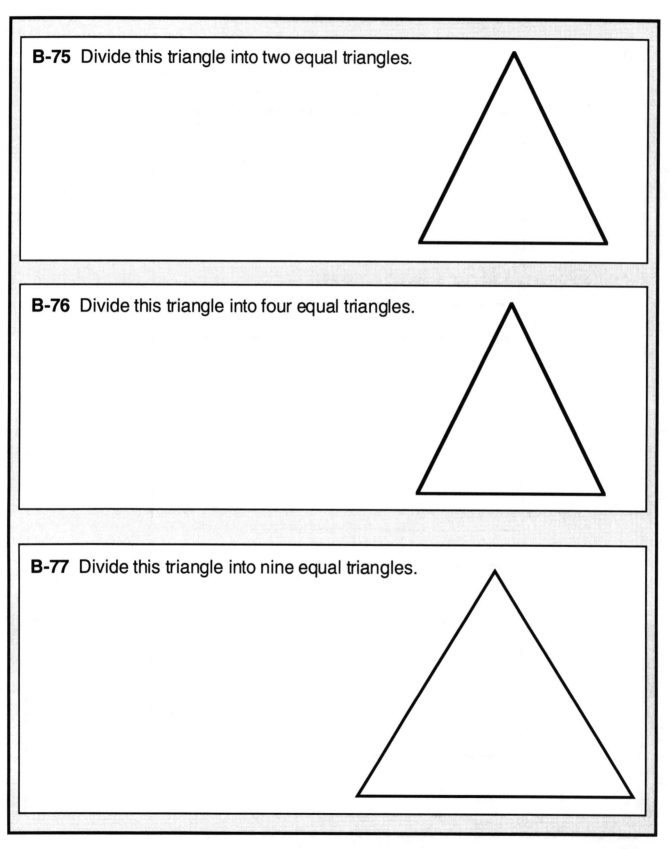

B-75 Divide this triangle into two equal triangles.

B-76 Divide this triangle into four equal triangles.

B-77 Divide this triangle into nine equal triangles.

PAPER FOLDING—SELECT

DIRECTIONS: The left side of each exercise shows an unfolded sheet of paper with holes punched in it. One of the drawings in the choice box shows how the paper will look when folded. Circle the correct answer.

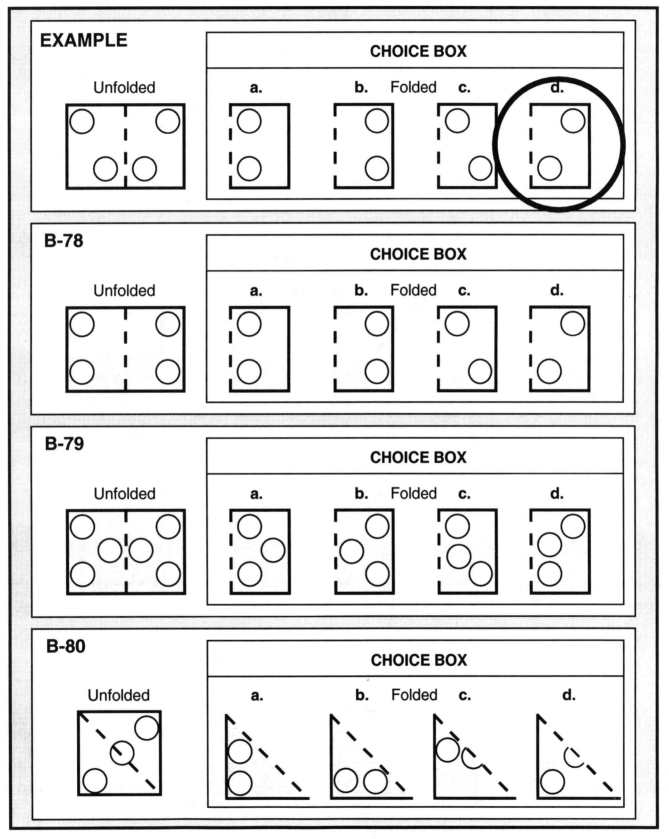

PAPER FOLDING—SELECT

DIRECTIONS: The left side of each exercise shows a folded sheet of paper with holes punched in it. One of the drawings in the choice box shows how the paper will look when unfolded. Circle the correct answer.

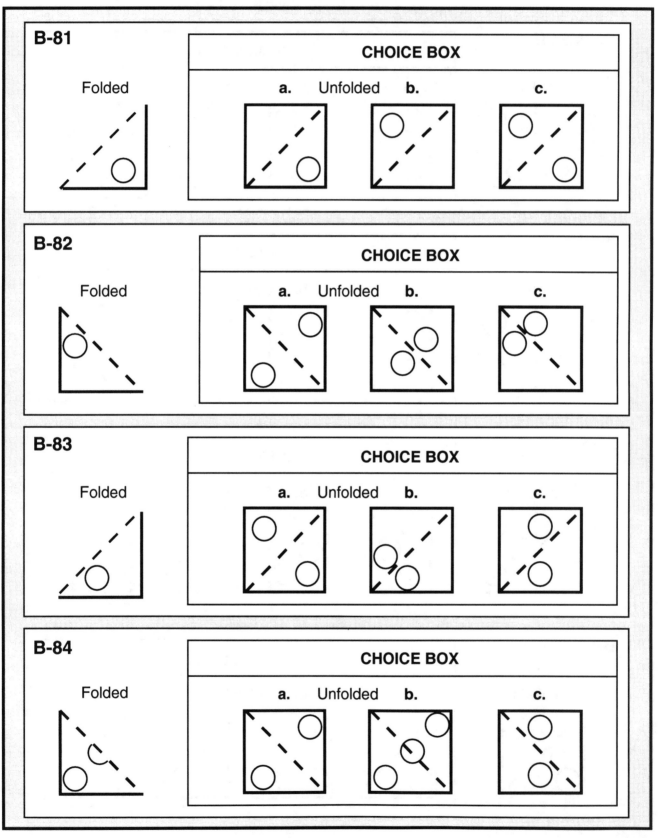

PAPER FOLDING—SUPPLY

DIRECTIONS: Here are four sheets of paper with holes punched in them. They are to be folded along the dotted line. Draw how each sheet will look after it is folded.

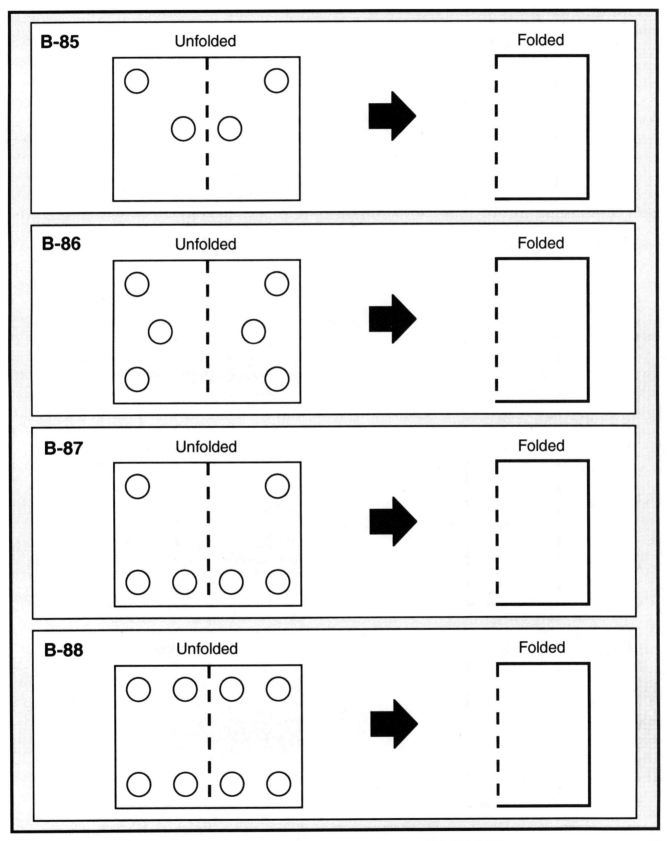

PAPER FOLDING—SUPPLY

DIRECTIONS: Here are four sheets of paper with holes punched in them. They are folded along the dotted line. Draw how each sheet will look when unfolded.

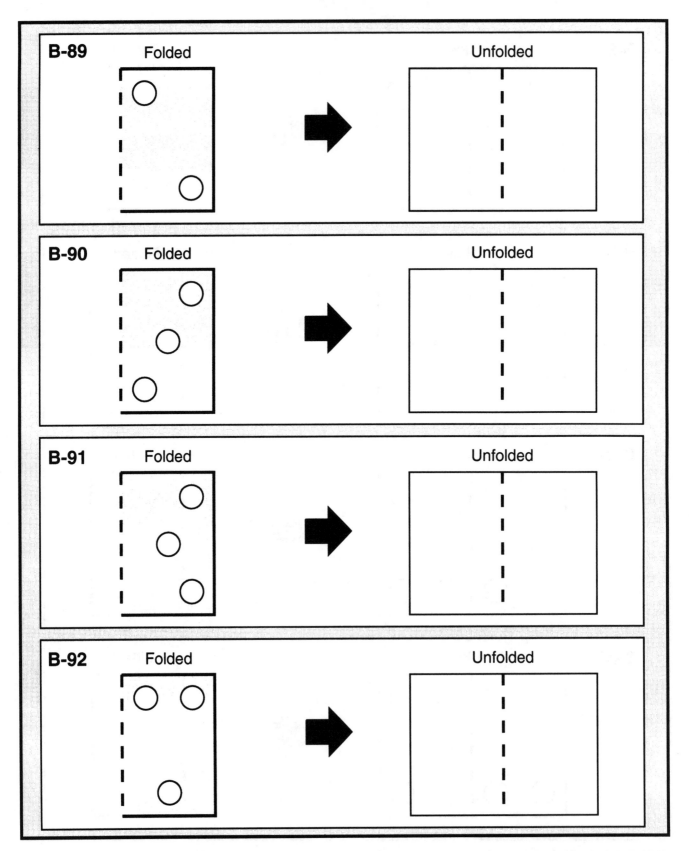

SYMMETRICAL PATTERNS—SUPPLY

DIRECTIONS: Here are four symmetrical patterns. They are to be folded along the dotted line of symmetry. Draw how each pattern will look when folded.

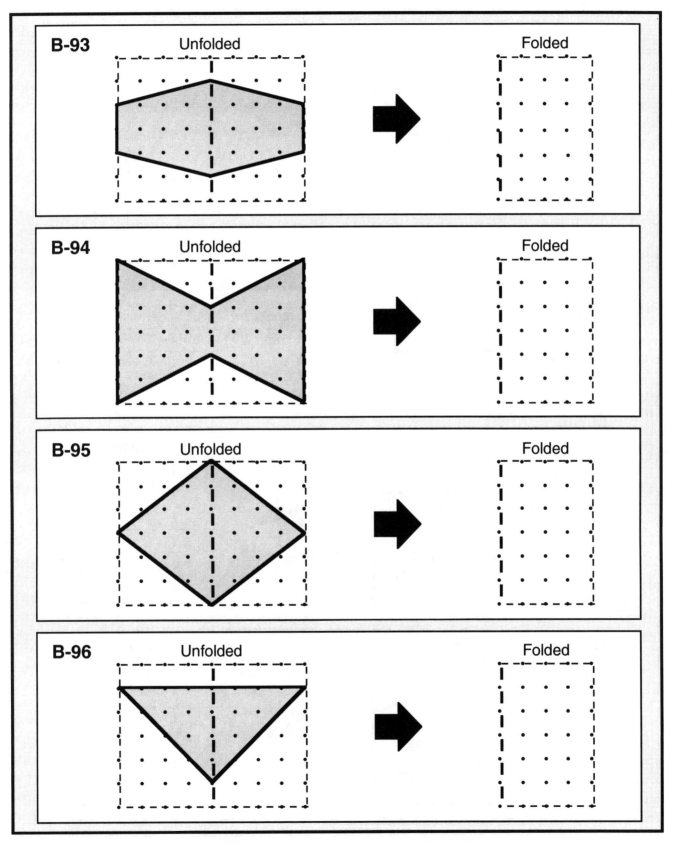

SYMMETRICAL PATTERNS—SUPPLY

DIRECTIONS: Here are four symmetrical patterns. They are to be folded along the dotted line of symmetry. Draw how each pattern will look when folded.

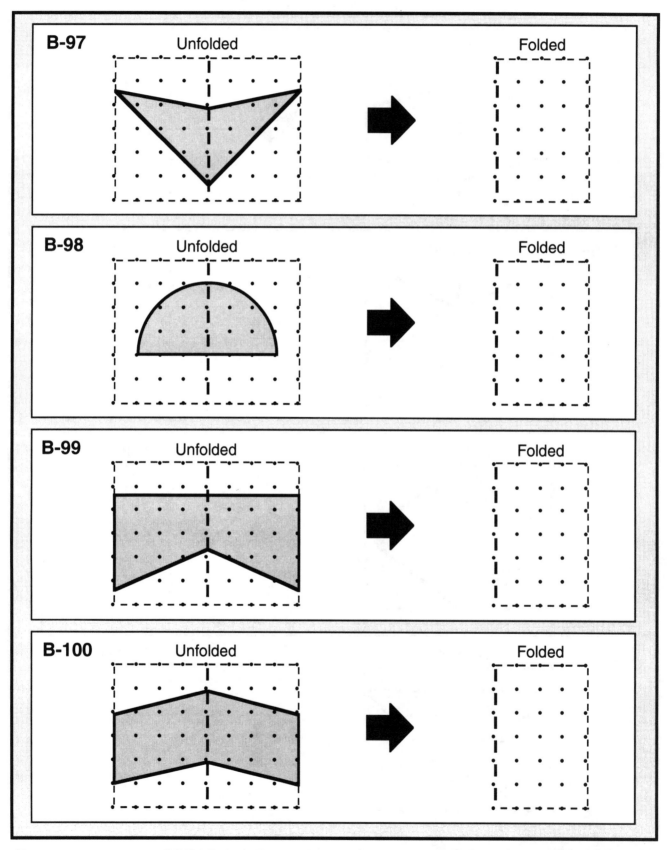

SYMMETRICAL PATTERNS—SUPPLY

DIRECTIONS: Here are four folded patterns. They are to be unfolded along the dotted line of symmetry. Draw how each unfolded symmetrical pattern will look.

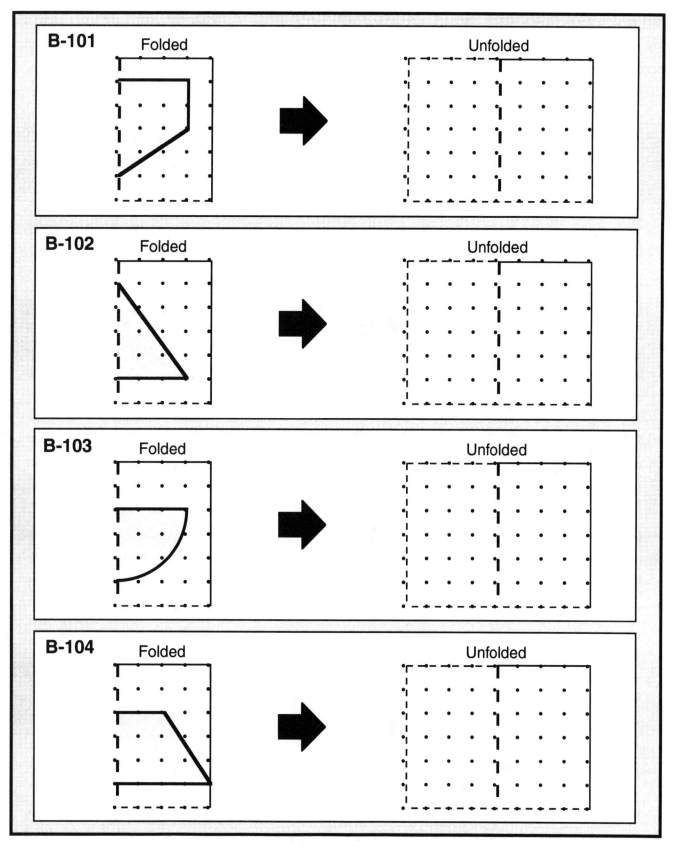

SYMMETRICAL PATTERNS—SUPPLY

DIRECTIONS: Here are four folded patterns. They are to be unfolded along the dotted line of symmetry. Draw how each unfolded symmetrical pattern will look.

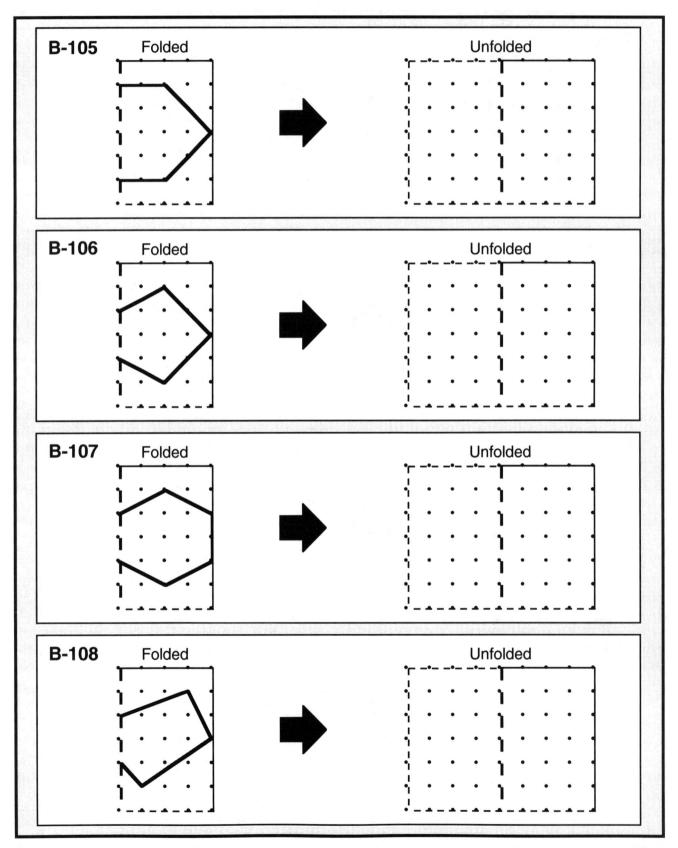

SYMMETRICAL PATTERNS—SUPPLY

DIRECTIONS: Complete each of the six patterns below so that each is symmetrical about the dashed line of symmetry.

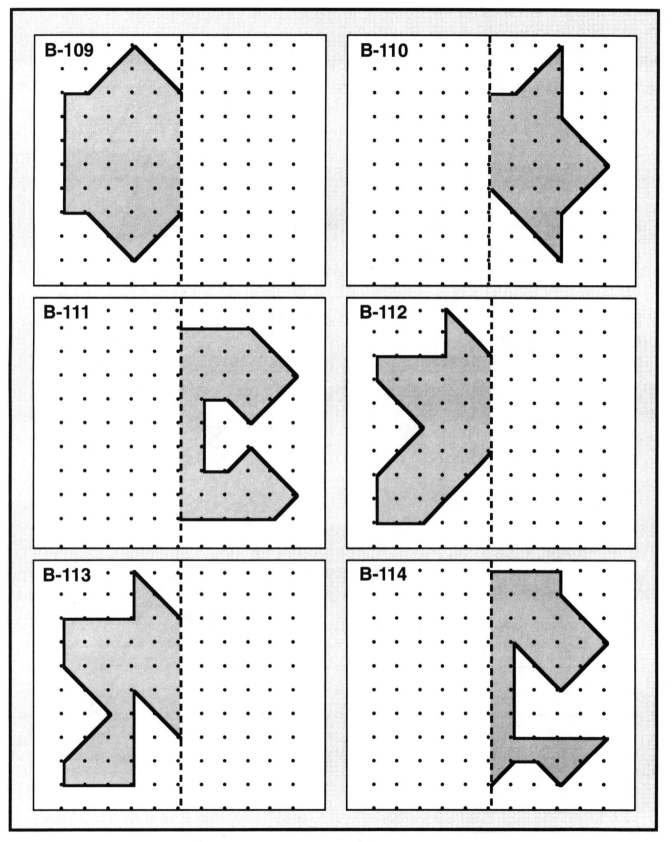

AXIS OF SYMMETRY—SUPPLY

DIRECTIONS: An axis of symmetry is a line which divides a design into two equal parts. Draw an axis of symmetry on each of the drawings below.

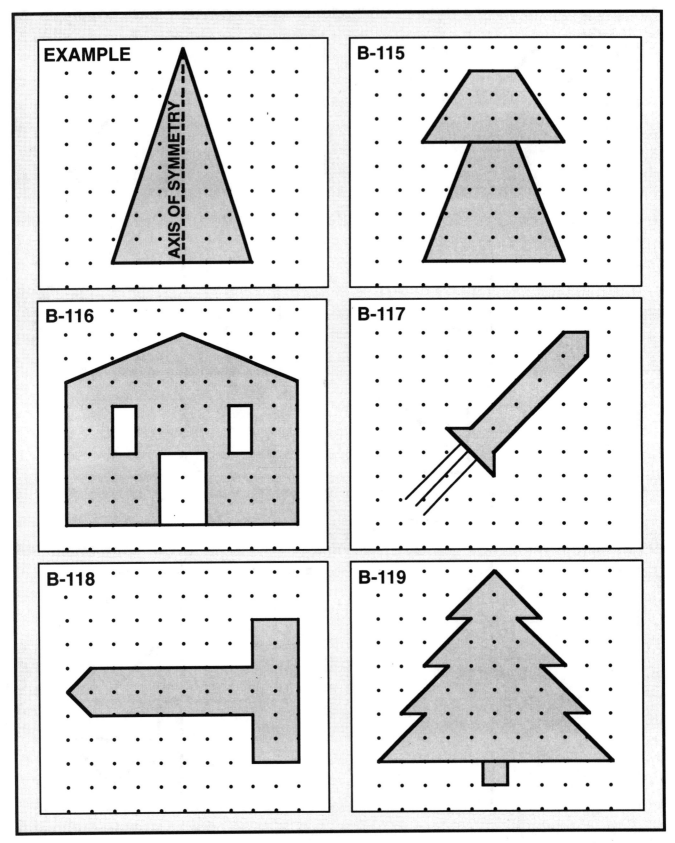

EXAMPLE

AXIS OF SYMMETRY

B-115

B-116

B-117

B-118

B-119

AXIS OF SYMMETRY—SUPPLY

DIRECTIONS: An axis of symmetry is a line which divides a design into two equal parts. Draw an axis of symmetry on each of the drawings below.

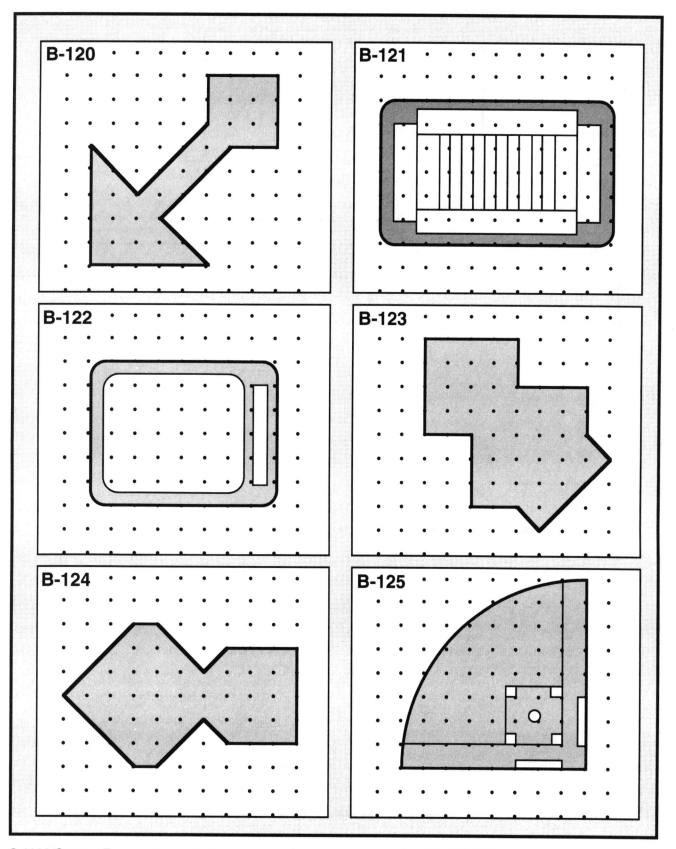

B-120

B-121

B-122

B-123

B-124

B-125

COVERING A SURFACE

DIRECTIONS: Draw the top rectangle on the lower grid of dots as many times as needed to cover the whole grid. There should be no empty space left on the grid.

B-126

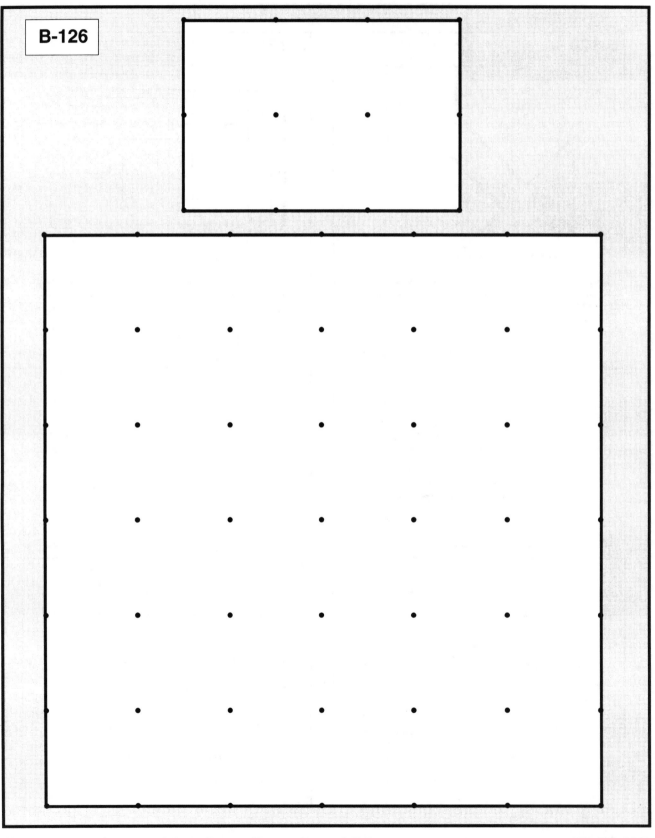

COVERING A SURFACE

DIRECTIONS: Draw the top triangle on the lower grid of dots as many times as needed to cover the whole grid. There should be no empty space left on the grid.

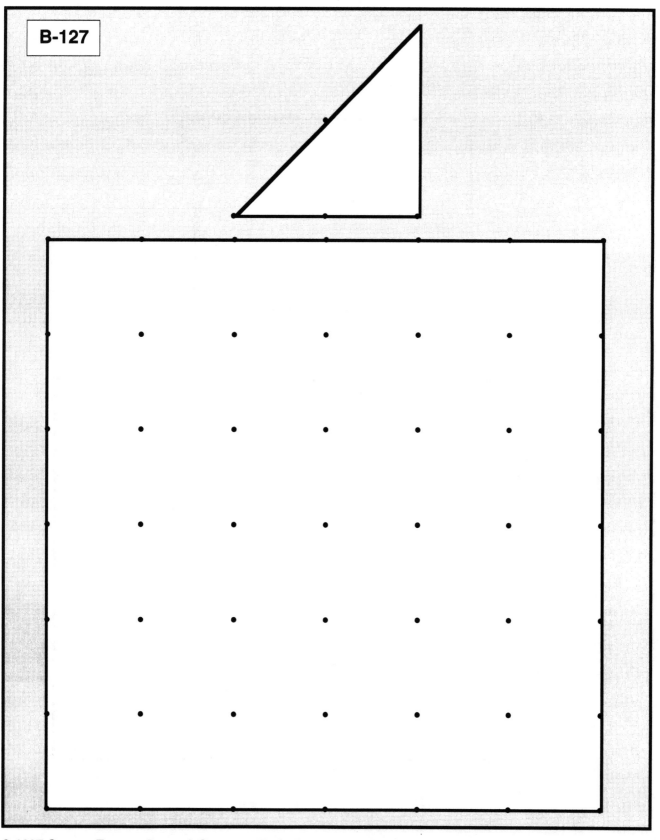

B-127

COVERING A SURFACE

DIRECTIONS: Draw the top figure on the lower grid of dots as many times as needed to cover the whole grid. There should be no empty space left on the grid.

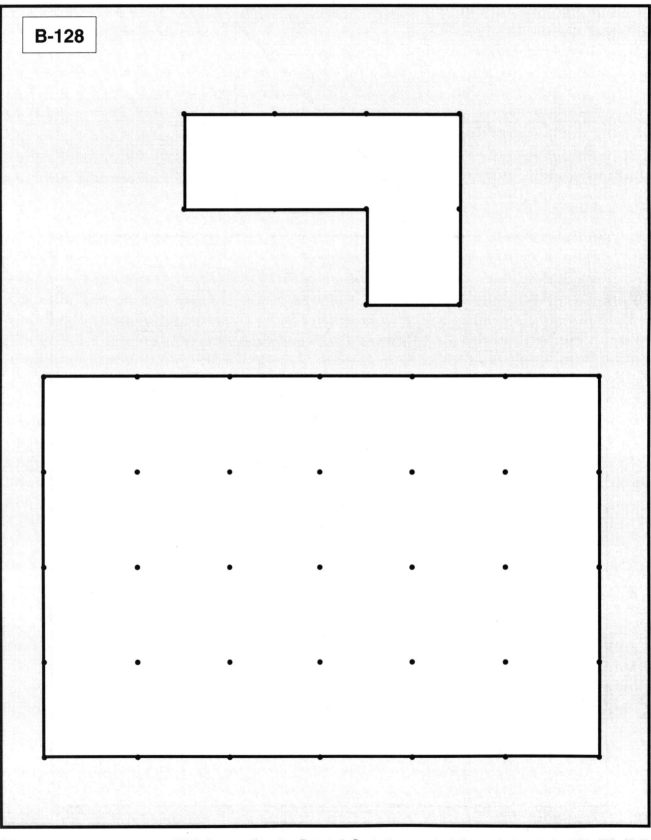

B-128

COVERING A SURFACE

DIRECTIONS: Draw the top figure on the lower grid of dots as many times as needed to cover the whole grid. There should be no empty space left on the grid.

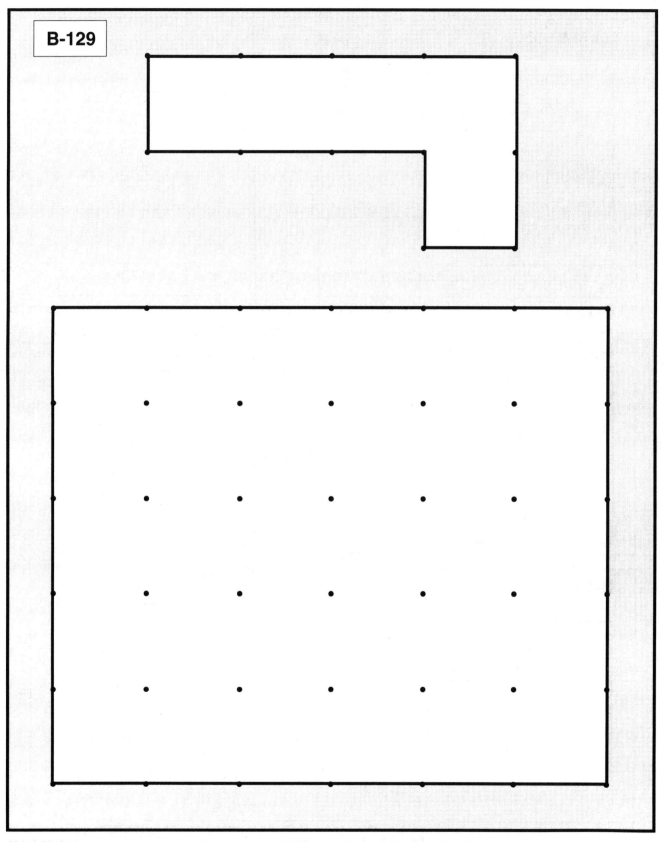

B-129

WHICH SHAPE COMPLETES THE SQUARE?

DIRECTIONS: Circle the shape that completes the big square.

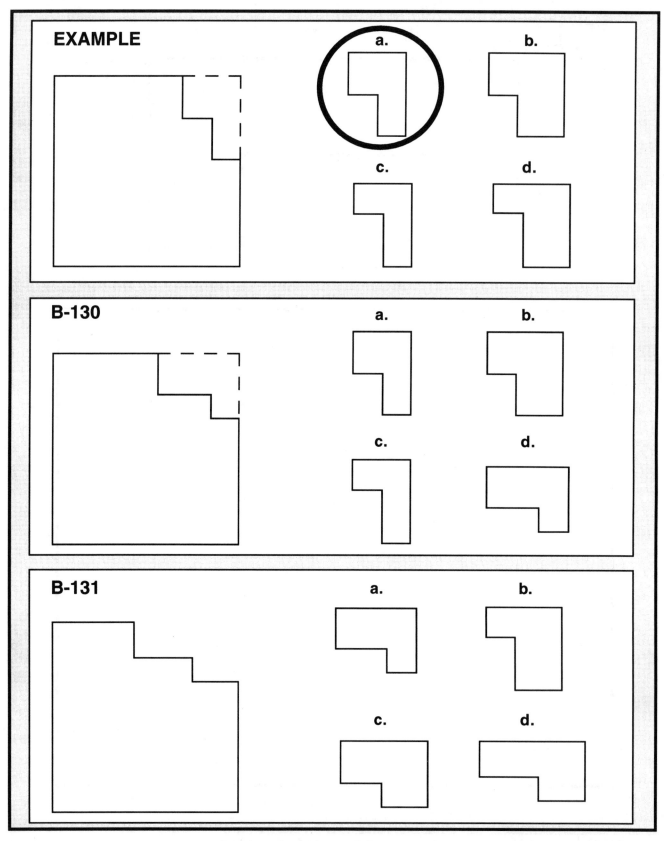

WHICH SHAPE COMPLETES THE SQUARE?

DIRECTIONS: Circle the shape that completes the big square.

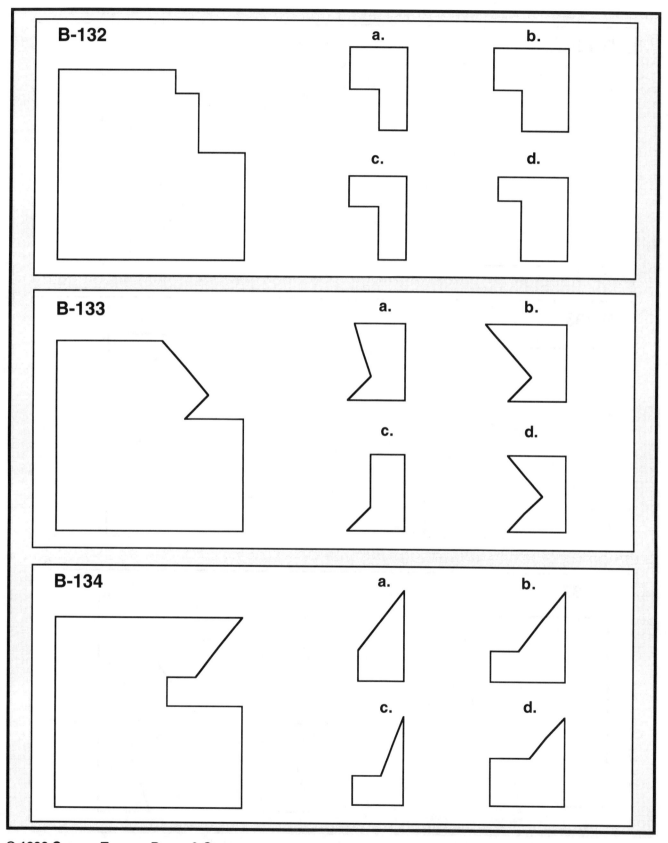

WHICH SHAPE COMPLETES THE SQUARE?

DIRECTIONS: Circle the shape that completes the big square.

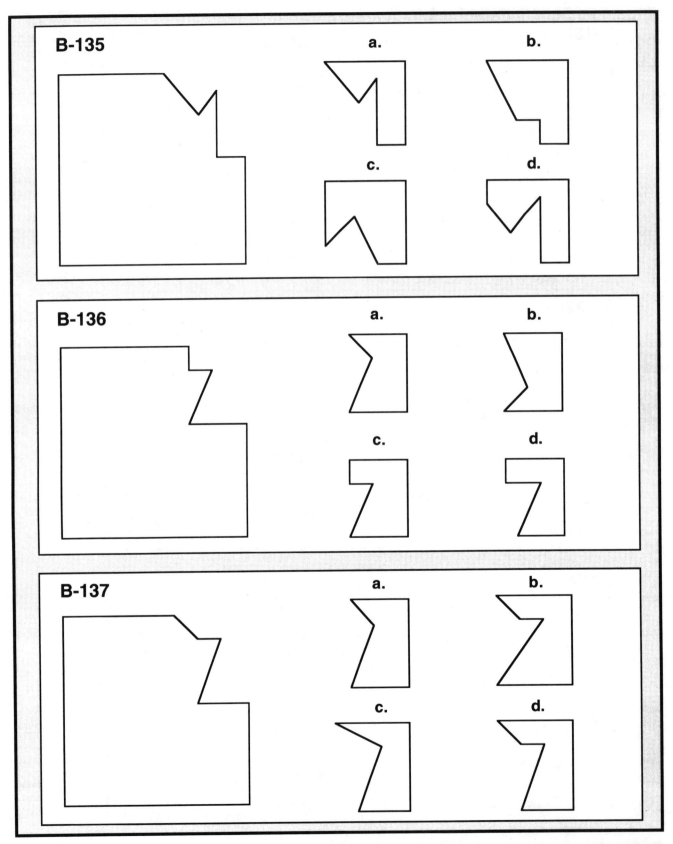

WHICH SHAPES COMPLETE THE SQUARE?

DIRECTIONS: Circle the two shapes that, together, complete the big square. Imagine rotating the shapes as necessary.

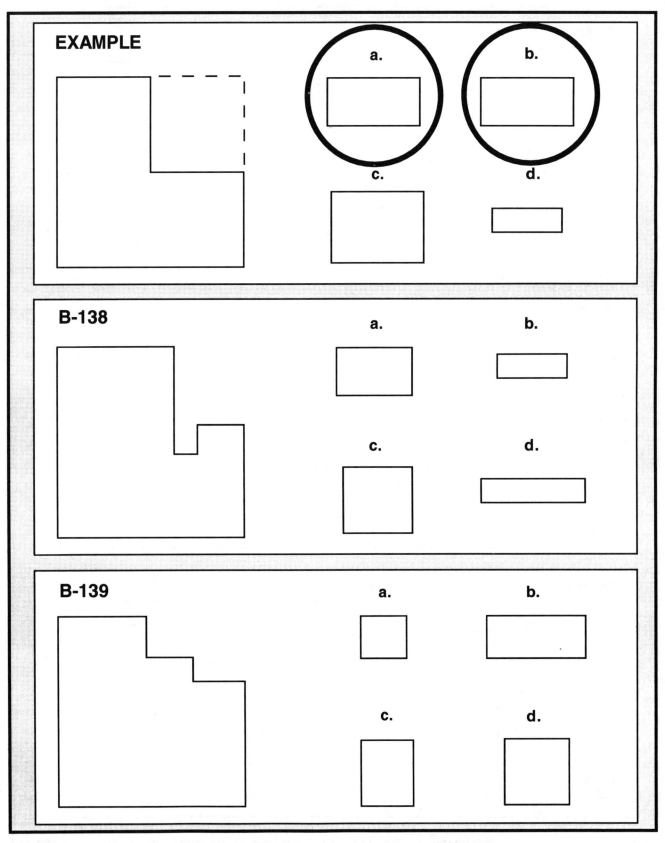

WHICH SHAPES COMPLETE THE SQUARE?

DIRECTIONS: Circle the two shapes that, together, complete the big square. Imagine rotating the shapes as necessary.

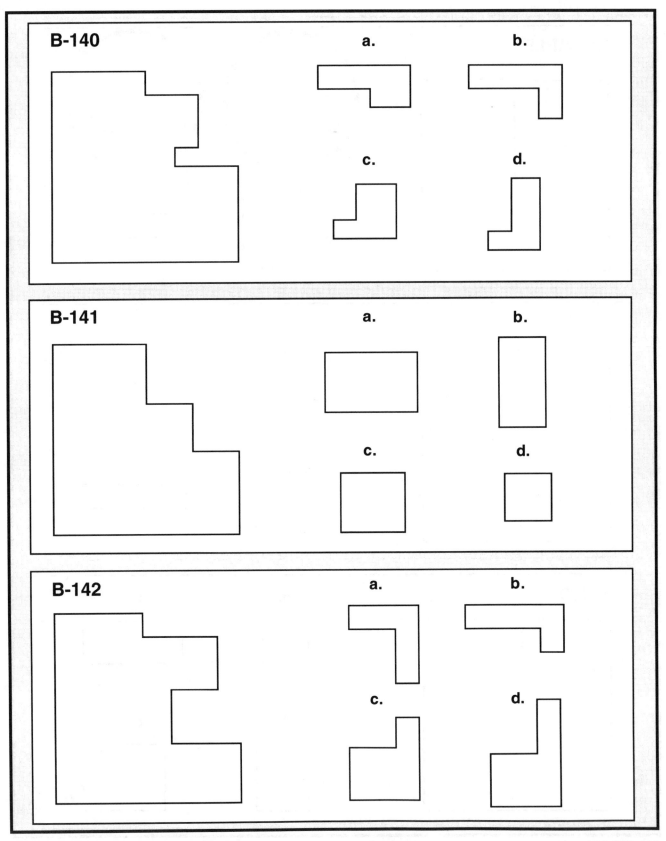

B-140   a.   b.   c.   d.

B-141   a.   b.   c.   d.

B-142   a.   b.   c.   d.

WHICH SHAPES COMPLETE THE SQUARE?

DIRECTIONS: Circle the two shapes that, together, complete the big square. Imagine rotating the shapes as necessary. More than one set of shapes may work.

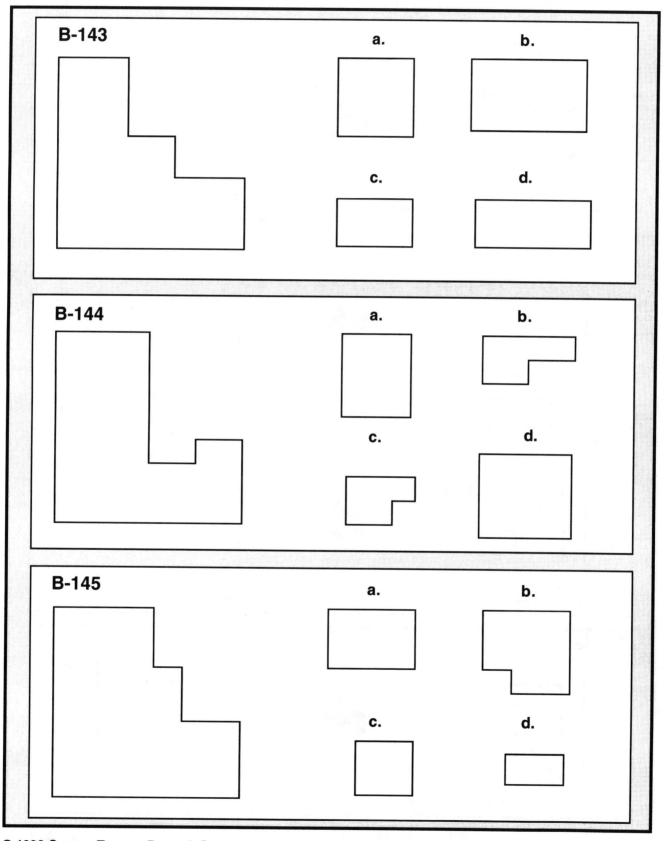

COPYING A FIGURE

DIRECTIONS: To copy a figure, count the number of spaces between the dots on each side of the figure. Count the spaces, not the dots. Use the dot grid to mark off the length of each side.

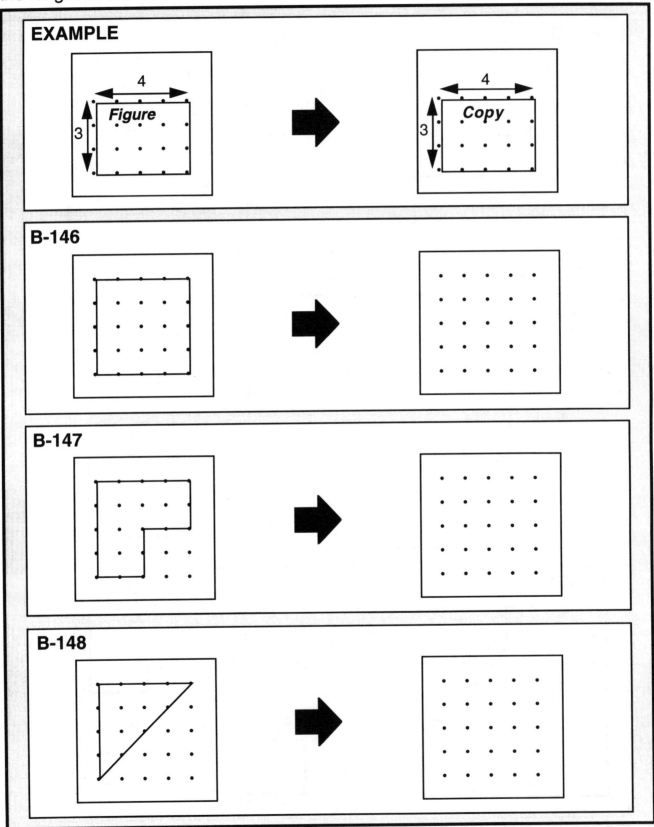

ENLARGING FIGURES

DIRECTIONS: To enlarge a figure so that each side is twice as long, count the number of spaces between the dots on each side of the figure and multiply by two. Count the spaces, not the dots. Use the dot grid to mark off the length of each side of the enlarged figure.

Enlarging a rectangle:

If the pattern is not a rectangle, then it is difficult to count the spaces directly. For example, the line from point A to point B does not pass through dots exactly.

The path from A to B can be replaced with lines AC and CB. Lines AC and CB do go through dots exactly; therefore, the dots can be used as a guide for measuring the lengths AC and CB. Count the spaces to measure the lengths. If the lengths of lines AC and CB are doubled, then line A'B' will be twice the length of line AB. This "triangle rule" will help you enlarge more complicated patterns.

ENLARGING FIGURES

DIRECTIONS: Use the dot grid to draw a figure with sides twice as long as the figure on the left.

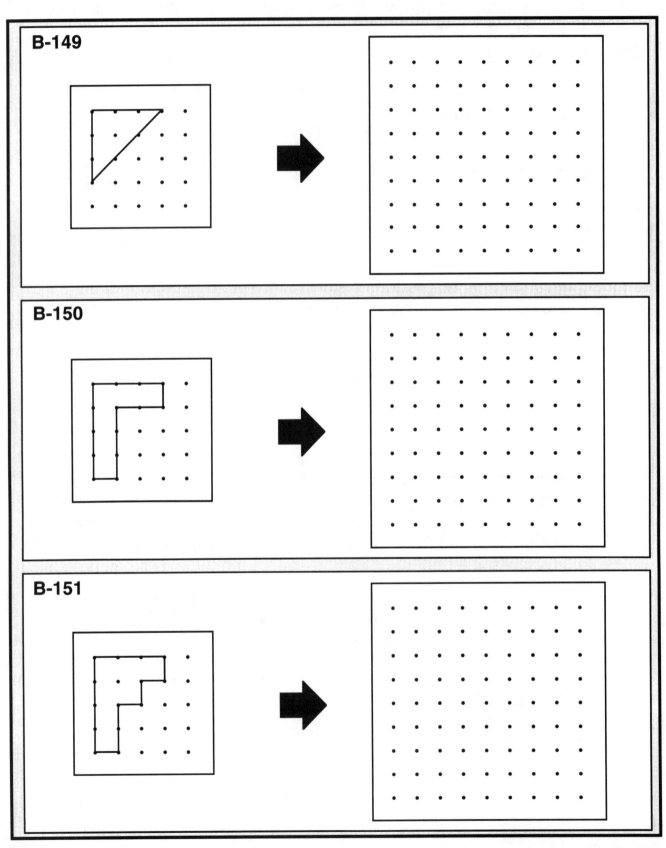

ENLARGING FIGURES

DIRECTIONS: Use the dot grid to draw a figure with sides twice as long as the figure on the left.

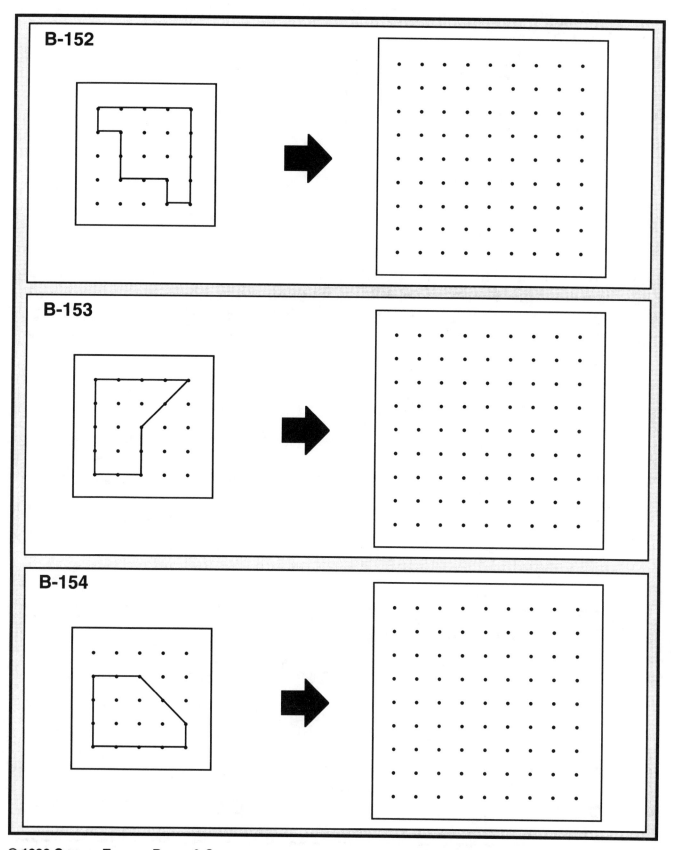

REDUCING FIGURES

DIRECTIONS: To reduce a figure so that each side is half as long, count the number of spaces between the dots on each side of the figure and divide by two. Count the spaces, not the dots. Use the dot grid to mark off the length of each side of the reduced figure.

Original Figure

Reduced Figure

If the pattern is not a rectangle, then the "triangle rule" may be used to reduce the size of a line drawn at an angle. Here is an example of the "triangle rule." Start at point A and go upward until your pencil is in line with point B. Then go over until your pencil is on point B. Next, count the spaces between the dots and divide by two. Finally, draw a reduced figure as shown.

becomes

B-155 Try the "triangle rule" on line CD.

Show your work here.

REDUCING FIGURES

DIRECTIONS: Use the dot grid to draw a figure with sides half as long as the figure on the left.

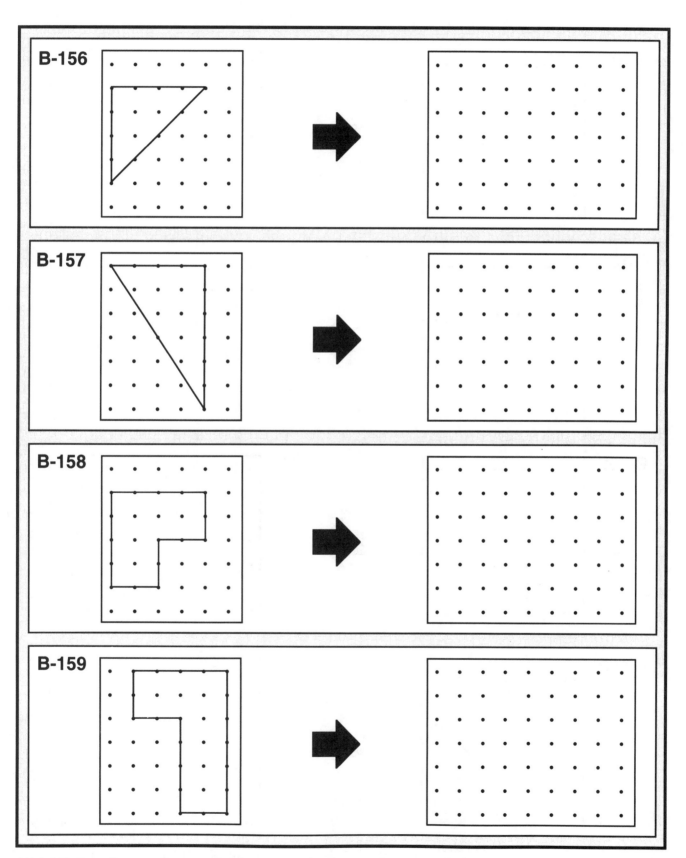

REDUCING FIGURES

DIRECTIONS: Use the dot grid to draw a figure with sides half as long as the figure on the left.

COMPARING SHAPES—EXPLAIN

DIRECTIONS: Use this diagram to organize your thinking about how a triangle and a trapezoid are alike and how they are different.

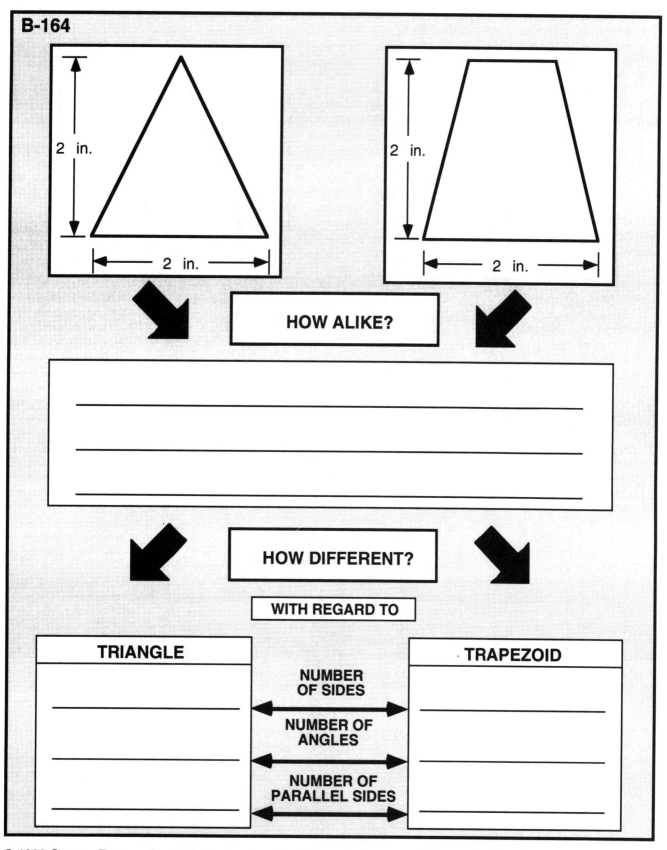

COMPARING SHAPES—EXPLAIN

DIRECTIONS: Use this diagram to organize your thinking about how a square and a parallelogram are alike and how they are different.

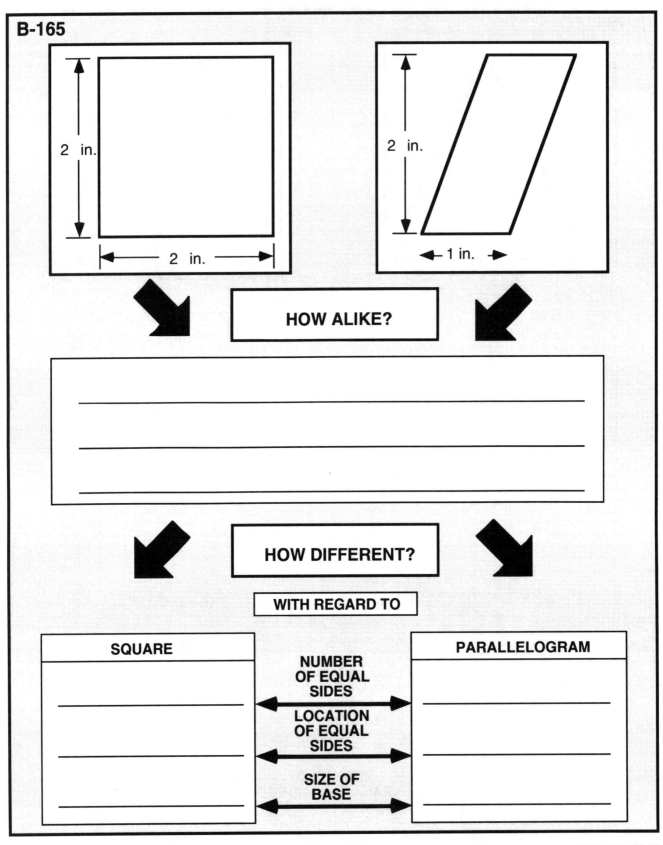

COMPARING SHAPES—EXPLAIN

DIRECTIONS: Use this diagram to organize your thinking about how a rectangle and a parallelogram are alike and how they are different.

CHAPTER THREE

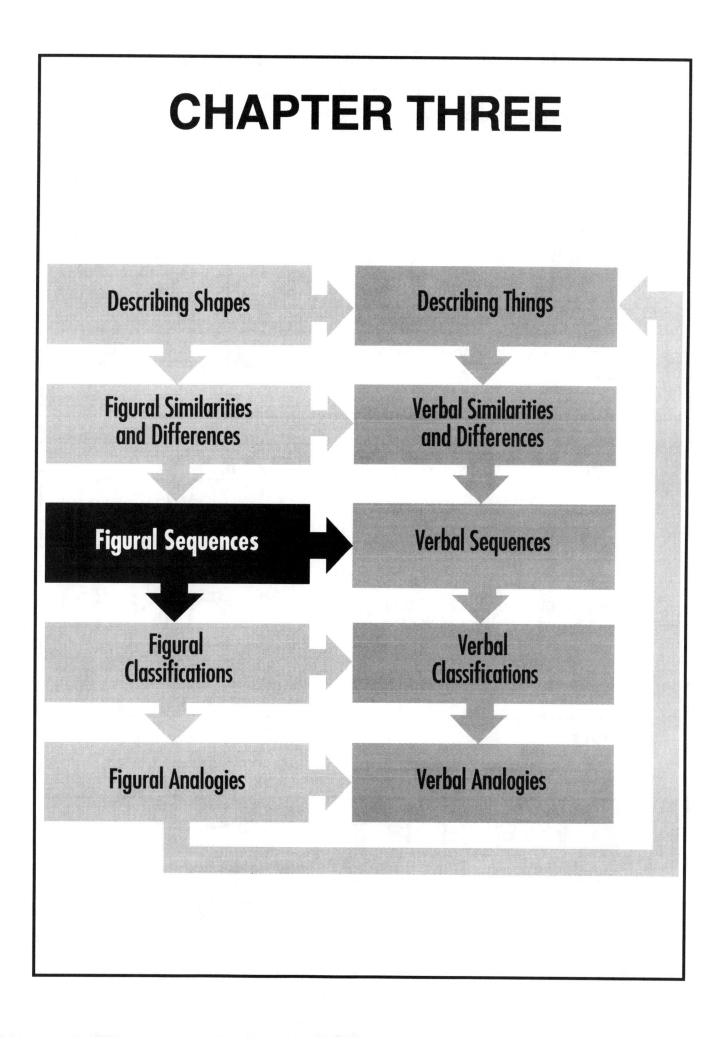

Describing Shapes → Describing Things

Figural Similarities and Differences → Verbal Similarities and Differences

Figural Sequences → Verbal Sequences

Figural Classifications → Verbal Classifications

Figural Analogies → Verbal Analogies

SEQUENCE OF FIGURES—SELECT

DIRECTIONS: Here are examples of three sequences. The correct figure that completes each sequence is circled and a description of the kind of sequence is given.

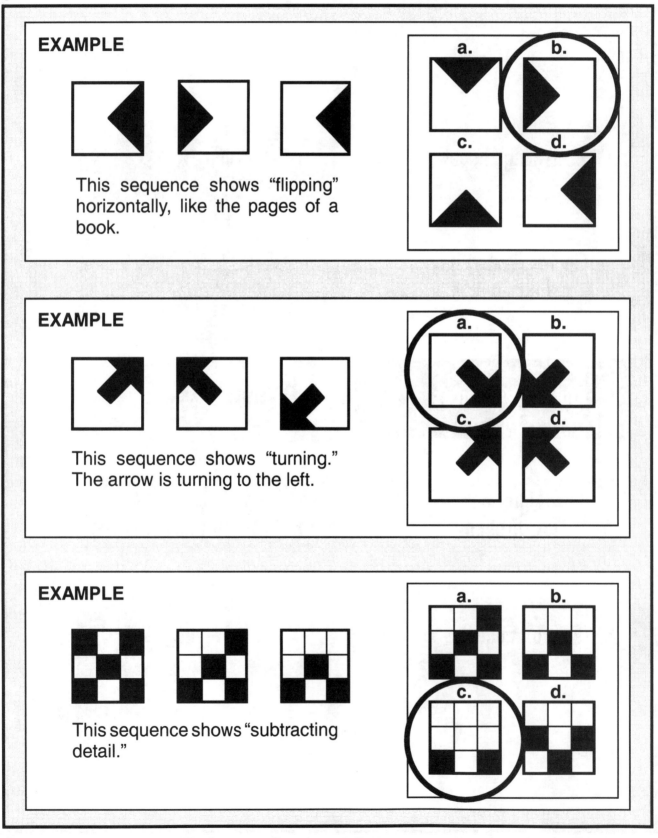

EXAMPLE

This sequence shows "flipping" horizontally, like the pages of a book.

EXAMPLE

This sequence shows "turning." The arrow is turning to the left.

EXAMPLE

This sequence shows "subtracting detail."

SEQUENCE OF FIGURES—SELECT

DIRECTIONS: Circle the figure that best continues the sequence.

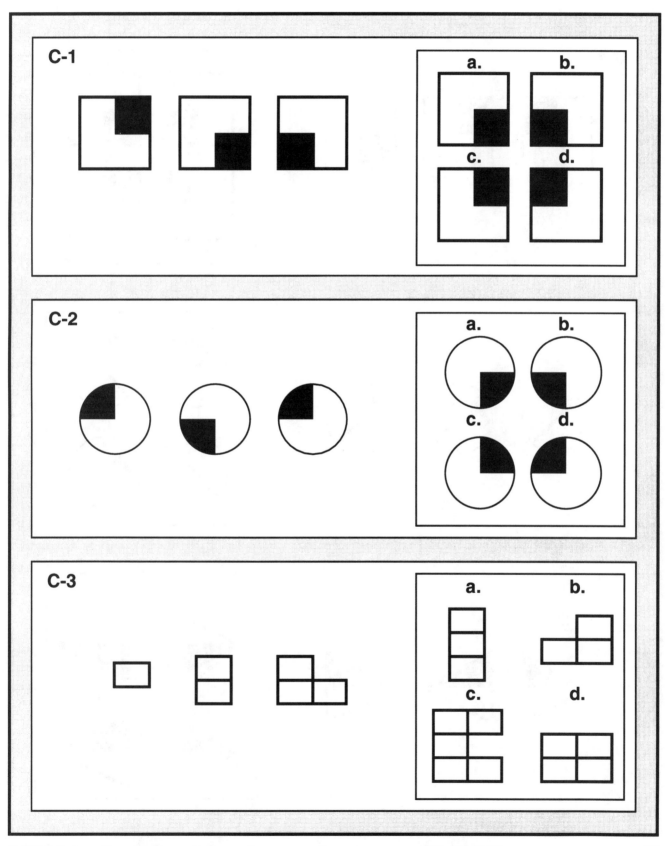

SEQUENCE OF FIGURES—SELECT

DIRECTIONS: Circle the figure that best continues the sequence.

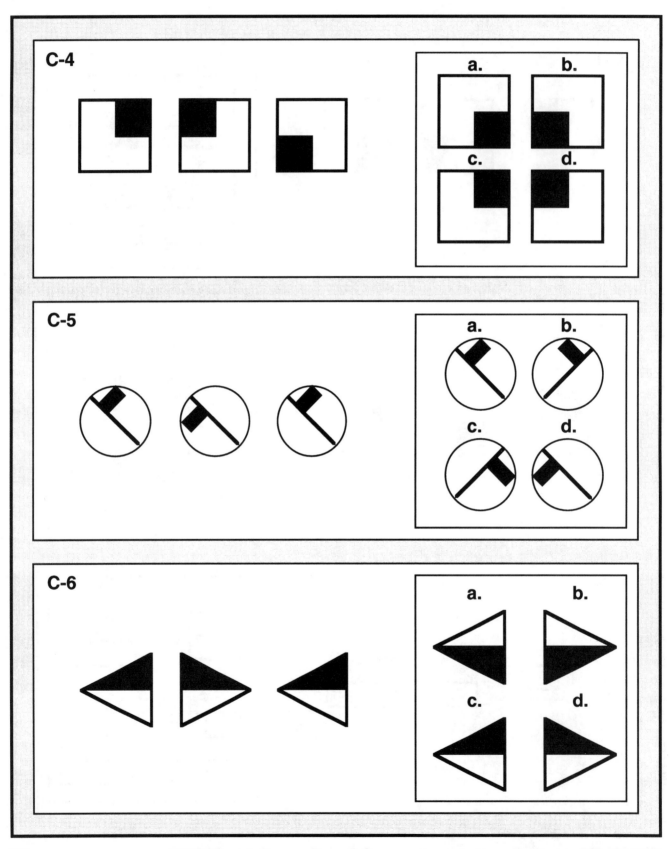

SEQUENCE OF FIGURES—SELECT

DIRECTIONS: Circle the figure that best continues the sequence.

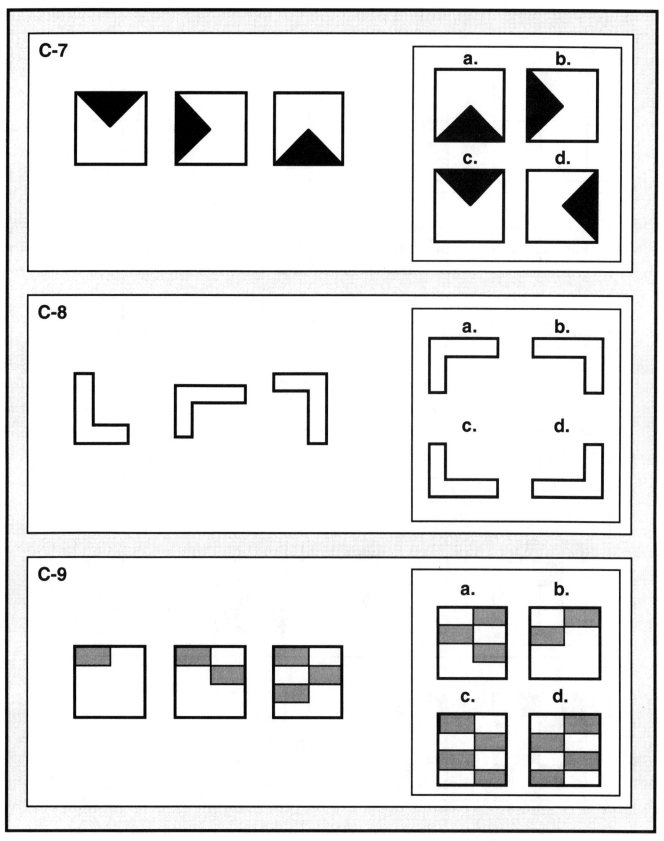

SEQUENCE OF FIGURES—SUPPLY

DIRECTIONS: Shade in the fourth shape in each row to continue each sequence.

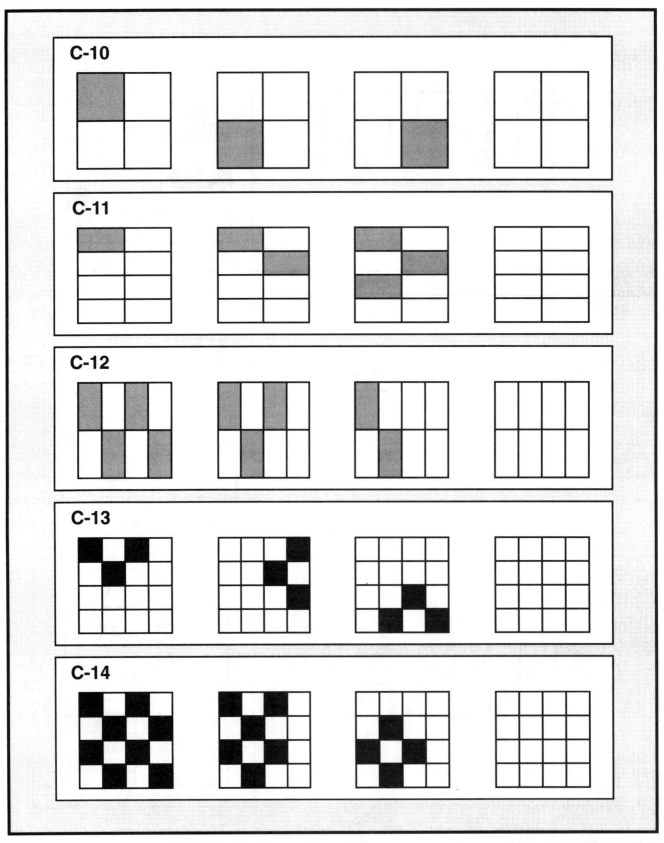

SEQUENCE OF FIGURES—SUPPLY

DIRECTIONS: Shade in the fourth shape in each row to continue each sequence.

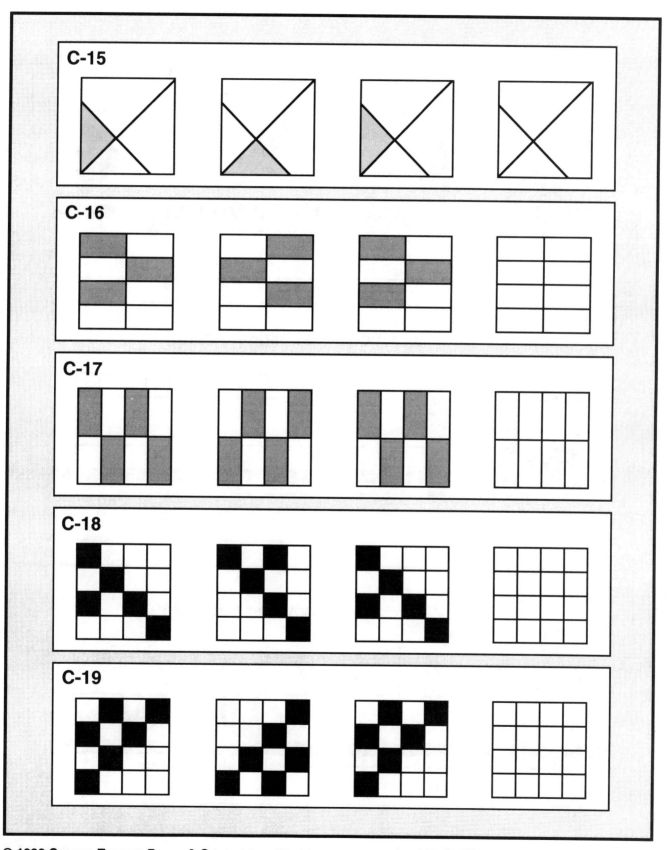

TUMBLING—SHADING

DIRECTIONS: As a shape tumbles along, the side that is on the ground changes. Darken the following figures to show how they look as they tumble across the page.

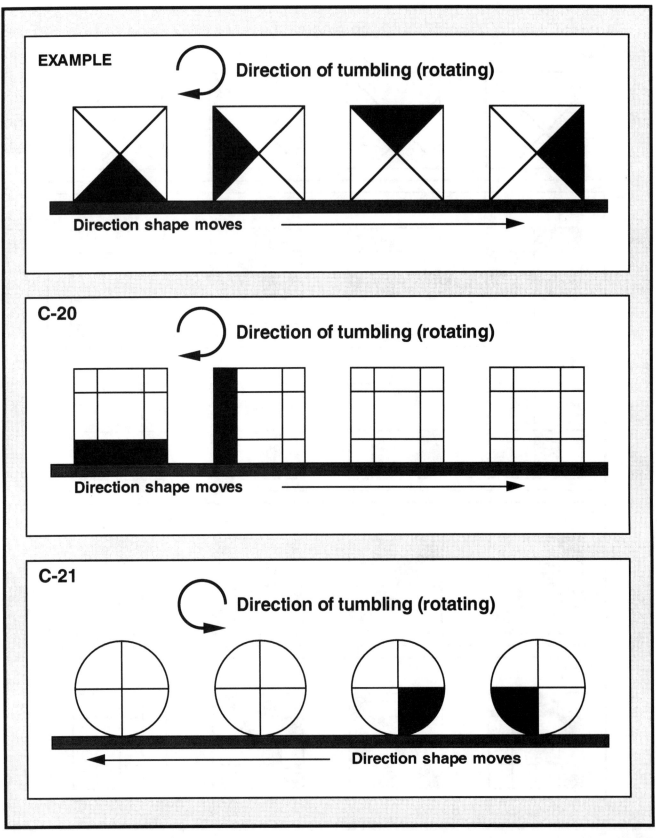

TUMBLING—SHADING

DIRECTIONS: As a shape tumbles along, the side that is on the ground changes. Darken the following figures to show how they look as they tumble across the page.

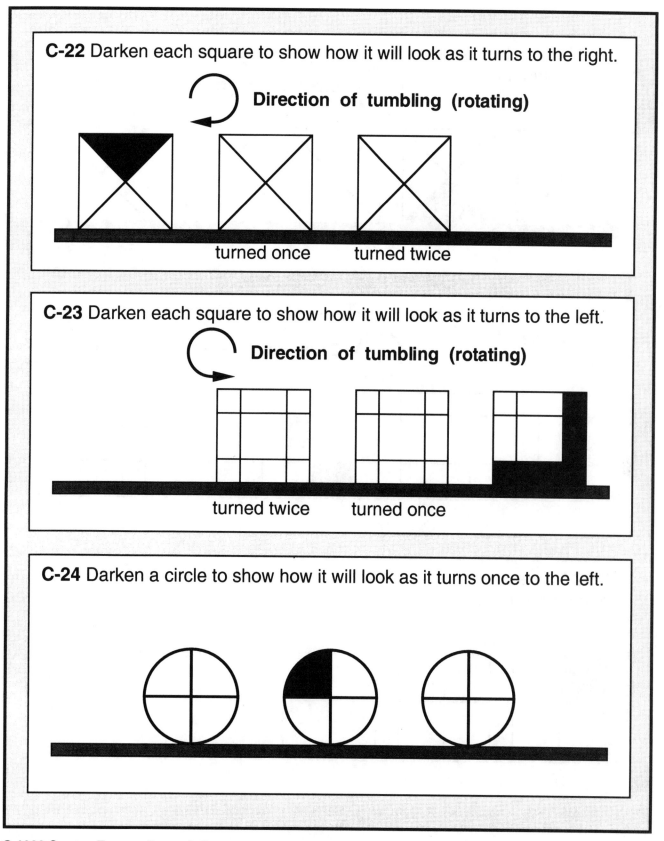

C-22 Darken each square to show how it will look as it turns to the right.

Direction of tumbling (rotating)

turned once   turned twice

C-23 Darken each square to show how it will look as it turns to the left.

Direction of tumbling (rotating)

turned twice   turned once

C-24 Darken a circle to show how it will look as it turns once to the left.

TUMBLING—SHADING

DIRECTIONS: As a shape tumbles along, the side that is on the ground changes. Darken the following figures to show how they look as they tumble across the page.

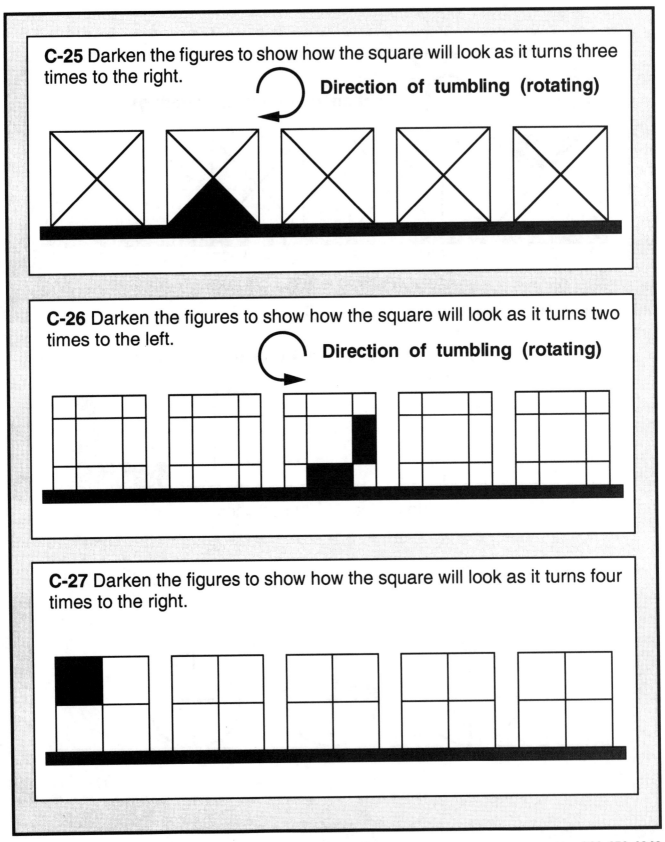

C-25 Darken the figures to show how the square will look as it turns three times to the right.

Direction of tumbling (rotating)

C-26 Darken the figures to show how the square will look as it turns two times to the left.

Direction of tumbling (rotating)

C-27 Darken the figures to show how the square will look as it turns four times to the right.

TURNING (ROTATING) FIGURES

DIRECTIONS: Explain how the first figure has been turned to produce the second by filling in the number of position changes and the direction of change.

EXAMPLE

Before turning   **After turning**

Direction of turning (rotating)

Turns _____1_____   Direction _____right_____

EXAMPLE

After turning   **Direction of turning**   **Before turning**

Turns _____2_____   Direction _____left_____

C-28

Before turning   **After turning**

Turns _____   Direction _____

TURNING (ROTATING) FIGURES

DIRECTIONS: Explain how the first figure has been turned to produce the second by filling in the number of position changes and the direction of change.

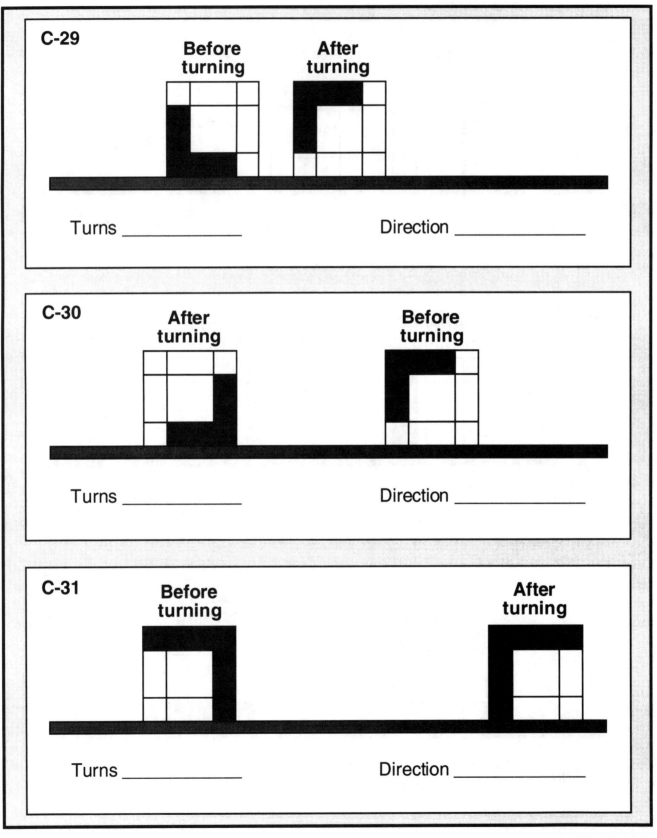

C-29

Before turning   **After turning**

Turns _____   Direction _____

C-30

After turning   **Before turning**

Turns _____   Direction _____

C-31

Before turning   **After turning**

Turns _____   Direction _____

PATTERN FOLDING—SELECT

DIRECTIONS: The pattern on the left is a wrapper for one of the solids on the right. Draw a circle around the correct solid.

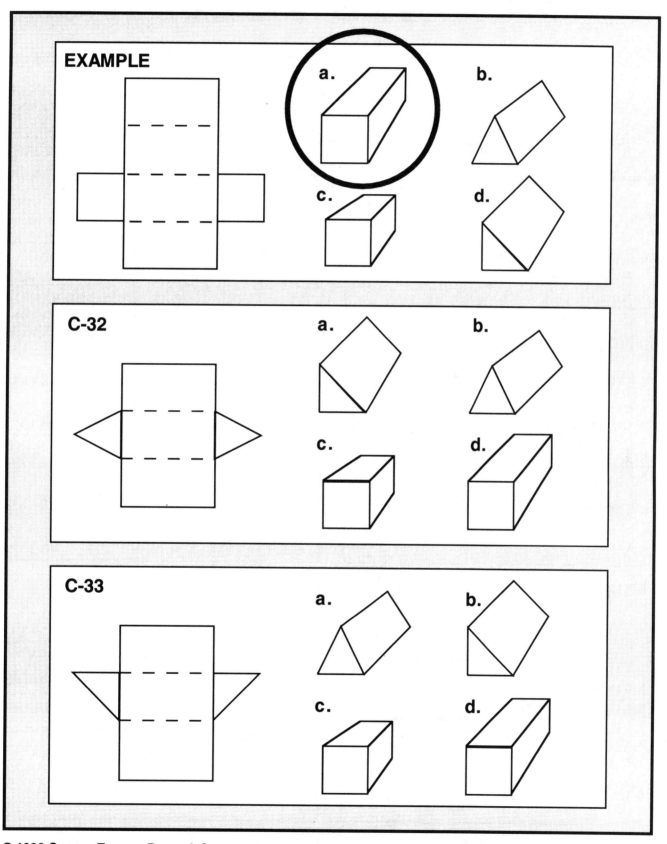

EXAMPLE

a.

b.

c.

d.

C-32

a.

b.

c.

d.

C-33

a.

b.

c.

d.

PATTERN FOLDING—SUPPLY

DIRECTIONS: The patterns at the bottom of the page, when folded, produce the cube at the top of the page. Fill in the blanks on the pattern with the correct position number for that face of the cube.

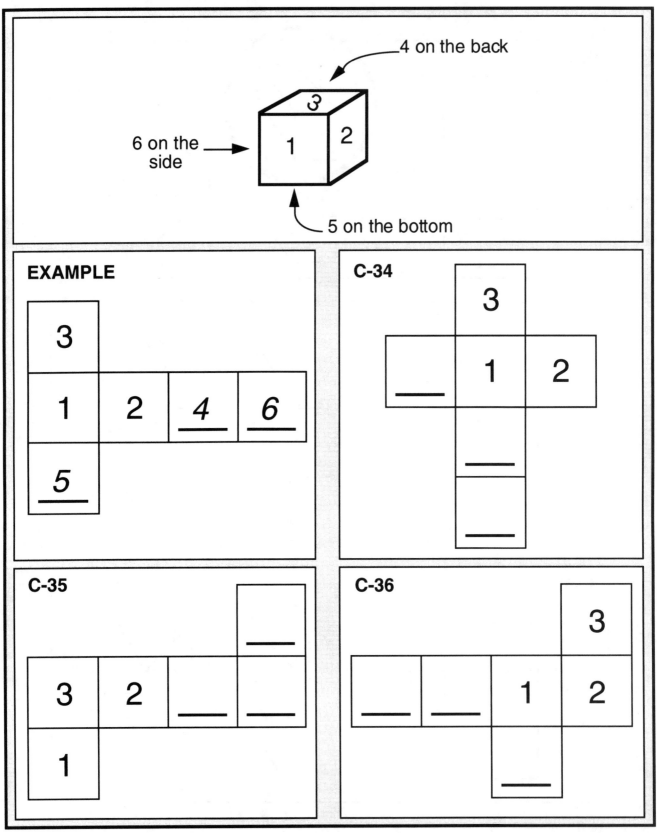

4 on the back

6 on the side

5 on the bottom

EXAMPLE

C-34

C-35

C-36

PATTERN FOLDING—SUPPLY

DIRECTIONS: The patterns at the bottom of the page, when folded, produce the cube at the top of the page. Fill in the blanks on the pattern with the correct position number for that face of the cube.

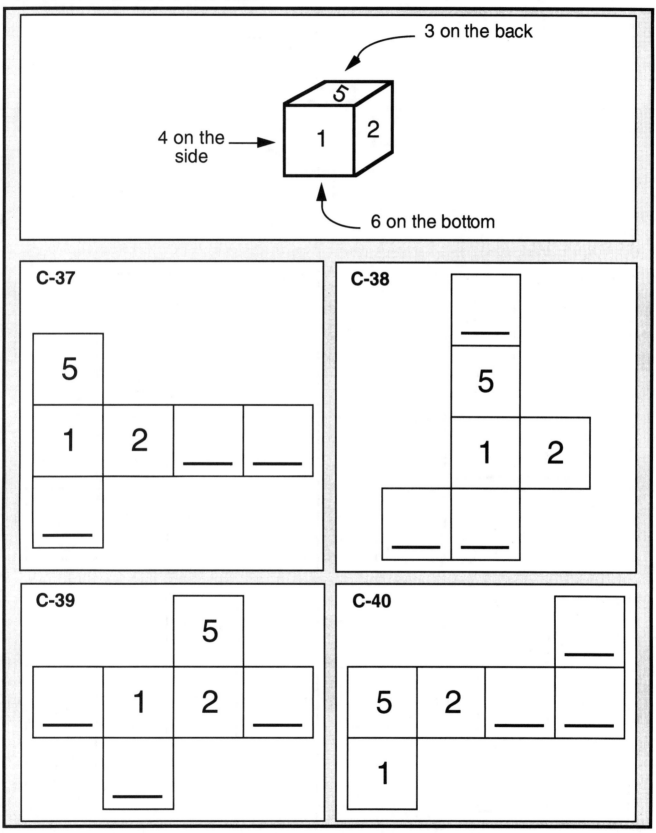

PATTERN FOLDING—SUPPLY

DIRECTIONS: The patterns at the bottom of the page, when folded, produce the cube at the top of the page. Fill in the blanks on the pattern with the correct position number for that face of the cube.

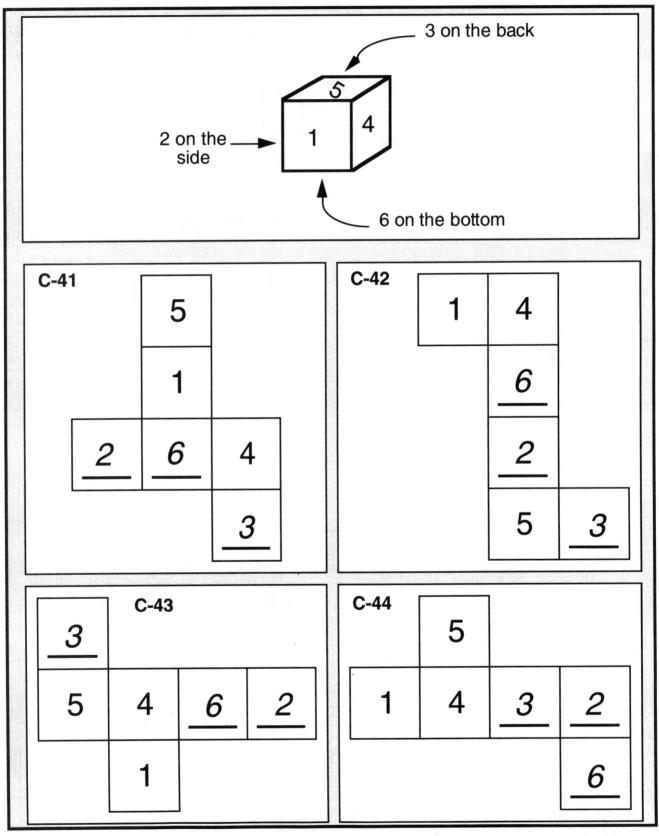

STACKING SHAPES—SELECT

DIRECTIONS: Look at the four shapes in the top box. At the bottom of the page are six combinations formed by placing one shape on another. Select the stack that fits each description.

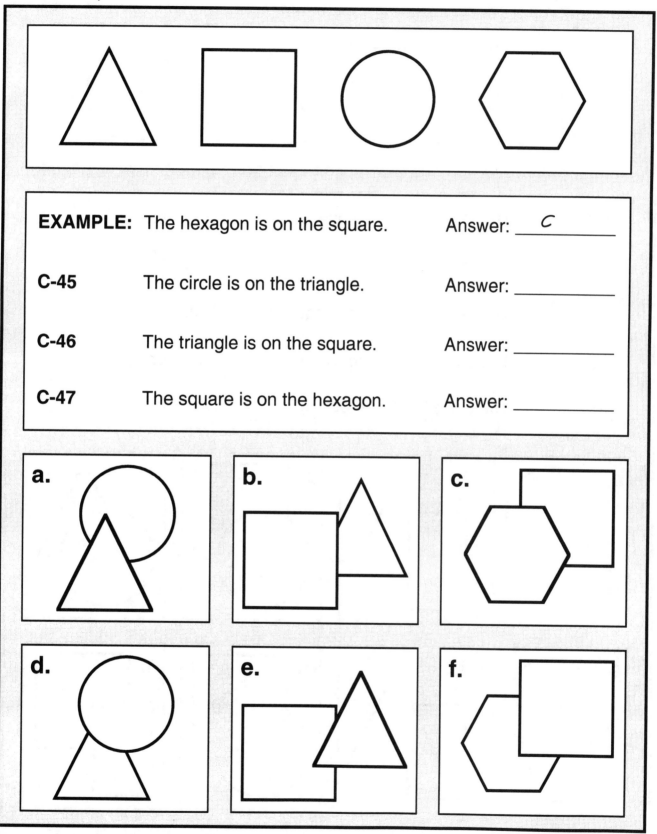

EXAMPLE: The hexagon is on the square.   Answer: _____C_____

C-45   The circle is on the triangle.   Answer: _____

C-46   The triangle is on the square.   Answer: _____

C-47   The square is on the hexagon.   Answer: _____

a.

b.

c.

d.

e.

f.

STACKING SHAPES—SELECT

DIRECTIONS: Look at the four shapes in the top box. At the bottom of the page are eight combinations formed by placing one shape on another. Select the stack that fits each description.

C-48	The circle is on the square.	Answer: _____
C-49	The triangle is on the rectangle.	Answer: _____
C-50	The rectangle is on the square.	Answer: _____
C-51	The square is on the circle.	Answer: _____
C-52	The circle is on the rectangle.	Answer: _____

STACKING SHAPES—SUPPLY

DIRECTIONS: Draw how each pair of shapes will look after they are stacked according to the directions.

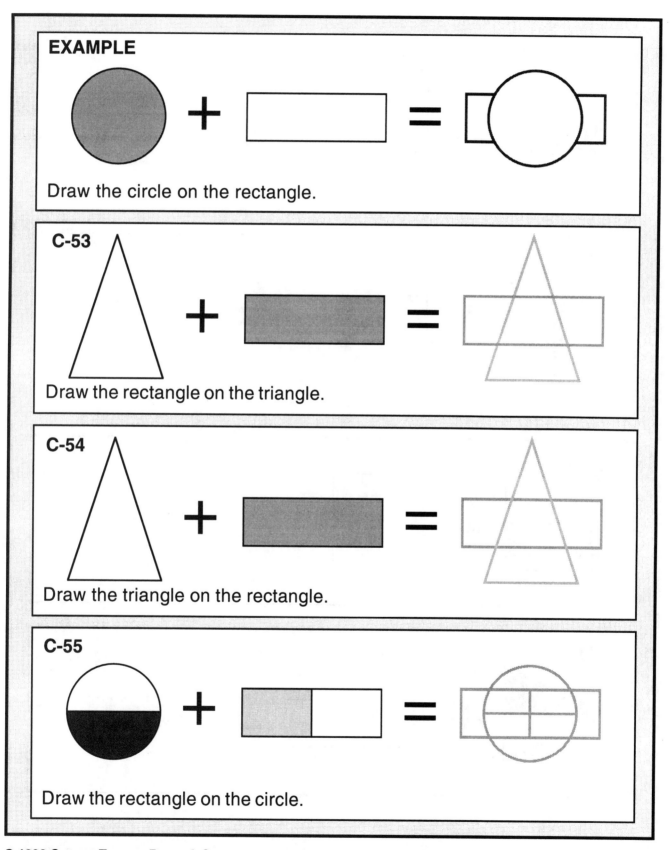

EXAMPLE

Draw the circle on the rectangle.

C-53

Draw the rectangle on the triangle.

C-54

Draw the triangle on the rectangle.

C-55

Draw the rectangle on the circle.

STACKING SHAPES—SUPPLY

DIRECTIONS: Draw how each pair of shapes will look after they are stacked according to the directions.

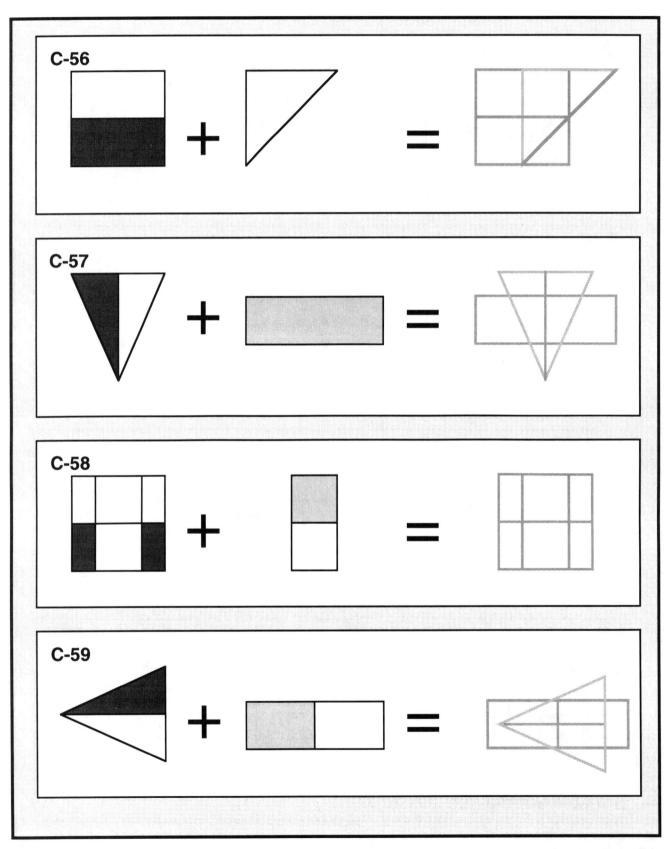

STACKING SHAPES—SUPPLY

DIRECTIONS: Draw how each group of three shapes will look after they are stacked according to the directions.

C-60

Darken some of the lines so that it appears that the rectangle and circle are both underneath the triangle.

C-61

Darken some of the lines so that it seems that the triangle is underneath both the circle and the rectangle.

C-62

Darken some of the lines so that the triangle will look like it is on top of the circle. The rectangle should appear to be on of the triangle.

C-63

Darken some of the lines so that the triangle will appear to be on top of the rectangle and underneath the circle.

STACKING SHAPES—SUPPLY

DIRECTIONS: Draw how each group of four shapes will look after they are stacked according to the directions.

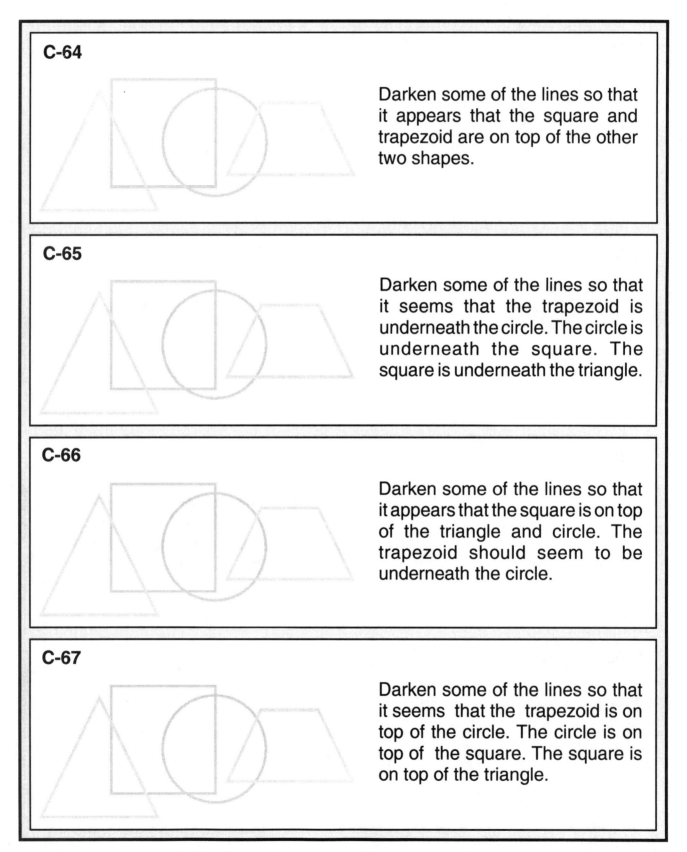

C-64

Darken some of the lines so that it appears that the square and trapezoid are on top of the other two shapes.

C-65

Darken some of the lines so that it seems that the trapezoid is underneath the circle. The circle is underneath the square. The square is underneath the triangle.

C-66

Darken some of the lines so that it appears that the square is on top of the triangle and circle. The trapezoid should seem to be underneath the circle.

C-67

Darken some of the lines so that it seems that the trapezoid is on top of the circle. The circle is on top of the square. The square is on top of the triangle.

STACKING SHAPES—EXPLAIN

DIRECTIONS: Supply the directions for stacking the shapes to make the figure on the right. If you need help in spelling, use the words in the word box at the bottom of the page.

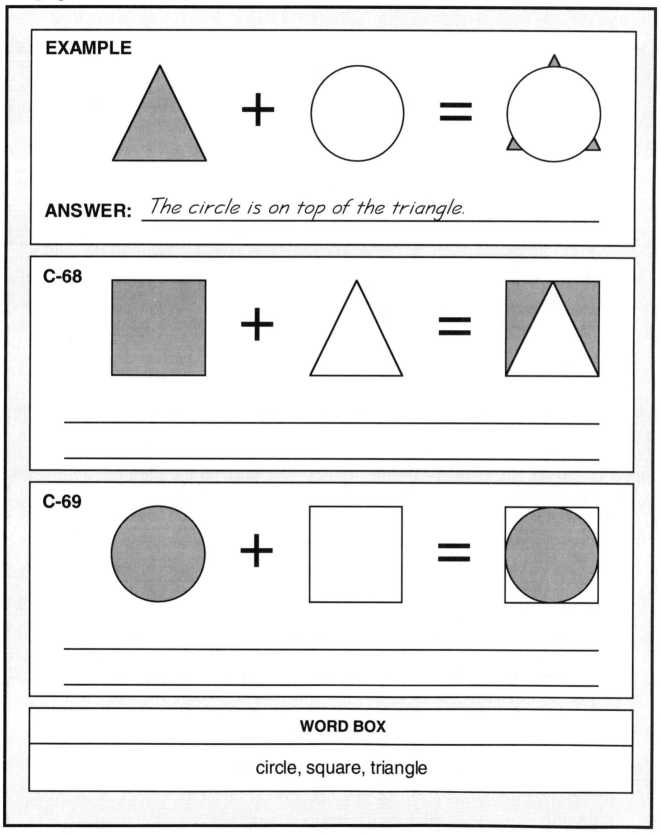

EXAMPLE

ANSWER: _The circle is on top of the triangle._

C-68

C-69

WORD BOX

circle, square, triangle

STACKING SHAPES—EXPLAIN

DIRECTIONS: Supply the directions for stacking the shapes to make the figure on the right. If you need help in spelling, use the words in the word box at the bottom of the page.

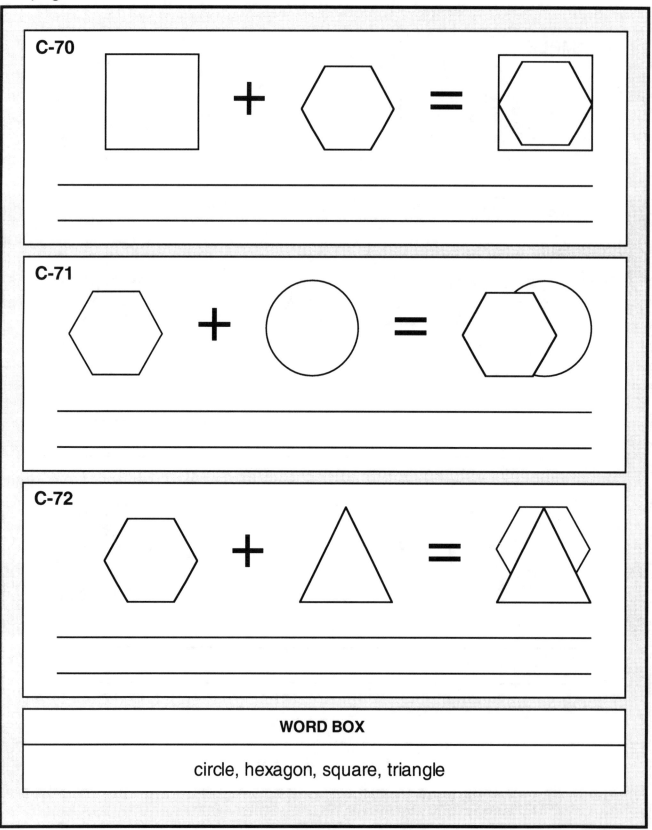

C-70

_____

_____

C-71

_____

_____

C-72

_____

_____

WORD BOX

circle, hexagon, square, triangle

STACKING SHAPES—EXPLAIN

DIRECTIONS: Supply the directions for stacking the shapes to make the figure on the left. If you need help in spelling, use the words in the word box at the bottom of the page.

EXAMPLE

The dark gray circle is on top of the white triangle. The white triangle is on top of the light gray square.

C-73

_____

_____

_____

_____

C-74

_____

_____

_____

_____

WORD BOX

circle, dark gray, light gray, square, triangle, white

STACKING SHAPES—EXPLAIN

DIRECTIONS: Supply the directions for stacking the shapes to make the figure on the left. If you need help in spelling, use the words in the word box at the bottom of the page.

C-75

_____

_____

_____

_____

C-76

_____

_____

_____

_____

C-77

_____

_____

_____

_____

WORD BOX

checked, circle, gray, square, striped, triangle

CHAPTER FOUR

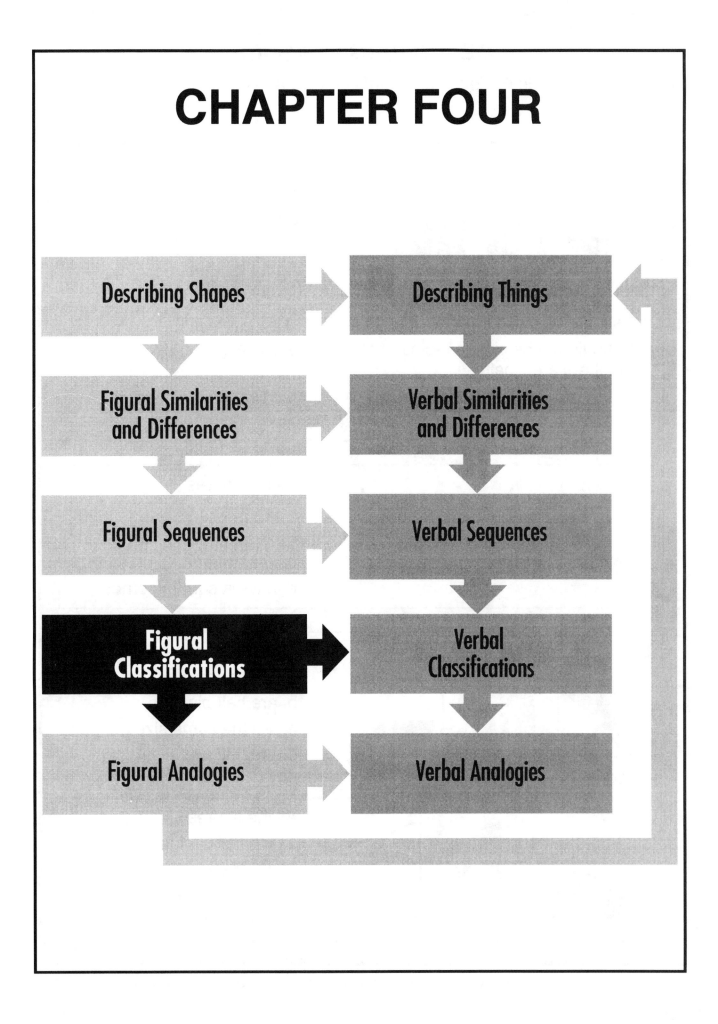

Describing Shapes → Describing Things

Figural Similarities and Differences → Verbal Similarities and Differences

Figural Sequences → Verbal Sequences

Figural Classifications → Verbal Classifications

Figural Analogies → Verbal Analogies

DESCRIBING CLASSES

DIRECTIONS: Circle the letter in front of each statement that is true.

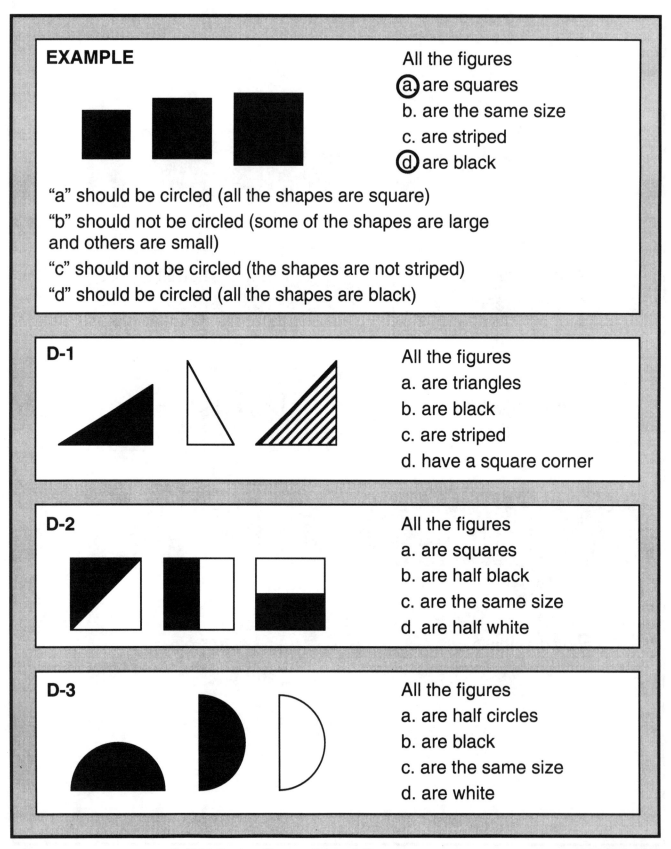

EXAMPLE

All the figures

ⓐ are squares

b. are the same size

c. are striped

ⓓ are black

"a" should be circled (all the shapes are square)

"b" should not be circled (some of the shapes are large and others are small)

"c" should not be circled (the shapes are not striped)

"d" should be circled (all the shapes are black)

D-1

All the figures

a. are triangles

b. are black

c. are striped

d. have a square corner

D-2

All the figures

a. are squares

b. are half black

c. are the same size

d. are half white

D-3

All the figures

a. are half circles

b. are black

c. are the same size

d. are white

DESCRIBING CLASSES

DIRECTIONS: Circle the letter in front of each true statement.

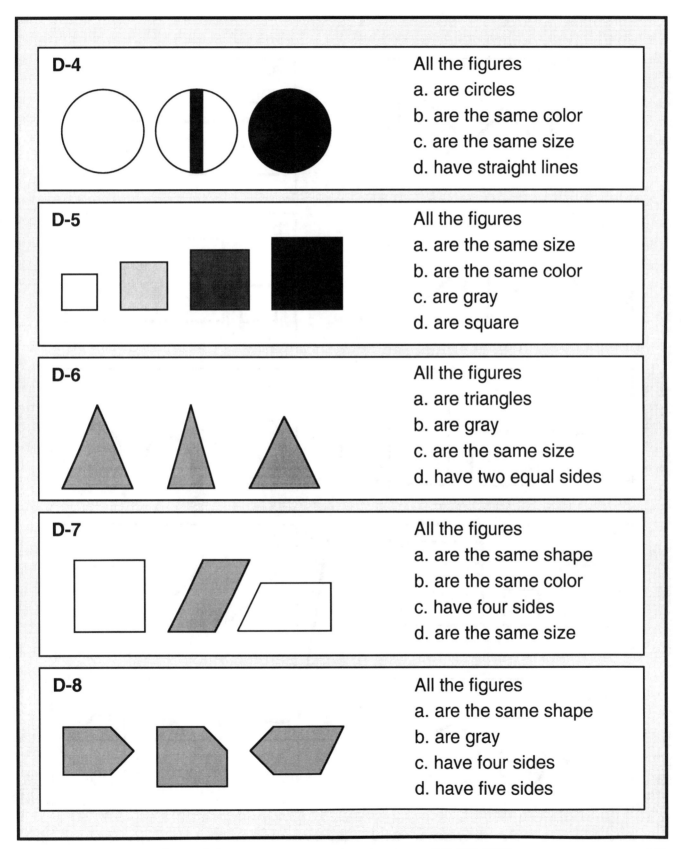

D-4

All the figures
a. are circles
b. are the same color
c. are the same size
d. have straight lines

D-5

All the figures
a. are the same size
b. are the same color
c. are gray
d. are square

D-6

All the figures
a. are triangles
b. are gray
c. are the same size
d. have two equal sides

D-7

All the figures
a. are the same shape
b. are the same color
c. have four sides
d. are the same size

D-8

All the figures
a. are the same shape
b. are gray
c. have four sides
d. have five sides

MATCHING CLASSES BY SHAPE

DIRECTIONS: Draw a line from each group of shapes on the left to a group on the right that belongs to the same class.

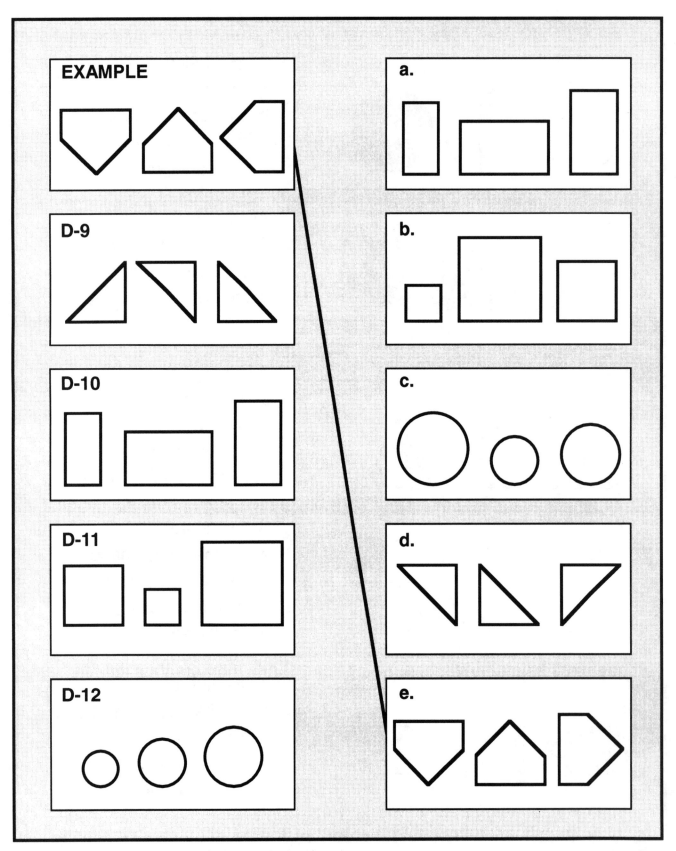

MATCHING CLASSES BY SHAPE

DIRECTIONS: Draw a line from each group on the left to a group on the right that belongs to the same class.

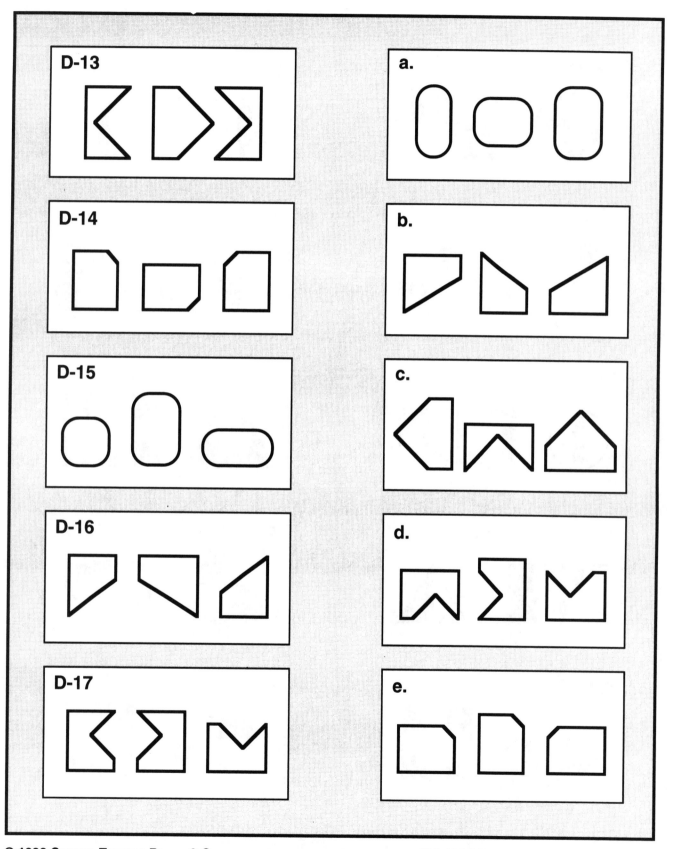

MATCHING CLASSES BY PATTERN

DIRECTIONS: Draw a line from each group on the left to a group on the right that belongs to the same class.

CLASSIFYING MORE THAN ONE WAY—MATCHING

DIRECTIONS: Match the figure in each box on the left to all the classes on the right to which it can belong. Write the letters of the correct classes on the line next to the figure. For example, the gray triangle in the example belongs to both class *c* (the white class) and class *f* (the triangle class).

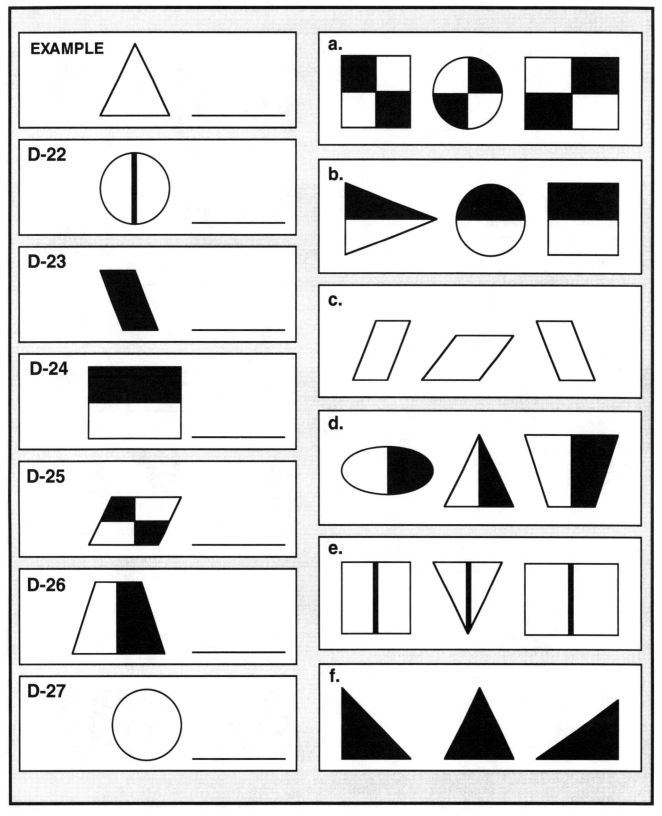

CLASSIFYING MORE THAN ONE WAY—MATCHING

DIRECTIONS: Match the figure in each box to all the classes on the right to which it can belong. You can match the figure by one or more characteristics. Write the letters of all the classes to which it can belong.

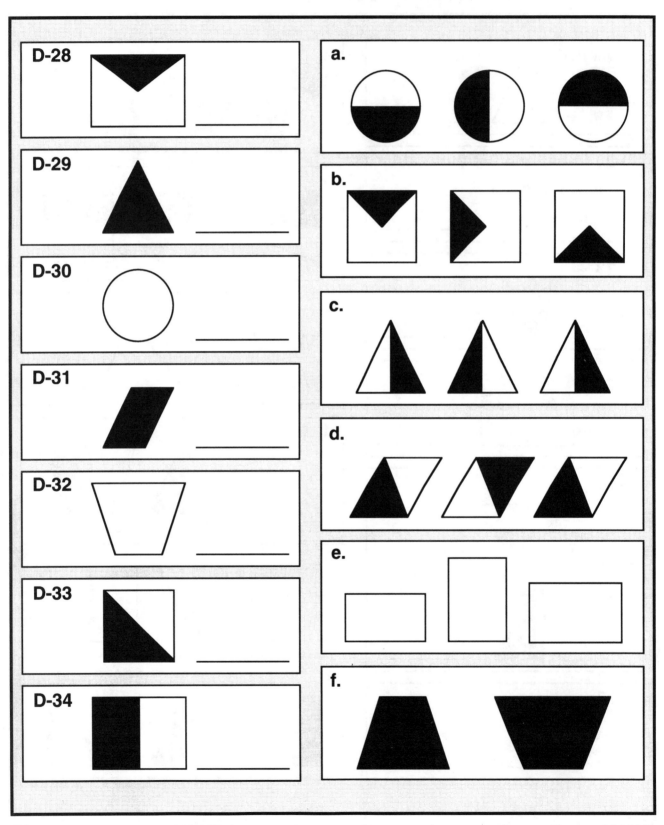

CHANGING CHARACTERISTICS—SELECT

DIRECTIONS: Look at each pair of figures below. In the answer column, circle "S" if the characteristic is the same for both figures. Circle "D" if the characteristic is different.

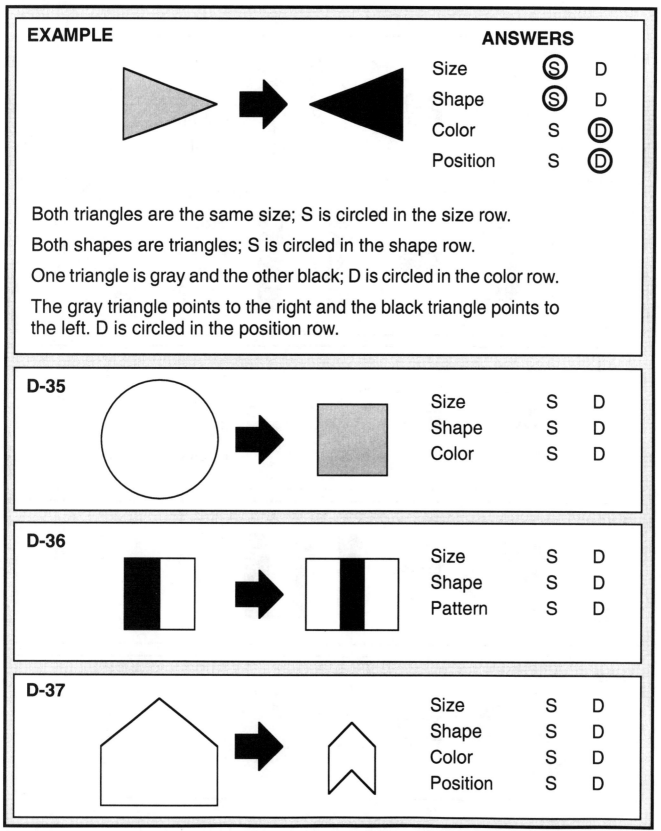

EXAMPLE   **ANSWERS**

Size   Ⓢ   D
Shape   Ⓢ   D
Color   S   Ⓓ
Position   S   Ⓓ

Both triangles are the same size; S is circled in the size row.

Both shapes are triangles; S is circled in the shape row.

One triangle is gray and the other black; D is circled in the color row.

The gray triangle points to the right and the black triangle points to the left. D is circled in the position row.

D-35

Size   S   D
Shape   S   D
Color   S   D

D-36

Size   S   D
Shape   S   D
Pattern S   D

D-37

Size   S   D
Shape   S   D
Color   S   D
Position S   D

CHANGING CHARACTERISTICS—SELECT

DIRECTIONS: Look at each pair of figures below. In the answer column, circle "S" if the characteristic is the same for both figures. Circle "D" if the characteristic is different.

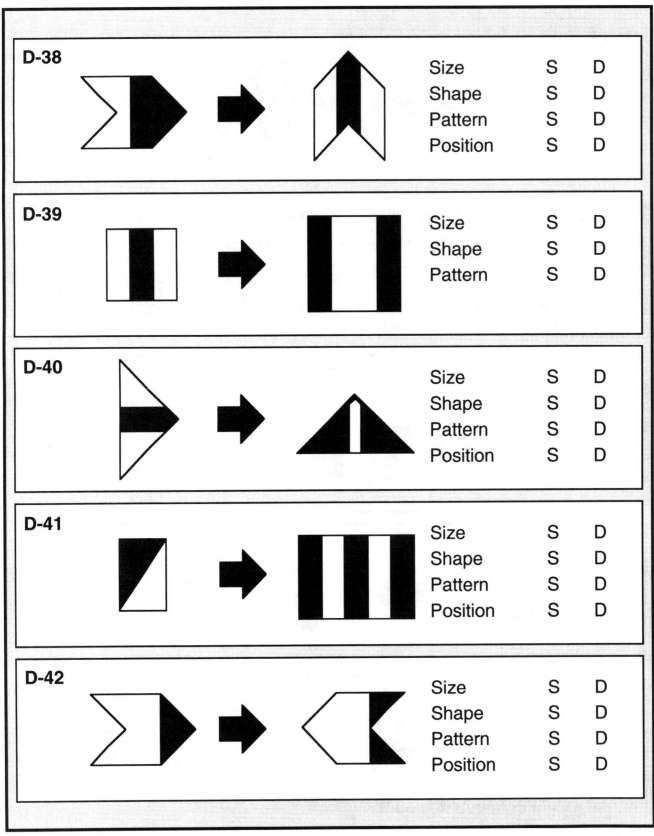

D-38			
	Size	S	D
	Shape	S	D
	Pattern	S	D
	Position	S	D

D-39			
	Size	S	D
	Shape	S	D
	Pattern	S	D

D-40			
	Size	S	D
	Shape	S	D
	Pattern	S	D
	Position	S	D

D-41			
	Size	S	D
	Shape	S	D
	Pattern	S	D
	Position	S	D

D-42			
	Size	S	D
	Shape	S	D
	Pattern	S	D
	Position	S	D

CHANGING CHARACTERISTICS—SUPPLY

DIRECTIONS: Look at the figure on the left. Read the directions and then draw another figure with the characteristics described in the instructions.

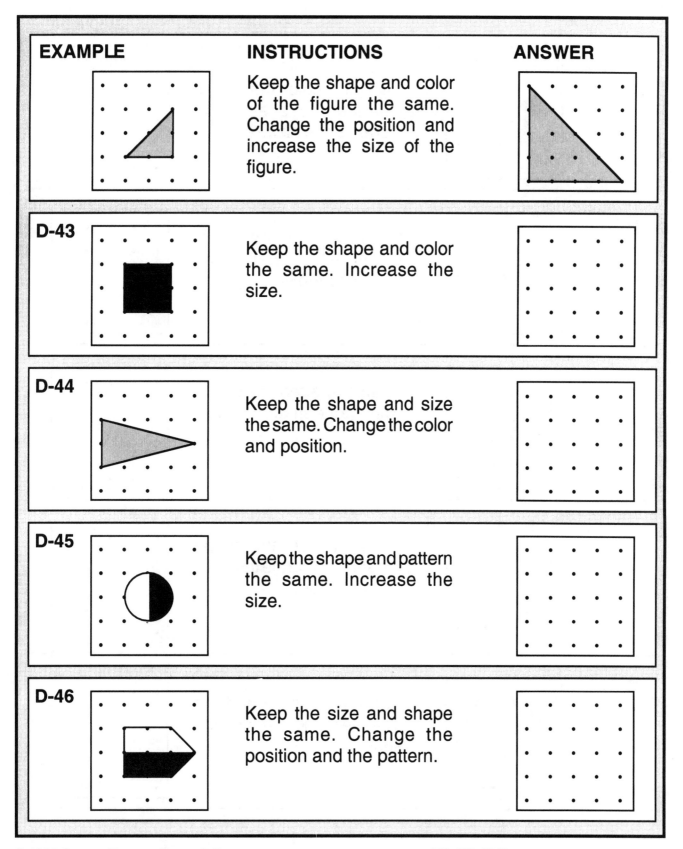

EXAMPLE	INSTRUCTIONS	ANSWER
	Keep the shape and color of the figure the same. Change the position and increase the size of the figure.	
D-43	Keep the shape and color the same. Increase the size.	
D-44	Keep the shape and size the same. Change the color and position.	
D-45	Keep the shape and pattern the same. Increase the size.	
D-46	Keep the size and shape the same. Change the position and the pattern.	

CHANGING CHARACTERISTICS—SUPPLY

DIRECTIONS: Look at the figure on the left. Read the directions and then draw another figure with the characteristics described in the instructions on the right.

D-47

Keep the color the same. Change the shape and increase the size.

D-48

Keep the color the same. Change the shape and decrease the size.

D-49

Keep the pattern the same. Change the shape and size.

D-50

Keep the size and shape the same. Change the color and direction.

D-51

Keep the pattern and the size the same. Change the shape.

DRAW ANOTHER

DIRECTIONS: In the box on the right, draw another figure that belongs to the group on the left.

DRAW ANOTHER

DIRECTIONS: In the box on the right, draw another figure that belongs to the group on the left.

D-57

D-58

D-59

D-60

D-61

CLASSIFYING BY SHAPE—SORTING

DIRECTIONS: Sort this group of shapes according to the number of sides each shape has. Copy the shapes in the correct boxes; use the dot grid to help you draw them accurately.

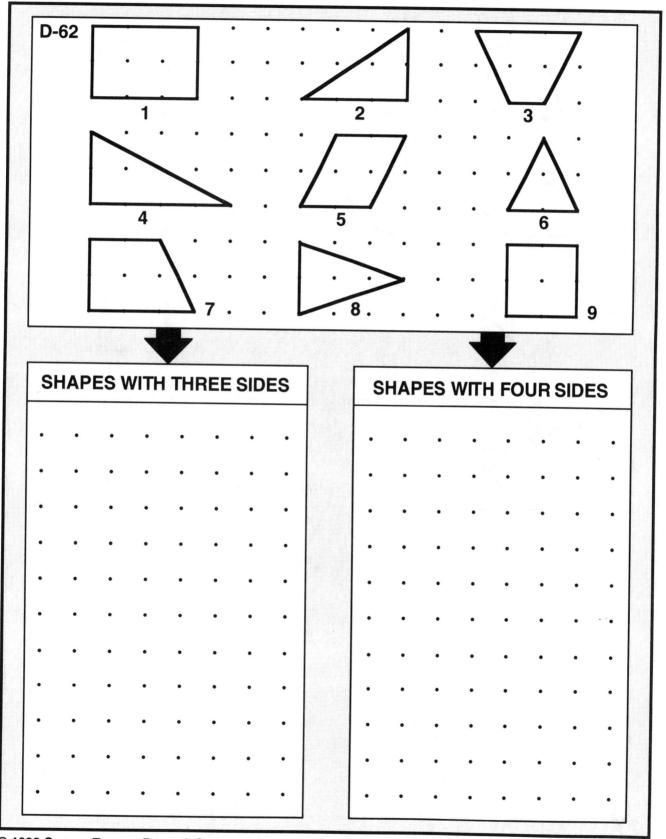

D-62

1
2
3
4
5
6
7
8
9

SHAPES WITH THREE SIDES

SHAPES WITH FOUR SIDES

CLASSIFYING BY SHAPE—SORTING

DIRECTIONS: Sort this group of shapes according to the number of sides each shape has. Below each shape is a number. Put the number of each shape in the correct box.

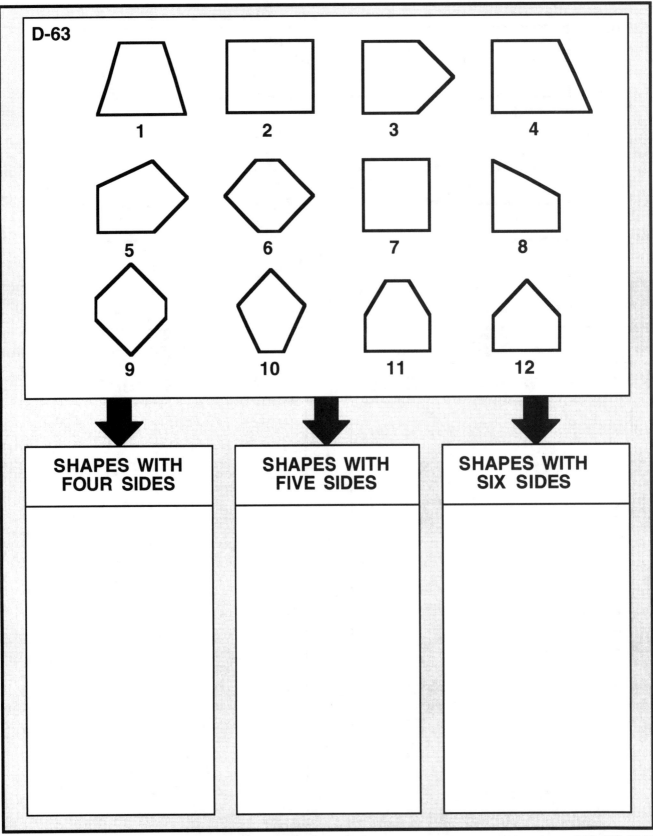

SHAPES WITH FOUR SIDES	SHAPES WITH FIVE SIDES	SHAPES WITH SIX SIDES

CLASSIFYING BY PATTERN—SORTING

DIRECTIONS: Sort this group of shapes according to the patterns drawn on the shapes. Below each shape is a number. Put the number for each shape in the box with the correct matching pattern.

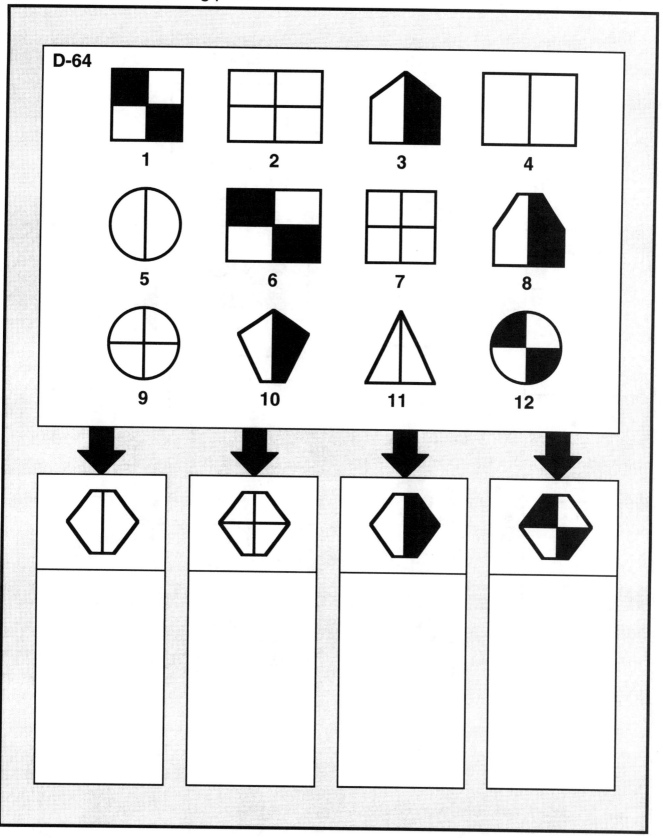

CLASSIFYING MORE THAN ONE WAY—SORTING

DIRECTIONS: Sort this group of shapes according to the number of sides each shape has. Below each shape is a number. Put the number for each shape in the correct sorting boxes; each shape number may go in more than one box.

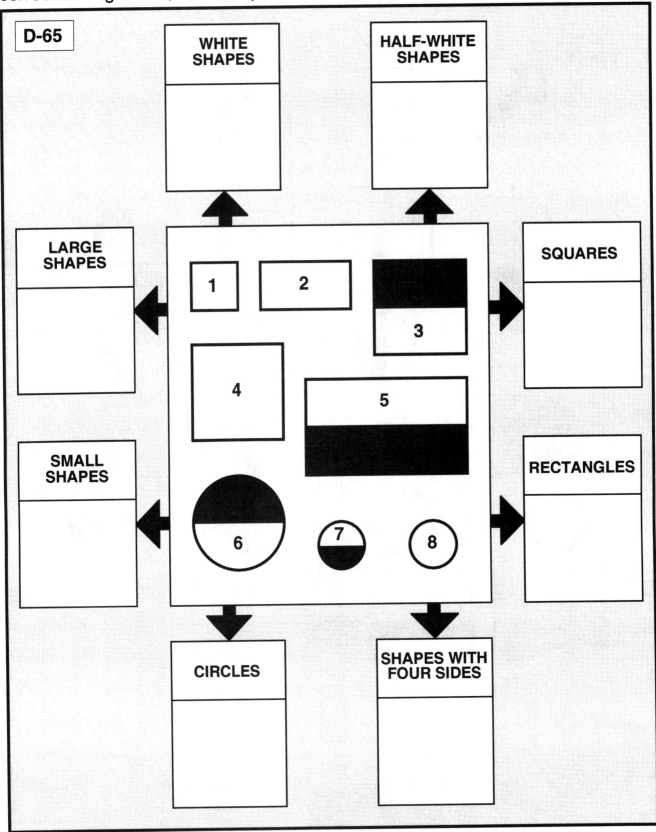

D-65

WHITE SHAPES

HALF-WHITE SHAPES

LARGE SHAPES

SQUARES

SMALL SHAPES

RECTANGLES

CIRCLES

SHAPES WITH FOUR SIDES

1 2 3 4 5 6 7 8

OVERLAPPING CLASSES—INTERSECTIONS

DIRECTIONS: Read the explanation of overlapping classes before going on to the next page.

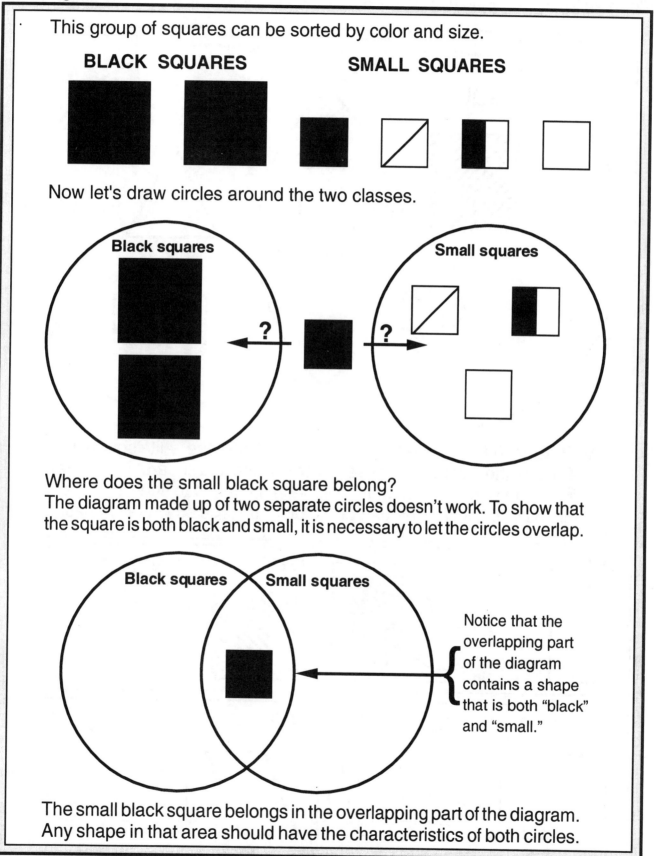

This group of squares can be sorted by color and size.

BLACK SQUARES   **SMALL SQUARES**

Now let's draw circles around the two classes.

Black squares   **Small squares**

?   ?

Where does the small black square belong?
The diagram made up of two separate circles doesn't work. To show that the square is both black and small, it is necessary to let the circles overlap.

Black squares   **Small squares**

Notice that the overlapping part of the diagram contains a shape that is both "black" and "small."

The small black square belongs in the overlapping part of the diagram. Any shape in that area should have the characteristics of both circles.

OVERLAPPING CLASSES—INTERSECTIONS

DIRECTIONS: Using the information in the top diagram, darken part of the small, overlapping circles diagram next to each figure to show where that figure would belong.

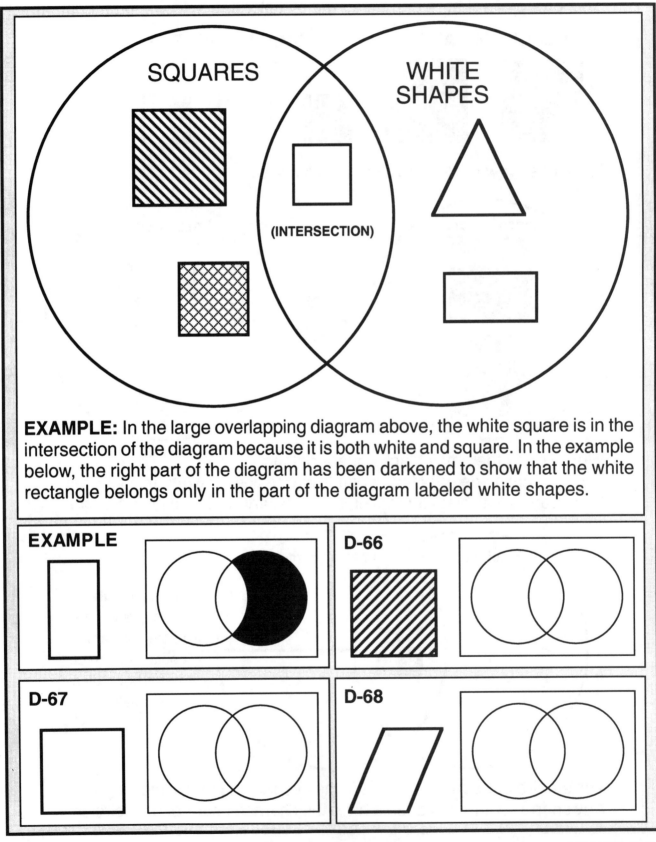

EXAMPLE: In the large overlapping diagram above, the white square is in the intersection of the diagram because it is both white and square. In the example below, the right part of the diagram has been darkened to show that the white rectangle belongs only in the part of the diagram labeled white shapes.

© 1998 CRITICAL THINKING BOOKS & SOFTWARE• WWW.CRITICALTHINKING.COM • 800-458-4849

OVERLAPPING CLASSES—INTERSECTIONS

DIRECTIONS: Three regions are labeled on the large overlapping classes diagram. "I" is the overlapping part or intersection. On the line next to each small shape below, write an "A," "B," or "I" to indicate where the shape belongs. In the example, the striped triangle belongs in the left ("A") region of the diagram.

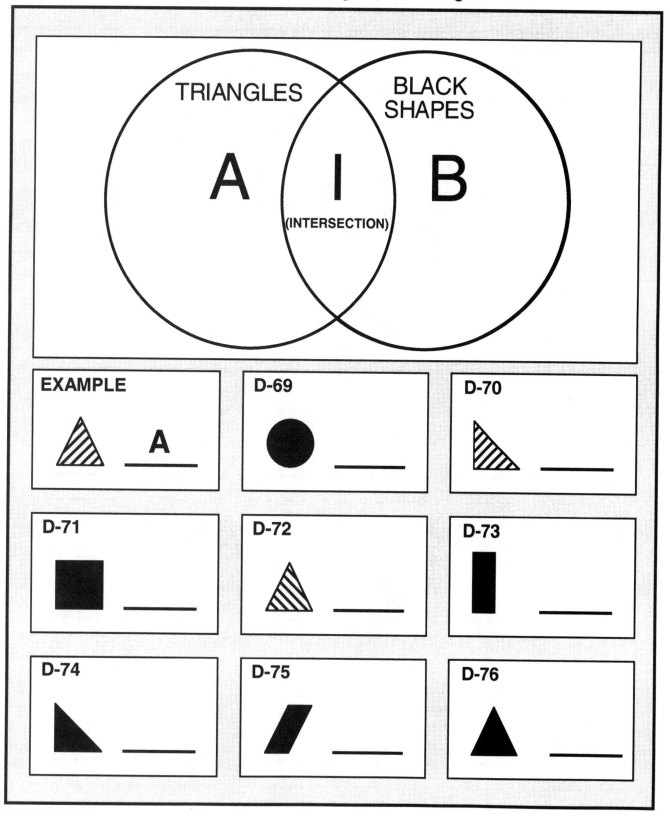

OVERLAPPING CLASSES—INTERSECTIONS

DIRECTIONS: Four regions are labeled on the large overlapping classes diagram. "O" is outside the overlapping circles. On the line next to each small shape below, write an "A," "B," "I," or "O" to indicate where the shape belongs. In the example, the black triangle belongs in the outside ("O") region of the diagram because it is not striped and has three sides, not four.

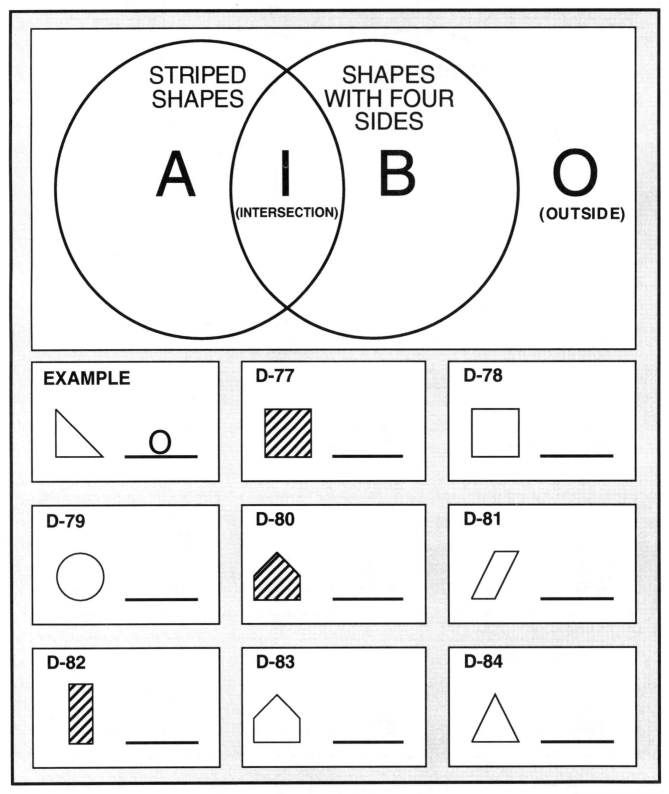

OVERLAPPING CLASSES—INTERSECTIONS

DIRECTIONS: Look at the shapes in circles 1 and 2 to answer questions **D-85** through **D-87**. In exercises **D-88** to **D-93**, write an "A," "B," "I," or "O" on the line to indicate where each shape belongs.

D-85 Circle 1 contains the class _____.

D-86 Circle 2 contains the class _____.

D-87 The intersection contains the class _____.

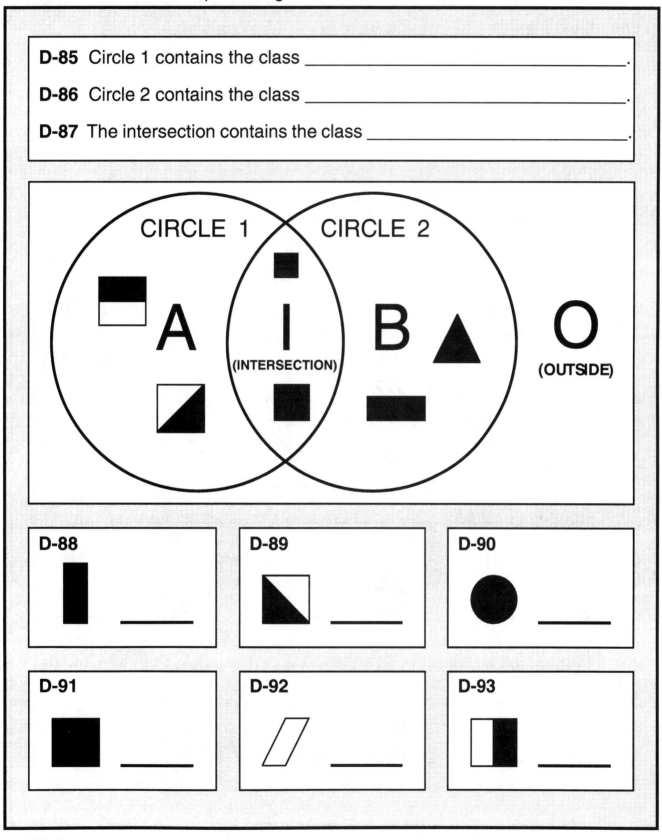

OVERLAPPING CLASSES—INTERSECTIONS

DIRECTIONS: Look at the shapes in the intersection (I) and Circle 2 to answer questions **D-94** through **D-96**. In exercises **D-97** to **D-102**, write an "A," "B," "I," or "O" on the line next to indicate where each shape belongs.

D-94 Circle 1 contains the class _____.

D-95 Circle 2 contains the class _____.

D-96 The intersection contains the class _____.

OVERLAPPING CLASSES—INTERSECTIONS

DIRECTIONS: Look at the shapes in the intersection (I) and Circle 2 to answer questions **D-103** through **D-105**. In exercises **D-106** to **D-111**, write an "A," "B," " I," or "O" on the line to indicate where each shape belongs.

D-103 Circle 1 contains the class _____.

D-104 Circle 2 contains the class _____.

D-105 The intersection contains the class _____.

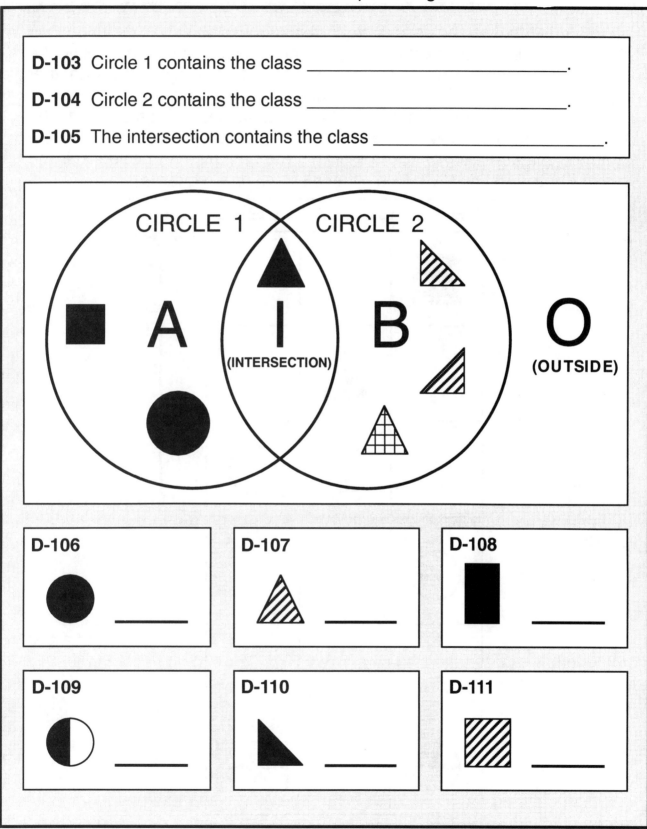

D-106 _____

D-107 _____

D-108 _____

D-109 _____

D-110 _____

D-111 _____

OVERLAPPING CLASSES—MATRIX

DIRECTIONS: Using the given figures as clues, decide which characteristic is true for each row and which characteristic is true for each column. Draw in the missing figures.

A matrix diagram can be used to organize a group of objects to describe their characteristics in more than one way. All the objects in a row must have the same characteristic, and all the objects in a column must share another characteristic. (Note: Rows go across and columns go up and down.)

Each figure has two characteristics. For example, in the first matrix the figure in the top corner is square and black. The figures in each row share a common characteristic, as do the figures in each column. So the figures in the top row of the first matrix will be either all black or all squares.

Rows ⟶

Columns

D-112

D-113

OVERLAPPING CLASSES—MATRIX

DIRECTIONS: Complete each matrix.

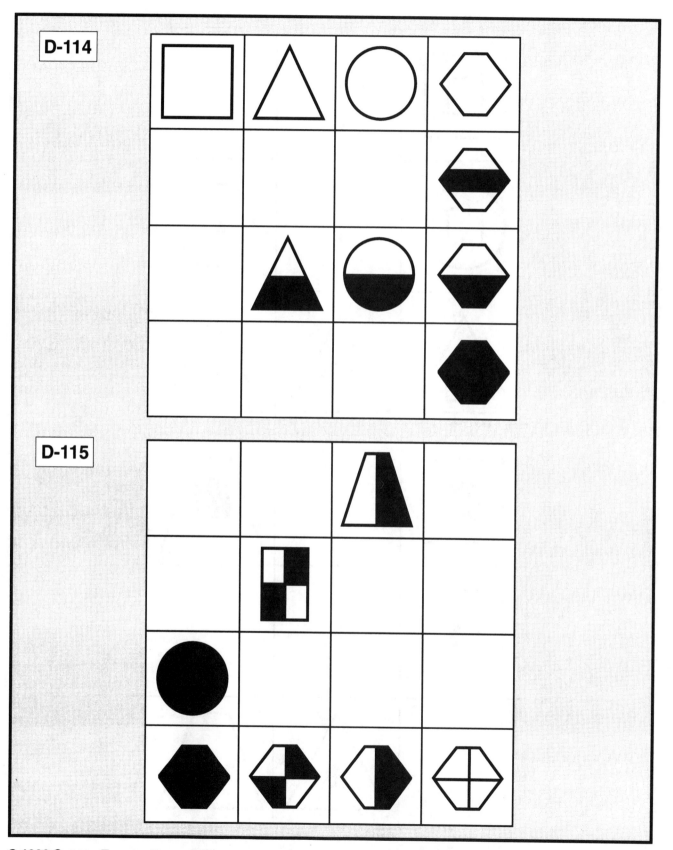

OVERLAPPING CLASSES—MATRIX

DIRECTIONS: Complete each matrix.

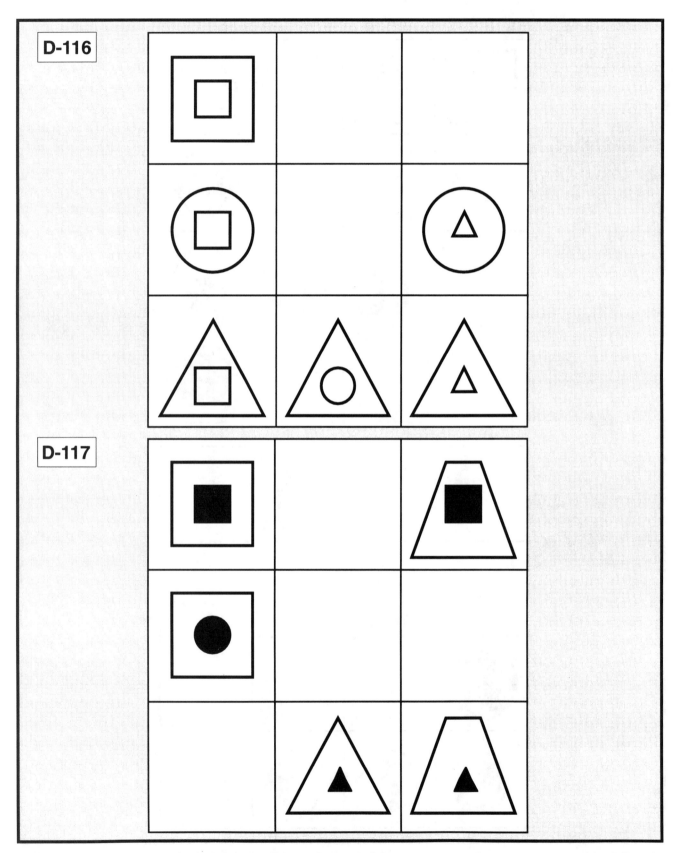

DEDUCE THE CLASS

DIRECTIONS: In the next group of exercises, you will continue to classify figures, but now you must determine the characteristics of the class. Look at the figures that belong to the class. Then look at the figures that do **not** belong to that class.

By looking at the clue figures, decide what is true of the members of the group or class. You may wish to look at the number of straight lines and the number of curved lines in each figure.

After you have decided (deduced) the characteristics of the class, you will decide which of the given figures belong to that class.

HERE ARE THE STEPS:

1. Carefully study the "clue" figures.

2. Decide (deduce) the characteristics of the "clue figures" by asking yourself:

   a. How are the clue figures alike?

   b. How are the clue figures different?

3. Look at the figures in the questions and decide if they belong in the class.

DEDUCE THE CLASS

DIRECTIONS: Use the five clue figures to deduce what a quad is. Then answer the questions yes or no.

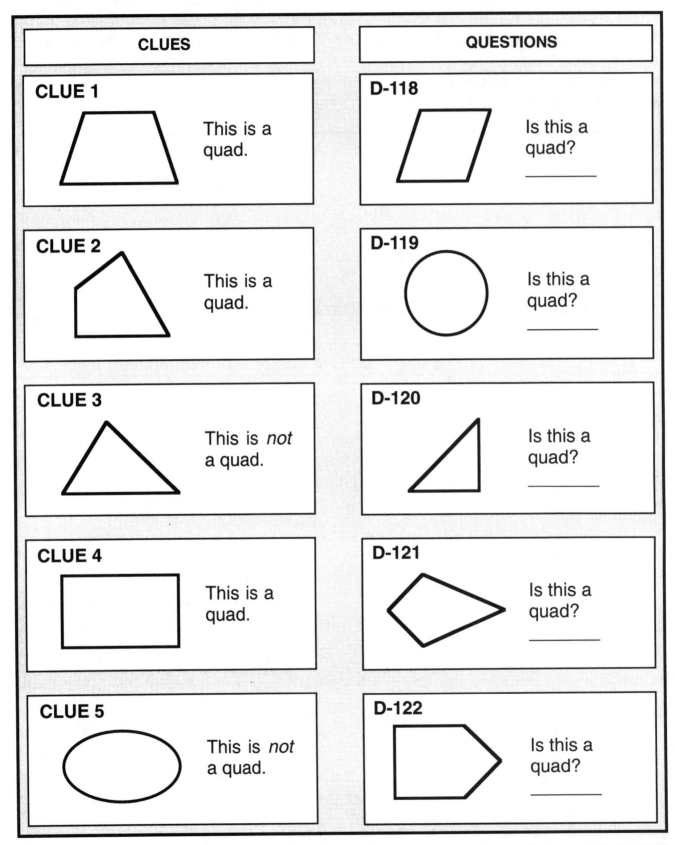

CLUES	QUESTIONS
CLUE 1 This is a quad.	**D-118** Is this a quad? _____
CLUE 2 This is a quad.	**D-119** Is this a quad? _____
CLUE 3 This is *not* a quad.	**D-120** Is this a quad? _____
CLUE 4 This is a quad.	**D-121** Is this a quad? _____
CLUE 5 This is *not* a quad.	**D-122** Is this a quad?

DEDUCE THE CLASS

DIRECTIONS: Use the five clue figures to deduce what a penta is. Then answer the questions yes or no.

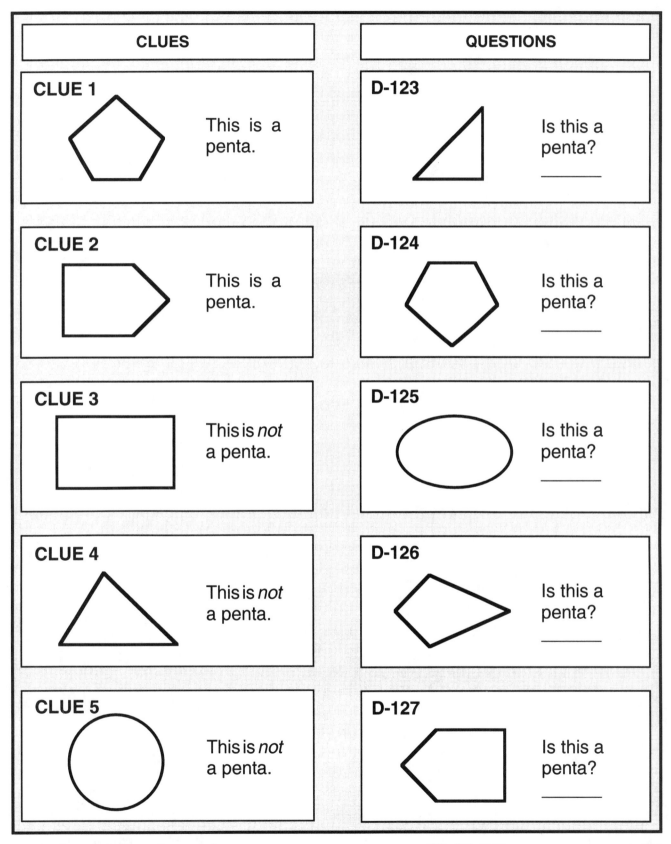

CLUES	QUESTIONS
CLUE 1 This is a penta.	**D-123** Is this a penta? _____
CLUE 2 This is a penta.	**D-124** Is this a penta? _____
CLUE 3 This is *not* a penta.	**D-125** Is this a penta? _____
CLUE 4 This is *not* a penta.	**D-126** Is this a penta? _____
CLUE 5 This is *not* a penta.	**D-127** Is this a penta? _____

CHAPTER FIVE

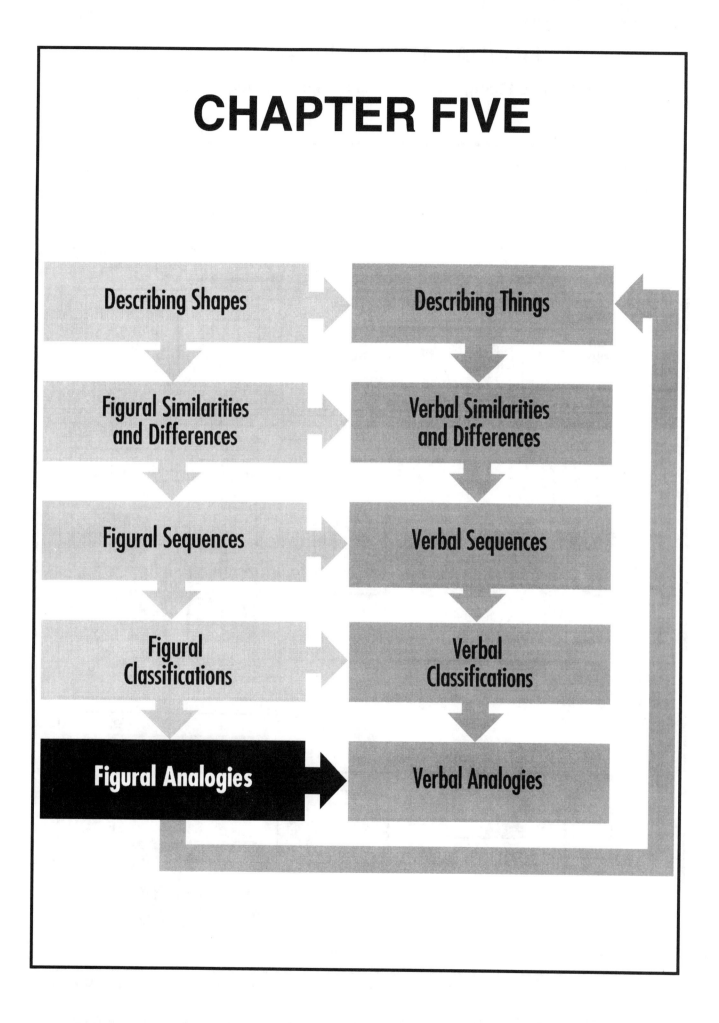

Describing Shapes → Describing Things

Figural Similarities and Differences → Verbal Similarities and Differences

Figural Sequences → Verbal Sequences

Figural Classifications → Verbal Classifications

Figural Analogies → Verbal Analogies

FIGURAL ANALOGIES—SELECT

DIRECTIONS: Circle the figure that completes the analogy.

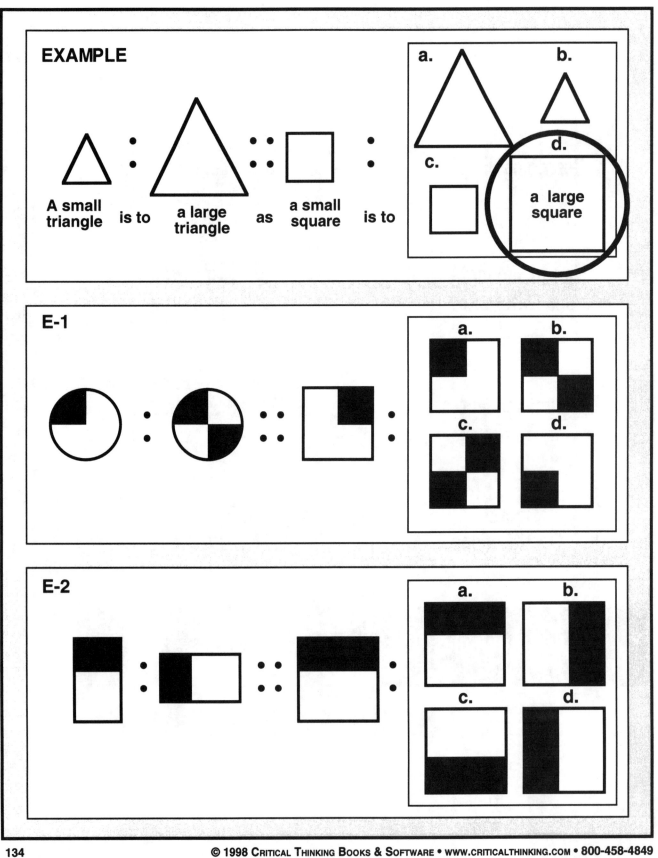

FIGURAL ANALOGIES—SELECT

DIRECTIONS: Circle the figure that completes the analogy.

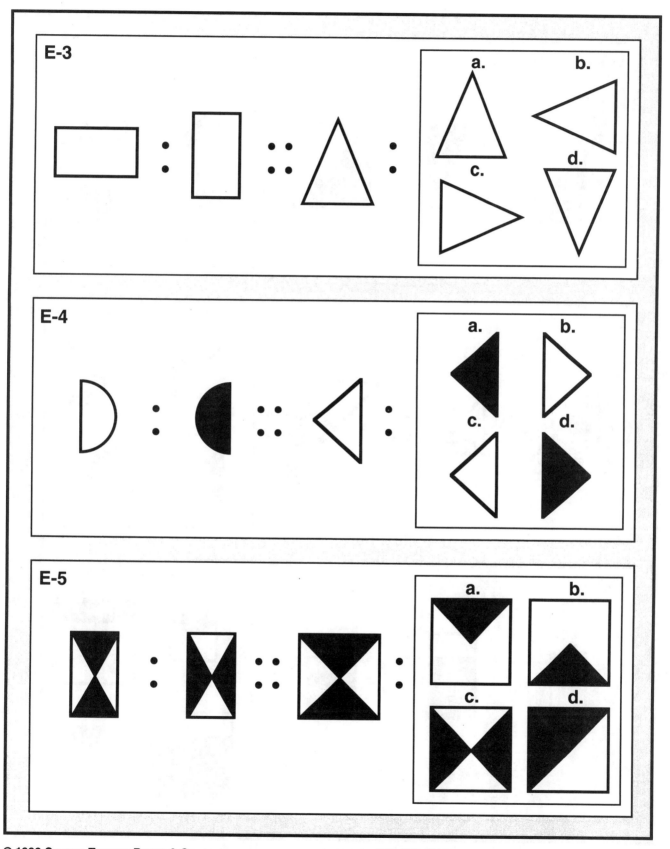

FIGURAL ANALOGIES—SELECT

DIRECTIONS: Circle the figure that completes the analogy.

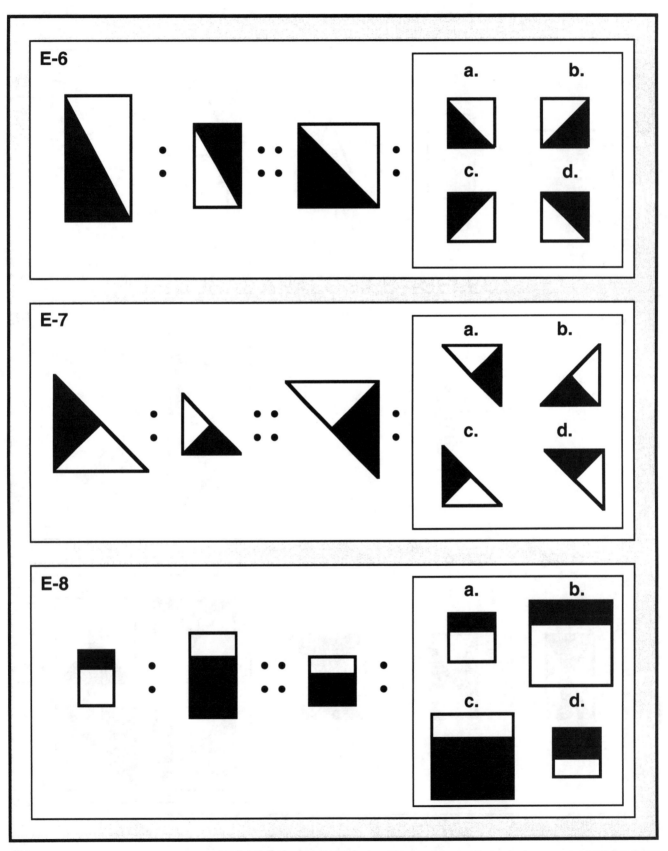

FIGURAL ANALOGIES—SELECT

DIRECTIONS: Circle the figure that completes the analogy.

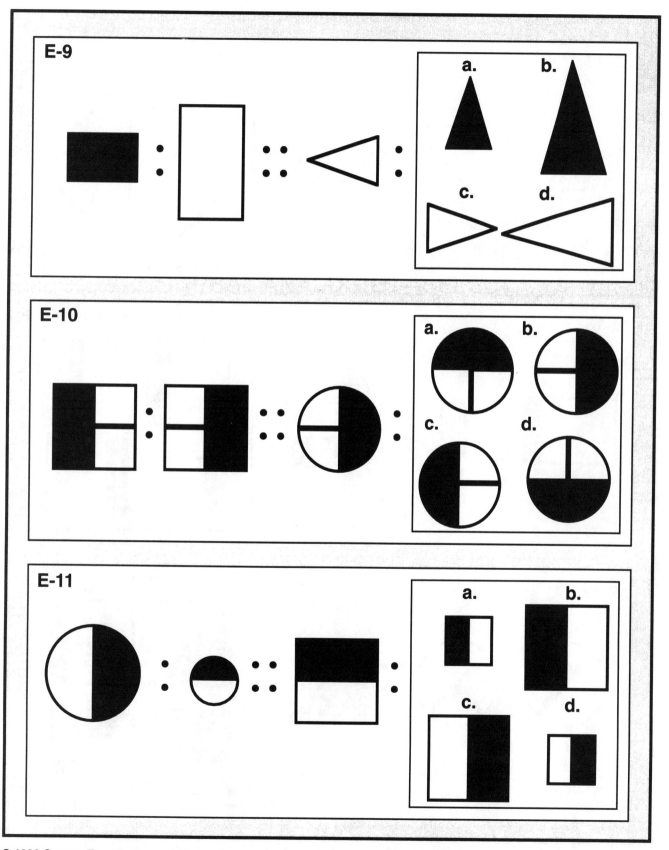

FIGURAL ANALOGIES—SELECT

DIRECTIONS: Circle the figure that completes the analogy.

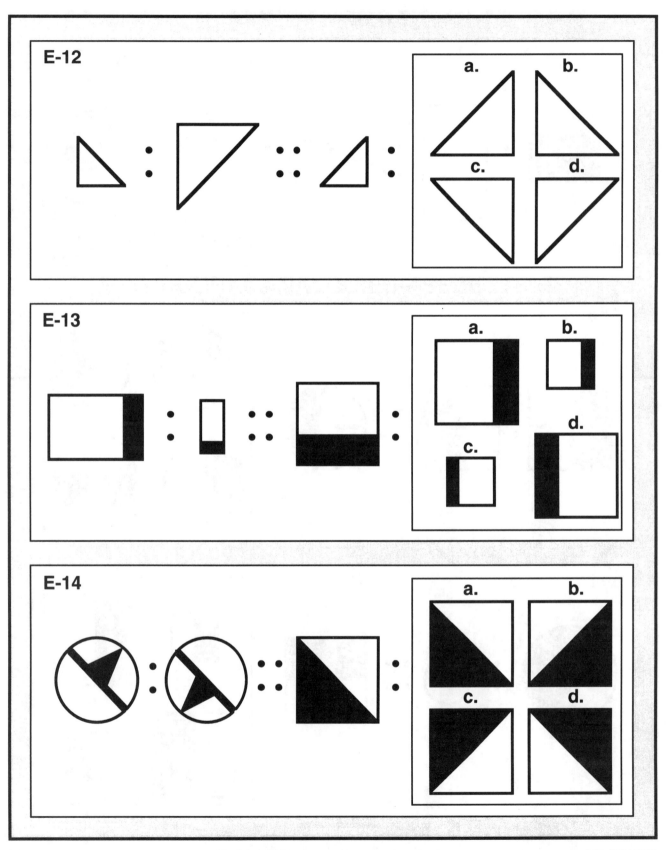

FIGURAL ANALOGIES—SELECT A PAIR

DIRECTIONS: Draw a line between the pairs that correctly form an analogy, A : B :: C : D. Remember, in an analogy both pairs must be related in the same way.

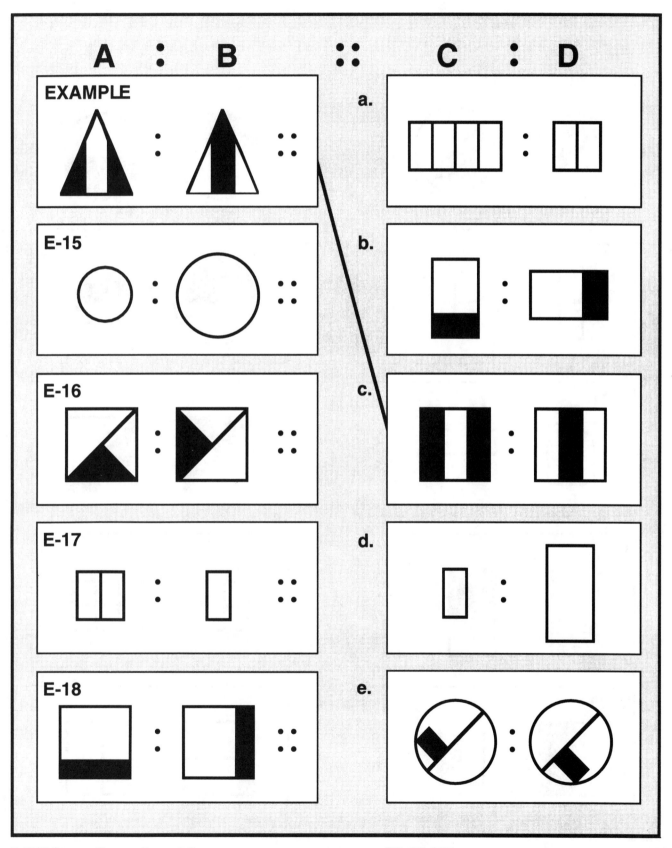

FIGURAL ANALOGIES—SELECT A PAIR

DIRECTIONS: Draw a line between the pairs that correctly form an analogy, A : B ::
C : D. Remember, in an analogy both pairs must be related in the same way.

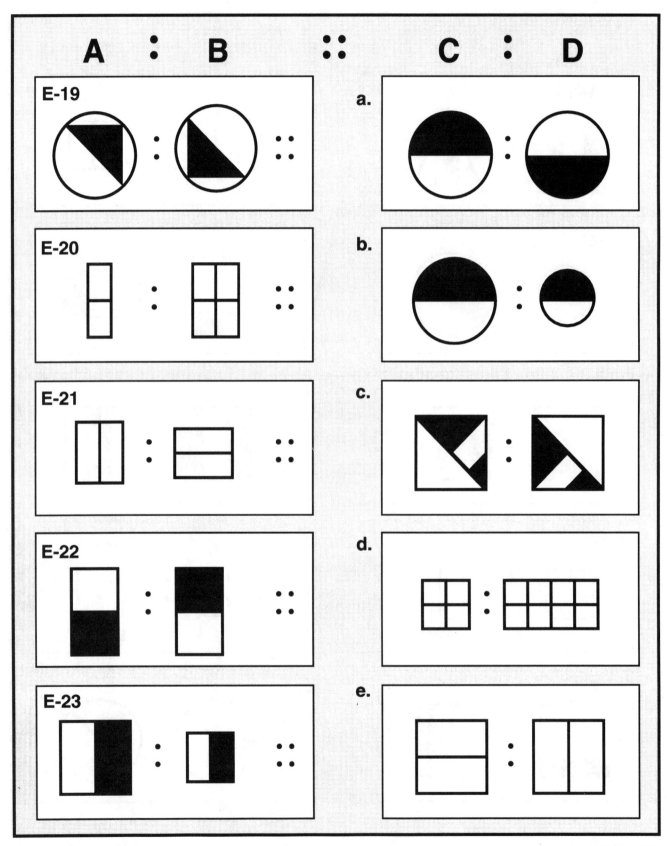

DESCRIBING TYPES OF FIGURAL ANALOGIES

DIRECTIONS: In the exercises you have just done, there are several types of analogous relationships. These relationships can be described as follows:

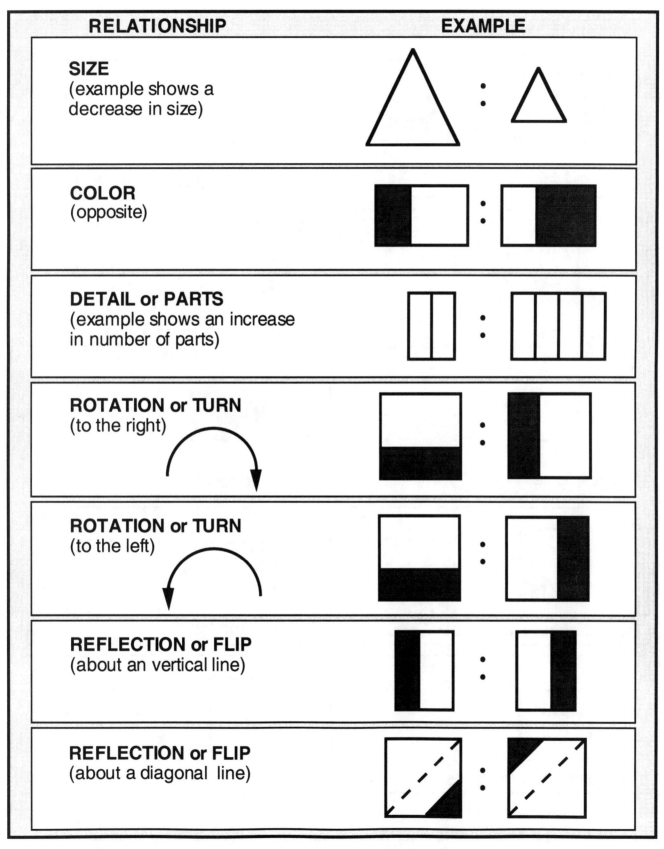

COMPLETE THE PAIR

DIRECTIONS: Using the grid as a guideline, draw a figure which illustrates the relationship written below each box.

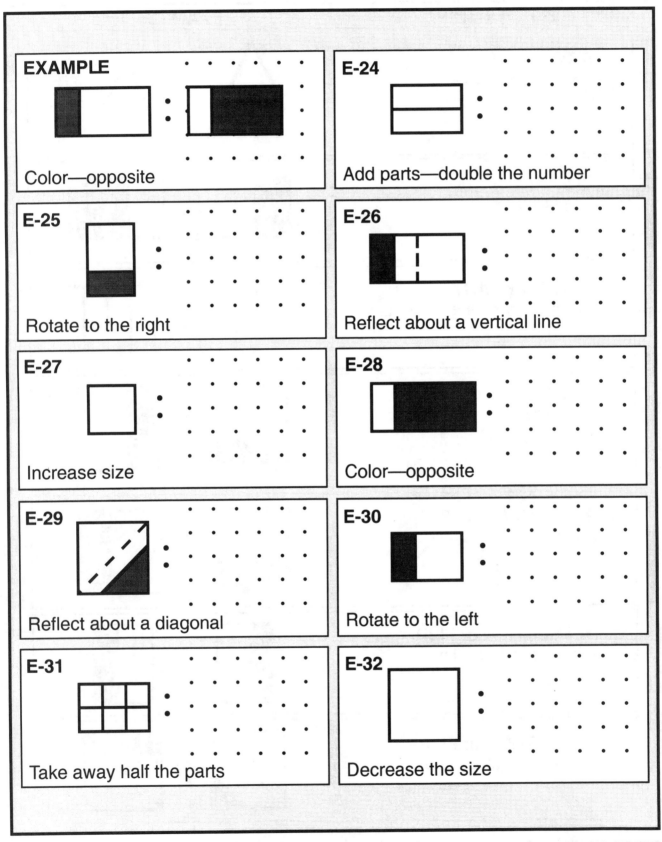

EXAMPLE

Color—opposite

E-24

Add parts—double the number

E-25

Rotate to the right

E-26

Reflect about a vertical line

E-27

Increase size

E-28

Color—opposite

E-29

Reflect about a diagonal

E-30

Rotate to the left

E-31

Take away half the parts

E-32

Decrease the size

FIGURAL ANALOGIES—COMPLETE

DIRECTIONS: Shade in the last figure in each row so that the figural analogies are complete.

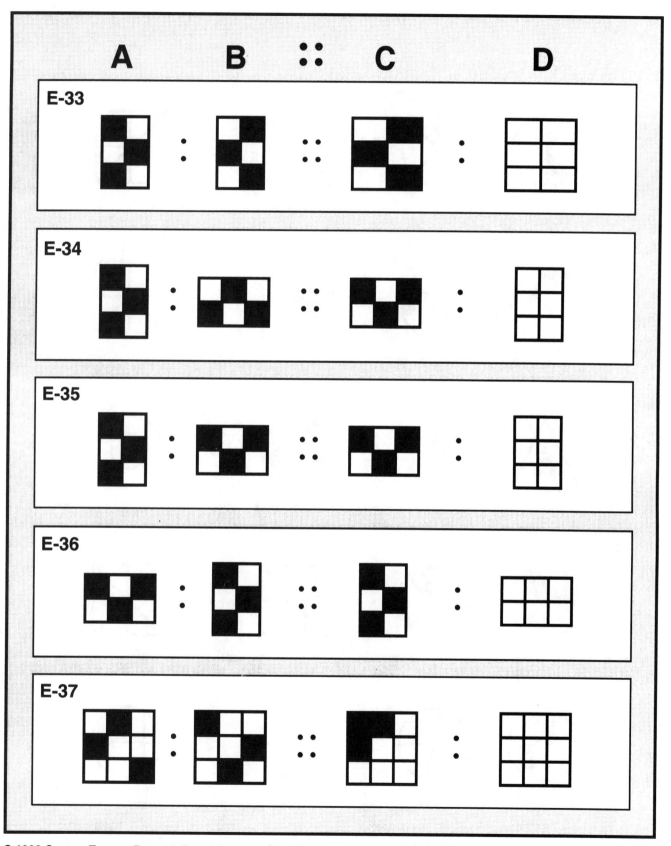

FIGURAL ANALOGIES—COMPLETE

DIRECTIONS: Shade in the last figure in each row so that the analogies are complete.

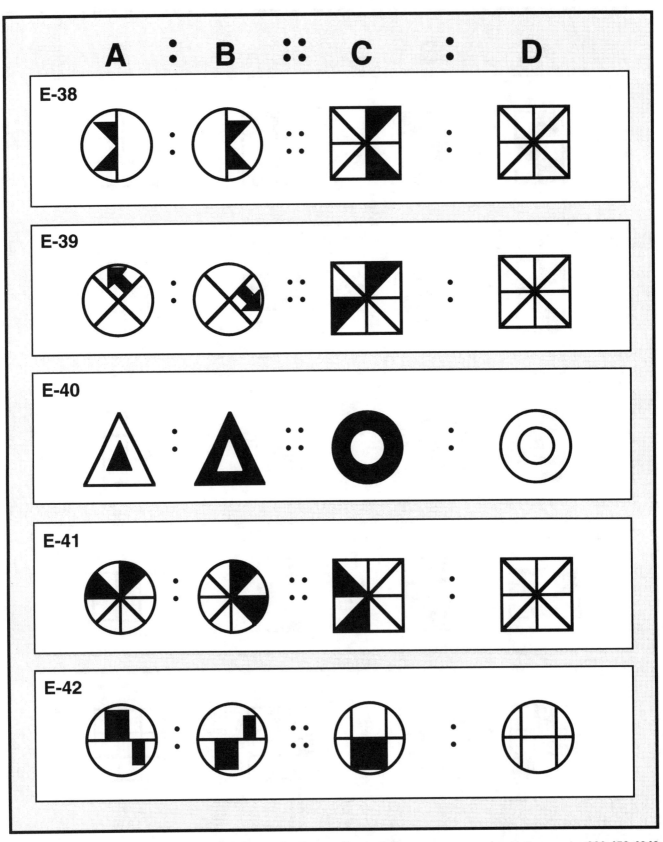

FIGURAL ANALOGIES—COMPLETE

DIRECTIONS: Shade in the last figure in each row so that the analogies are complete.

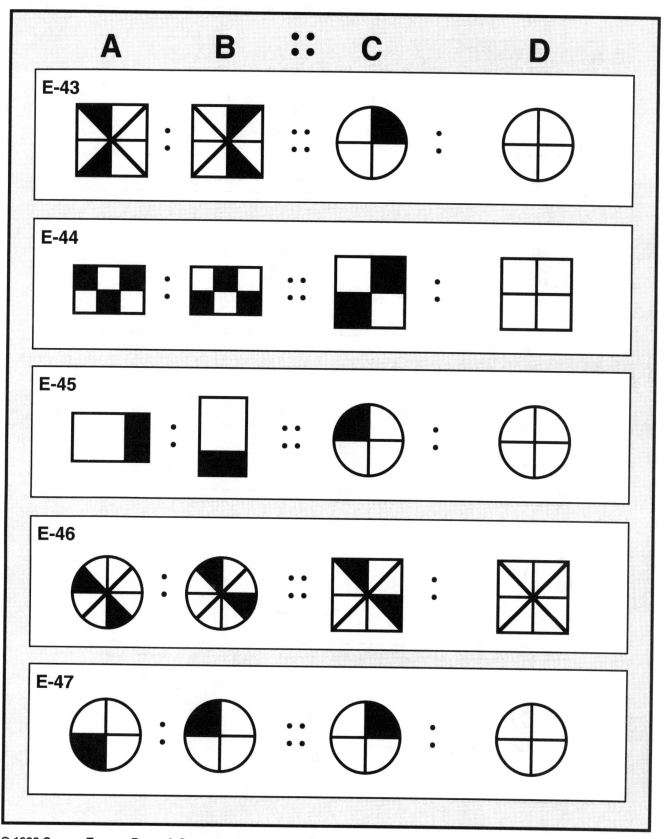

FIGURAL ANALOGIES—SUPPLY

DIRECTIONS: Using the dot grid, draw in a figure to complete each analogy.

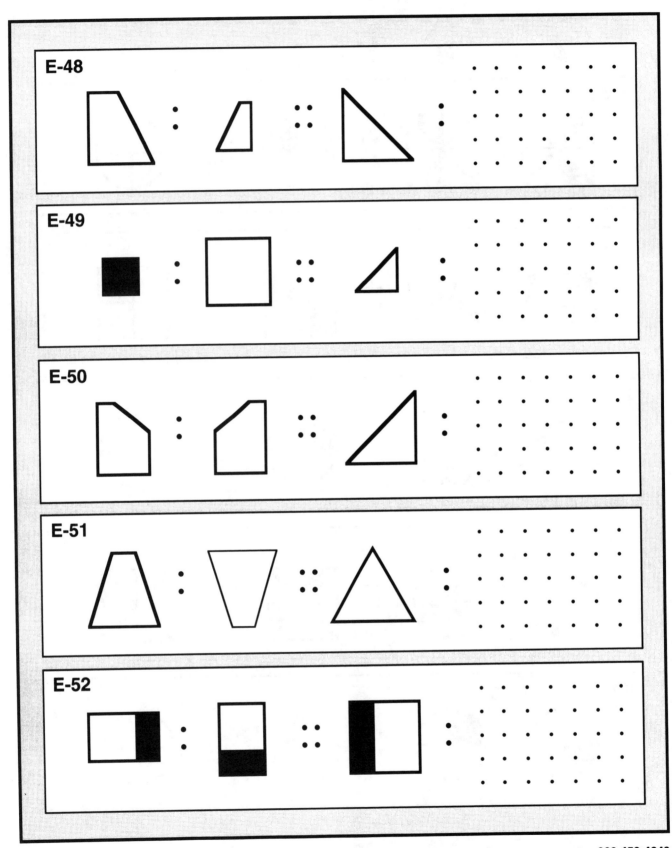

FIGURAL ANALOGIES—SUPPLY

DIRECTIONS: Using the dot grid, draw in a figure to complete each analogy.

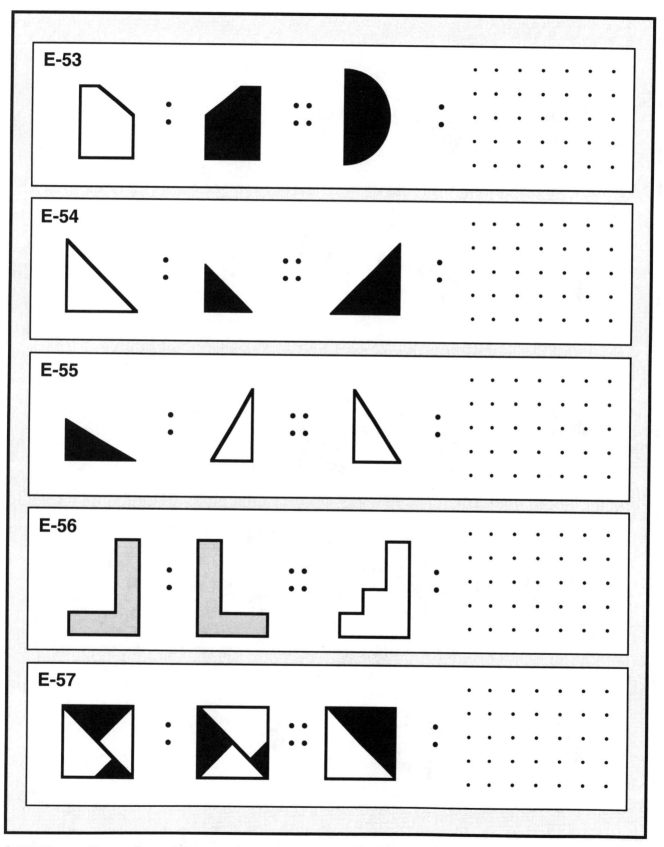

FIGURAL ANALOGIES—SUPPLY

DIRECTIONS: Using the dot grid, draw in a figure to complete each analogy.

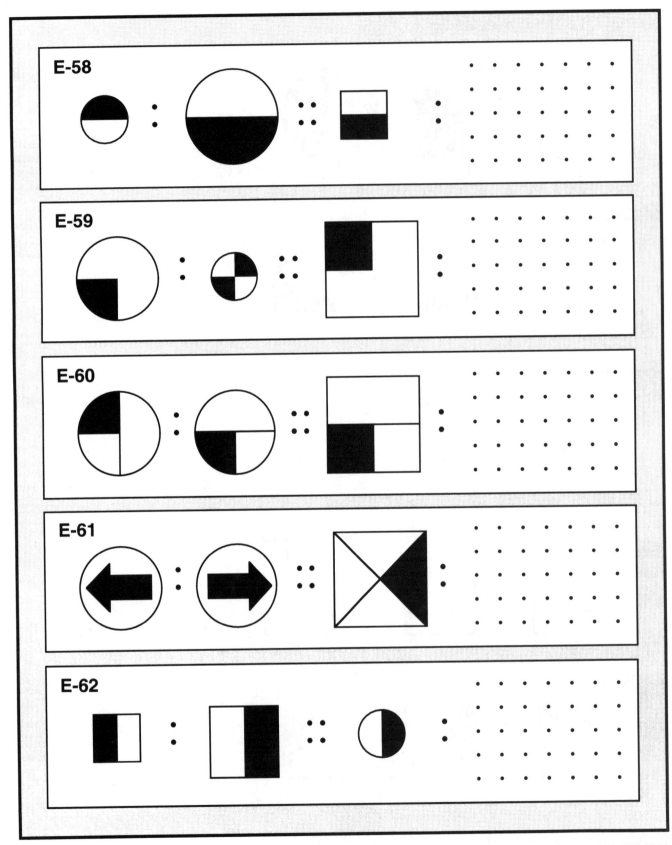

FIGURAL ANALOGIES—SUPPLY A PAIR

DIRECTIONS: Using the dot grid, draw the last two figures, "C" and "D," to complete the analogy. Figures "C" and "D" should be related to each other in the same way that the first two figures, "A" and "B," are related.

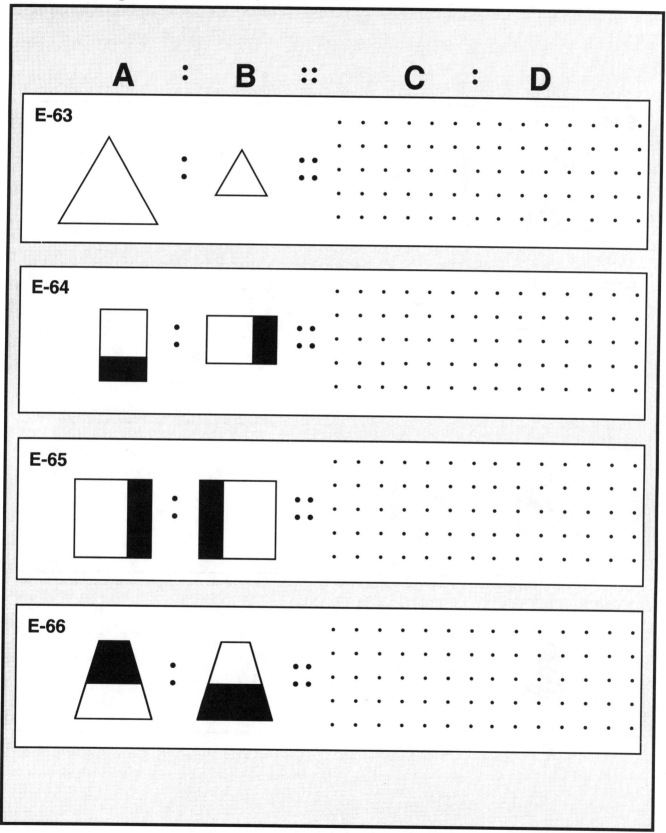

FIGURAL ANALOGIES—SUPPLY A PAIR

DIRECTIONS: Using the dot grid, draw the last two figures, "C" and "D," to complete the analogy. Figures "C" and "D" should be related to each other in the same way that the first two figures, "A" and "B," are related.

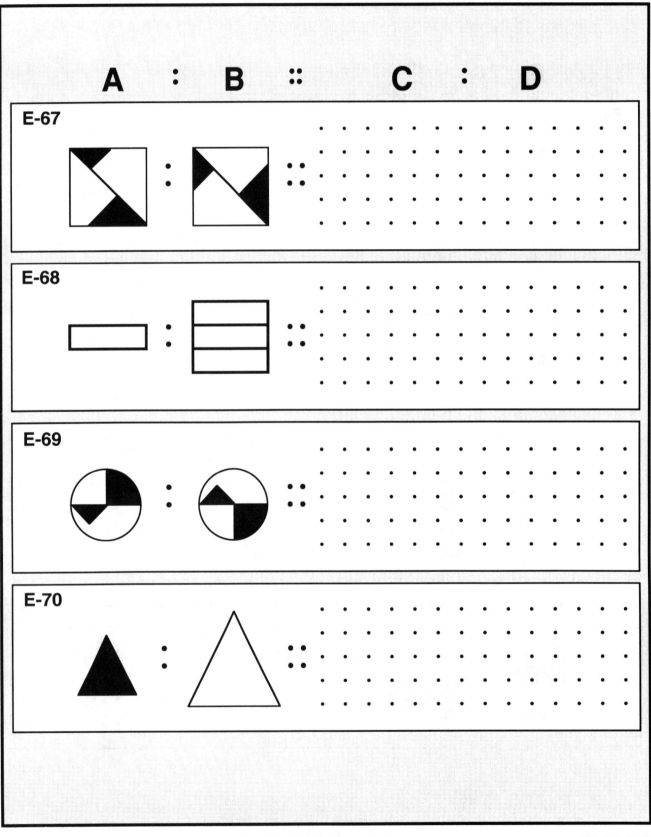

FIGURAL ANALOGIES—FOLLOW THE RULE

DIRECTIONS: Read the rule in each box. Complete each pair in these analogies by drawing shapes which follow that rule.

E-71 Increase detail by doubling the number of parts.

E-72 Illustrate color-opposites.

E-73 Reflect about an up-down (vertical) line.

E-74 Rotate in the direction of the arrow (counterclockwise).

FIGURAL ANALOGIES—FOLLOW THE RULE

DIRECTIONS: Read the rule in each box. Complete each pair in these analogies by drawing shapes which follow that rule.

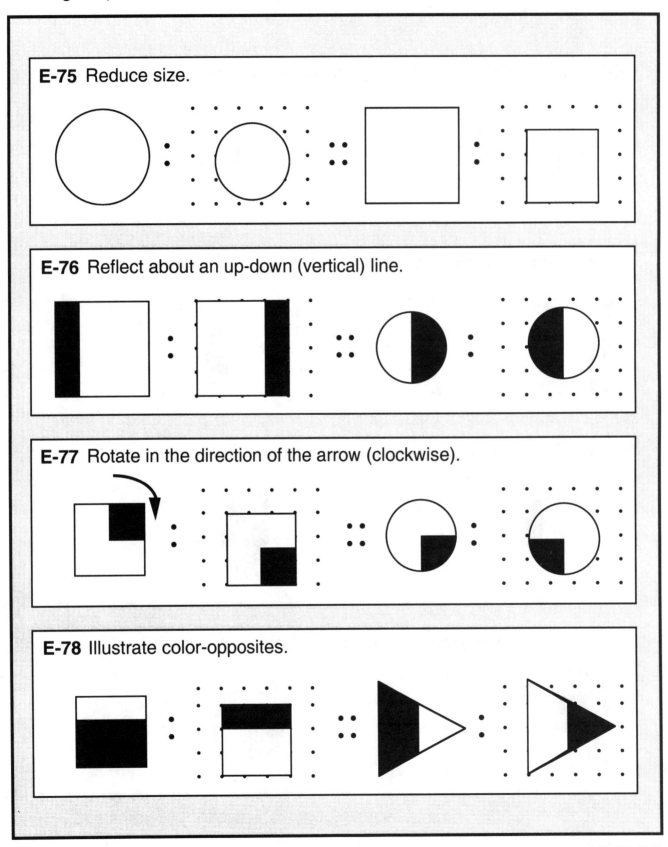

FIGURAL ANALOGIES—FOLLOW THE RULE

DIRECTIONS: Read the rule in each box. Complete each pair in these analogies by drawing shapes which follow that rule.

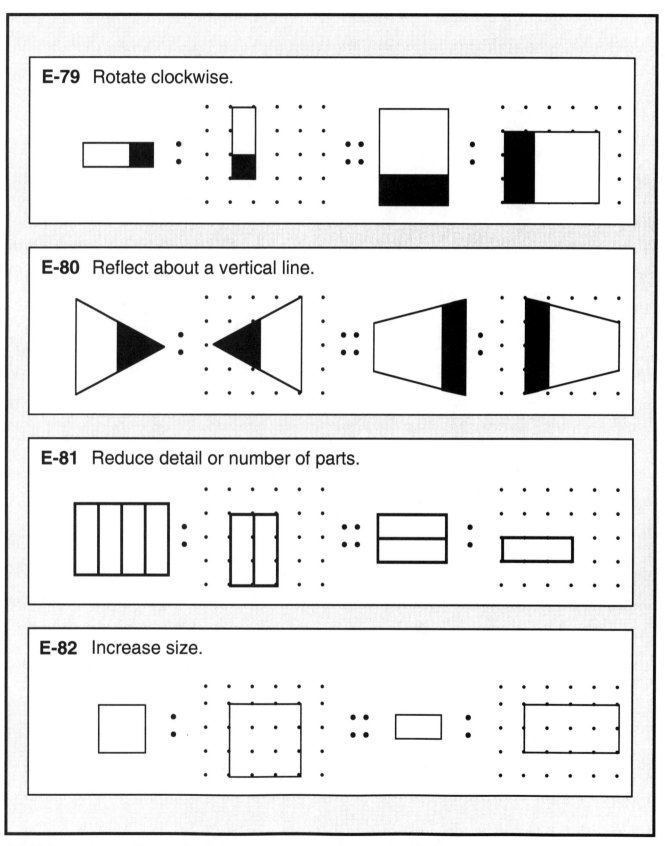

E-79 Rotate clockwise.

E-80 Reflect about a vertical line.

E-81 Reduce detail or number of parts.

E-82 Increase size.

CHAPTER SIX

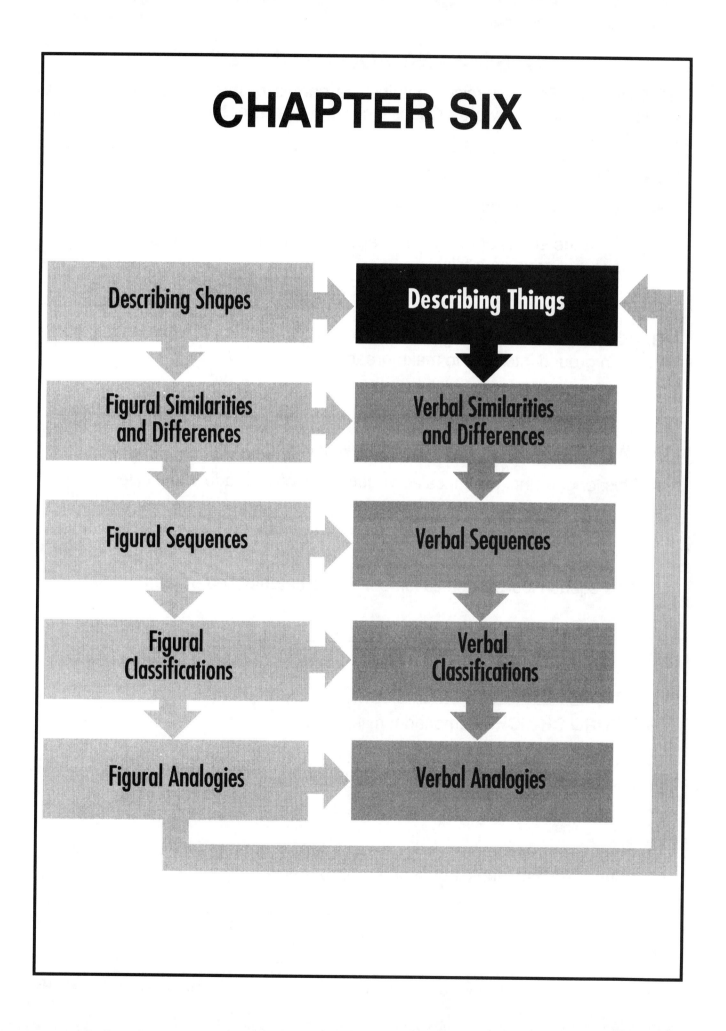

Describing Shapes

Describing Things

Figural Similarities and Differences

Verbal Similarities and Differences

Figural Sequences

Verbal Sequences

Figural Classifications

Verbal Classifications

Figural Analogies

Verbal Analogies

DESCRIBING FOODS—SELECT

DIRECTIONS: Each exercise contains the names of three foods, followed by descriptions of two of the words. Choose the word that fits each description and write it in the blank.

EXAMPLE

WORD CHOICES: corn, rice, wheat

A. We eat the seeds of this yellow vegetable. The seeds are protected by husks that grow on a tall stalk.

corn

B. We eat the seeds of this grain, which grows as a tall grass. The seeds are often ground into flour to make bread.

wheat

F-1 WORD CHOICES: cucumber, yellow squash, zucchini

A. This long, round, green, salad vegetable is often made into pickles.

_____

B. This squash looks like a cucumber and is eaten boiled or fried.

_____

F-2 WORD CHOICES: lemonade, milk, water

A. This liquid has no nutritional value, but we need to drink 6 to 8 glasses of it each day. It makes up most of our body.

_____

B. This liquid is an important source of calcium to build strong teeth and bones. You can drink it or pour it on your cereal.

_____

DESCRIBING ANIMALS—SELECT

DIRECTIONS: Each exercise contains the names of three animals followed by descriptions of two of the words. Choose the word that fits each description and write it in the blank.

F-3 WORD CHOICES: deer, elk, moose

A. The largest member of the deer family, this animal has a very large head and a long flap of skin, called a bell, that hangs under its throat. The males have large, broad, spoon-shaped antlers.

_____

B. A medium-sized member of the deer family, this animal's coat is grayish brown with a white patch on its rump. In the United States, it is only found in the Rocky Mountains and in the Central Valley of California.

_____

F-4 WORD CHOICES: butterfly, moth, wasp

A. This insect is dull in color, has large wings, and flies at night.

_____

B. Groups of these stinging insects build large, paperlike, "woven" nests.

_____

F-5 WORD CHOICES: seal, sea lion, walrus

A. This member of the seal family has ears and flippers that are larger than those of true seals. Its long, tapered body is covered with thin, short, coarse hair. This animal can turn its hind flippers forward to move about on land.

_____

B. This large marine mammal lives in the open water at the edge of the Arctic ice pack. It lacks external ears, has long tusks and thick, nearly hairless, skin, except for long bristles on the cheek pads. It has reversible hind flippers for moving over ice.

_____

DESCRIBING VEHICLES—SELECT

DIRECTIONS: Each exercise contains the names of three vehicles followed by descriptions of two of the words. Choose the word that fits each description and write it in the blank.

F-6 WORD CHOICES: bicycle, moped, motorcycle

A. This two-wheeled vehicle can be pedaled or driven by a small engine. Its top speed is about 30 miles per hour.

_____

B. This two-wheeled vehicle is powered by a gasoline engine that can propel it at speeds up to 100 miles per hour. Because it is often driven at high speeds, it is a very dangerous vehicle, and accidents on it often result in injuries or death.

_____

F-7 WORD CHOICES: backhoe, bulldozer, crane

A. This very large vehicle moves short distances on rolling tracks. A motor-driven cable runs over the end of a long, necklike boom. A hook at the end of the cable is used to lift heavy objects.

_____

B. This large vehicle has a large, movable scoop shovel on the back that is used to dig ditches and trenches.

_____

F-8 WORD CHOICES: all-terrain vehicle, motocross bicycle, snowmobile

A. This vehicle has large, fat tires that allow it to move over almost any land or marshy area.

_____

B. This two-wheeled vehicle is small and tough. It is built to fly over dirt jumps and race around tracks. It has special tires and a rugged frame.

_____

DESCRIBING GEOGRAPHIC TERMS—SELECT

DIRECTIONS: Each exercise contains the names of three landforms or bodies of water, followed by descriptions of two of the words. Choose the word that fits each description and write it in the blank.

F-9 WORD CHOICES: canal, channel, stream

A. A natural, narrow waterway connecting two bodies of water.

_____

B. A manmade, narrow waterway connecting two bodies of water.

_____

F-10 WORD CHOICES: basin, canyon, mesa

A. A flat-topped hill with steep sides, common in deserts.

_____

B. A broad flat area surrounded by hills or mountains.

_____

F-11 WORD CHOICES: island, isthmus, peninsula

A. A narrow strip of land connecting two larger land areas.

_____

B. Land surrounded by water on three sides.

_____

DESCRIBING OCCUPATIONS—SELECT

DIRECTIONS: Each exercise contains the names of three occupations, followed by descriptions of two of the jobs. Choose the word that fits each description and write it in the blank.

F-12 WORD CHOICES: dental hygienist, dental assistant, dentist

A. This person gives dental examinations and cleans patients' teeth but does not fill or cap teeth.

_____

B. This person prepares a patient to see the dentist. He or she hands instruments and materials to the dentist during dental procedures, takes X-rays, takes impressions of the teeth, and performs other dental tasks.

_____

F-13 WORD CHOICES: inhalation therapist, nurse, physical therapist

A. This person helps hospitalized patients regain their ability to breathe.

_____

B. This person helps injured people learn to walk and/or use their arms and hands again.

_____

F-14 WORD CHOICES: computer engineer, data clerk, programmer

A. This person is responsible for entering the correct information into a computer.

_____

B. This person is responsible for designing and building computers.

_____

DESCRIBING COMPUTER DEVICES—SELECT

DIRECTIONS: Each exercise contains three computer terms, followed by descriptions of two of the terms. Choose the word that fits each description and write it in the blank.

F-15 WORD CHOICES: computer processing unit, computer memory, floppy disk

A. This computer component allows processed data to be stored within the computer.

_____

B. This computer component allows the operator to perform complex tasks such as calculations, word processing, drawing, and bookkeeping.

_____

F-16 WORD CHOICES: e-mail, internet, modem

A. This device connects a computer to the worldwide web.

_____

B. This system of interconnections between computers allows a computer operator to send and receive information (drawings, messages, or files) from other computer users.

_____

F-17 WORD CHOICES: CD ROM, Random Access Memory (RAM), Read Only Memory (ROM)

A. This integrated circuit allows a computer to access (find) and use the instructions (programs) stored or fed into a computer.

_____

B. This computer component allows a computer to read and store (remember) the calculations, written documents, and drawings produced by the computer operator.

_____

IDENTIFYING CHARACTERISTICS OF FOOD

DIRECTIONS: Read each passage about a food. Identify the characteristics of the food and write them in the blanks.

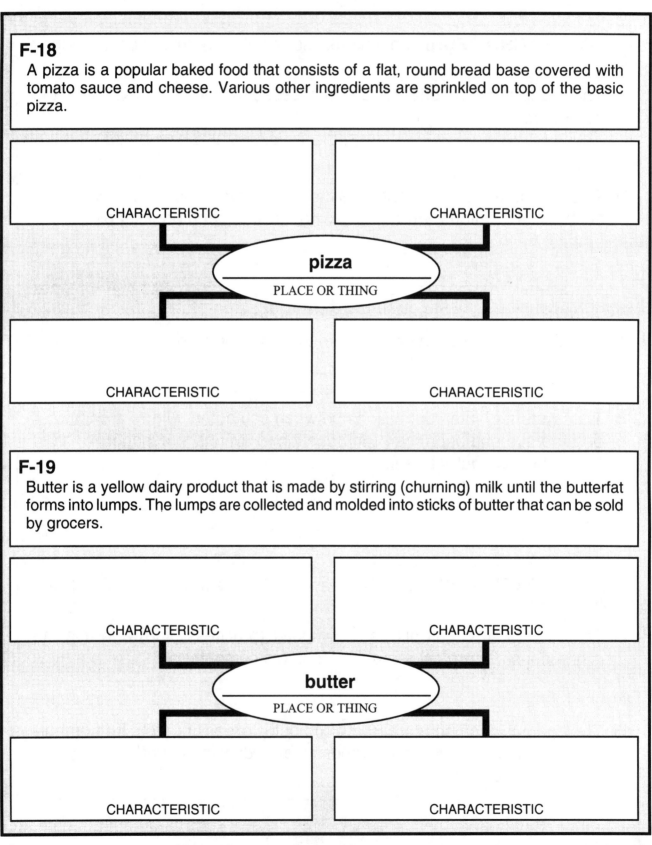

F-18

A pizza is a popular baked food that consists of a flat, round bread base covered with tomato sauce and cheese. Various other ingredients are sprinkled on top of the basic pizza.

CHARACTERISTIC

CHARACTERISTIC

pizza
PLACE OR THING

CHARACTERISTIC

CHARACTERISTIC

F-19

Butter is a yellow dairy product that is made by stirring (churning) milk until the butterfat forms into lumps. The lumps are collected and molded into sticks of butter that can be sold by grocers.

CHARACTERISTIC

CHARACTERISTIC

butter
PLACE OR THING

CHARACTERISTIC

CHARACTERISTIC

IDENTIFYING CHARACTERISTICS OF ANIMALS

DIRECTIONS: Read each passage about an animal. Identify the characteristics of the animal and write them in the blanks.

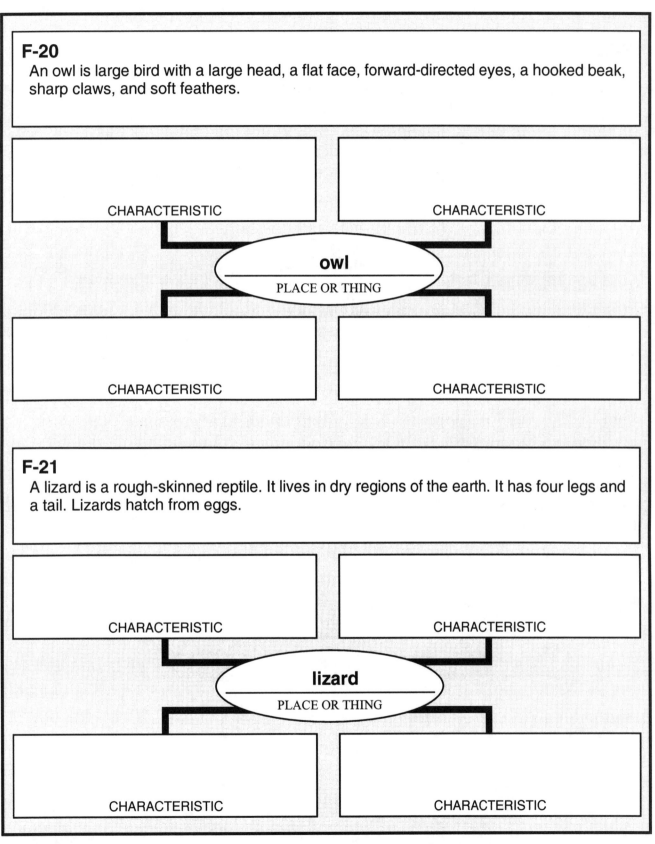

F-20
An owl is large bird with a large head, a flat face, forward-directed eyes, a hooked beak, sharp claws, and soft feathers.

CHARACTERISTIC

CHARACTERISTIC

owl
PLACE OR THING

CHARACTERISTIC

CHARACTERISTIC

F-21
A lizard is a rough-skinned reptile. It lives in dry regions of the earth. It has four legs and a tail. Lizards hatch from eggs.

CHARACTERISTIC

CHARACTERISTIC

lizard
PLACE OR THING

CHARACTERISTIC

CHARACTERISTIC

IDENTIFYING CHARACTERISTICS OF VEHICLES

DIRECTIONS: Read each passage about a vehicle. Identify the characteristics of the vehicle and write them in the blanks.

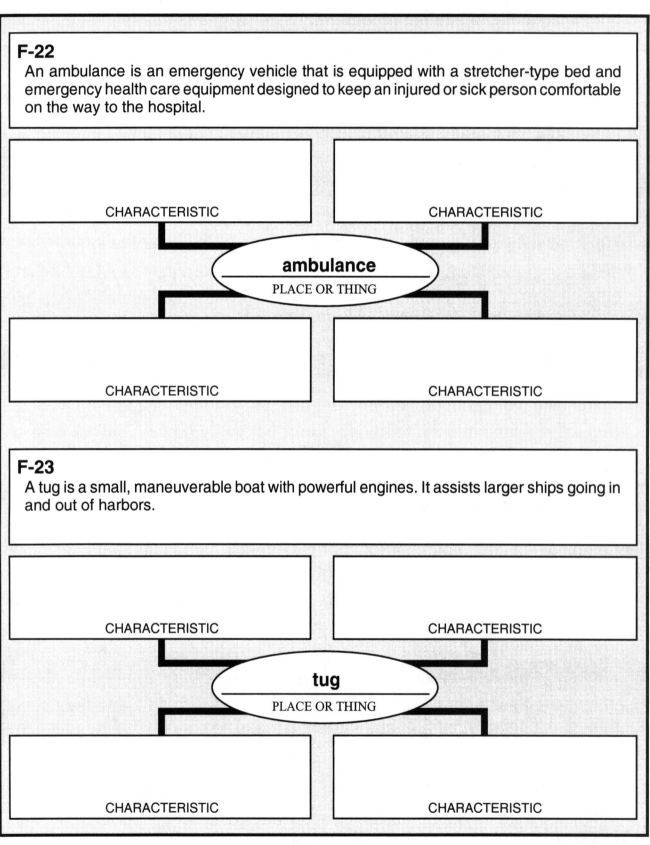

F-22
An ambulance is an emergency vehicle that is equipped with a stretcher-type bed and emergency health care equipment designed to keep an injured or sick person comfortable on the way to the hospital.

CHARACTERISTIC

CHARACTERISTIC

ambulance
PLACE OR THING

CHARACTERISTIC

CHARACTERISTIC

F-23
A tug is a small, maneuverable boat with powerful engines. It assists larger ships going in and out of harbors.

CHARACTERISTIC

CHARACTERISTIC

tug
PLACE OR THING

CHARACTERISTIC

CHARACTERISTIC

IDENTIFYING CHARACTERISTICS OF EARTH FEATURES

DIRECTIONS: Read each passage about an earth landform. Identify the characteristics of the landform and write them in the blanks.

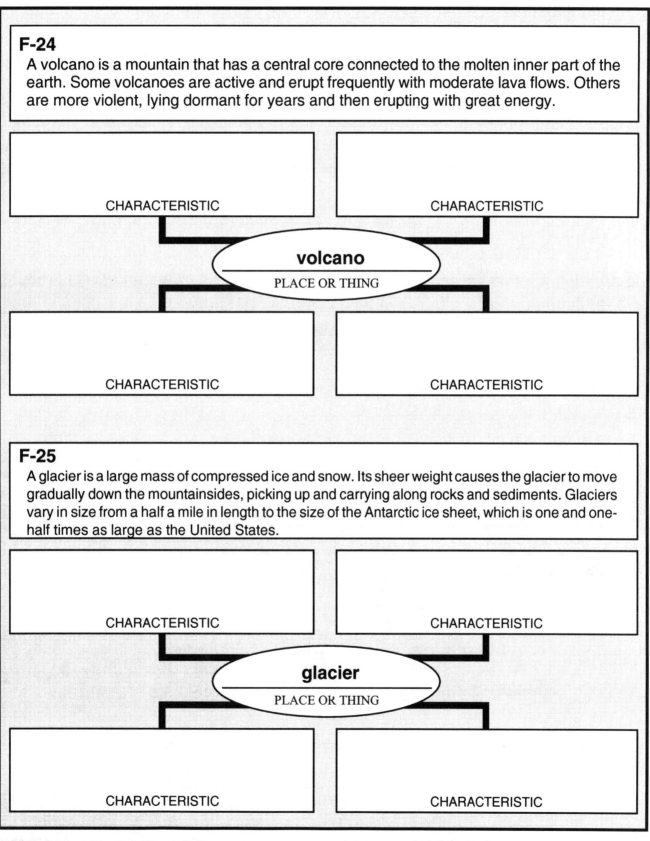

F-24

A volcano is a mountain that has a central core connected to the molten inner part of the earth. Some volcanoes are active and erupt frequently with moderate lava flows. Others are more violent, lying dormant for years and then erupting with great energy.

CHARACTERISTIC

CHARACTERISTIC

volcano
PLACE OR THING

CHARACTERISTIC

CHARACTERISTIC

F-25

A glacier is a large mass of compressed ice and snow. Its sheer weight causes the glacier to move gradually down the mountainsides, picking up and carrying along rocks and sediments. Glaciers vary in size from a half a mile in length to the size of the Antarctic ice sheet, which is one and one-half times as large as the United States.

CHARACTERISTIC

CHARACTERISTIC

glacier
PLACE OR THING

CHARACTERISTIC

CHARACTERISTIC

DESCRIBING FOODS—EXPLAIN

DIRECTIONS: In each box, describe the food that is named. Give specific characteristics.

F-26 rice

_____

_____

_____

_____

F-27 lettuce

_____

_____

_____

_____

F-28 strawberry

_____

_____

_____

_____

DESCRIBING ANIMALS—EXPLAIN

DIRECTIONS: In each box, describe the animal that is named. Give specific characteristics.

F-29 turtle

_____

_____

_____

_____

F-30 clam

_____

_____

_____

_____

F-31 hamster

_____

_____

_____

_____

DESCRIBING VEHICLES—EXPLAIN

DIRECTIONS: In each box, describe the vehicle that is named. Give specific characteristics.

F-32 pickup truck

_____

_____

_____

_____

F-33 ferry boat

_____

_____

_____

_____

F-34 helicopter

_____

_____

_____

_____

DESCRIBING PLACES ON EARTH—EXPLAIN

DIRECTIONS: In each box, describe the place or geographic feature that is named. Give specific characteristics.

F-35 tributary

_____

_____

_____

_____

F-36 plateau

_____

_____

_____

_____

F-37 equator

_____

_____

_____

_____

DESCRIBING OCCUPATIONS—EXPLAIN

DIRECTIONS: In each box, describe the occupation that is named. Give specific characteristics.

F-38 pilot

_____

_____

_____

_____

F-39 physician

_____

_____

_____

_____

F-40 architect

_____

_____

_____

_____

NAME THE ANIMAL—SUPPLY

DIRECTIONS: Each exercise contains a description of an animal. Read each description, then decide what is being described. Write the answer on the line.

F-41 This animal is the offspring of a male donkey and female horse. It is much like the horse in size and body shape but has the shorter, thicker head, long ears, and braying voice of the donkey. The male of this breed is not fertile.

_____

F-42 This land-dwelling, tailless, rough-skinned amphibian is often confused with a frog. It wards off enemies by secreting poison from its skin. Since it has warts on its skin, some people mistakenly believe that, if you handle one, you will get warts.

_____

F-43 This great ape is the largest of the living primates. A male can weigh about 600 pounds. It lives in family groups. It is found only in Africa and is being threatened with extinction.

_____

F-44 This long, smooth-skinned reptile has no arms or legs. It has a special jaw that opens very wide, allowing it to swallow large food items whole. Some varieties feed on mice and rats, making this reptile an asset in reducing the rodent population.

_____

F-45 This large, rough-skinned, amphibious reptile has short arms and legs and a long tail. It is distinguished from an alligator by the notch at the side of its snout, which exposes the teeth of its lower jaw.

_____

F-46 This largest living bird can grow up to 8 feet tall, but cannot fly. It runs with 12-foot strides at speeds up to 40 miles per hour. It lives in dry countries and feeds on plants, fruits, grasses, and leaves, as well as insects, lizards, birds, and mice.

_____

NAME THE PLANT–SUPPLY

DIRECTIONS: Each exercise contains a description of a plant. Read each description, then decide what is being described. Write the answer on the line.

F-47 This round fruit is about 8 inches in diameter and is a member of the cucumber family. Its rind has a "netted" skin which surrounds the light orange part that we eat. At its center is a large group of seeds that are scooped out before serving.

_____

F-48 This oval-shaped citrus fruit, between 2 and 3 inches in diameter, is similar to an orange. The thin orange skin is easy to peel. Its segments are easy to separate. It is named for the Moroccan seaport Tangier, from which the fruit was originally exported to Europe.

_____

F-49 This plant has large leafless, long-living stems of various shapes. Sharp spines grow on these stems. The plant is said to be succulent because of its ability to store water and survive in a dry climate.

_____

F-50 This vegetable is grown for its large bud, or head, which consists of many enfolded leaves closely spaced on a short stem. It is eaten fresh, cooked, or pickled as sauerkraut. It may be either green or purple.

_____

F-51 This tropical tree is tall with an unbranched trunk that is topped by a spreading crown of long-stalked, fanlike, pleated leaves. Some varieties produce coconuts. Other varieties produce a fruit that is used to produce an oil used in the manufacture of soap.

_____

F-52 This evergreen, cone-bearing tree has needles that are produced in groups of two, three, or five. The trees are a source of lumber, turpentine, resin, pitch, and tar. Many of these trees are grown as ornamentals for use at Christmas.

_____

NAME THE VEHICLE/PLACE—SUPPLY

DIRECTIONS: Each exercise contains a description of a vehicle or a place. Read each description, then decide what is being described. Write the answer on the line.

F-53 This vehicle is a railroad car supported by one rail. There are two types, saddlebag and suspended. The saddlebag type straddles a large rail or beamway, and is powered by vertical wheels on top of the beamway. The suspended type hangs from overhead rails.

_____

F-54 This aircraft is lifted by rotating blades set on top of the vehicle. It is capable of lifting vertically and hoveringin one place. This vehicle has been used for military maneuvers, agricultural purposes, and fire and rescue operations.

_____

F-55 This many-wheeled, motor vehicle is used to transport people along a fixed route within a city. It makes many stops along its route to pick up and discharge passengers. People pay a fare to ride this vehicle.

_____

F-56 This landform is very wet and usually near a larger body of water such as an ocean or a lake. This area supports grassy vegetation and is the breeding ground for many forms of aquatic life.

_____

F-57 A land mass that is completely surrounded by water is called a/an _____. A body of water completely surrounded by land is called a/an

_____

F-58 This landform occurs at the mouth of a river. When a river enters an ocean or lake, the sediments that have been carried along are dropped. These sediments pile up to form a triangular-shaped area named for the Greek letter that has a triangular shape.

_____

WRITING DESCRIPTIONS

DIRECTIONS: Follow the directions given in the example.

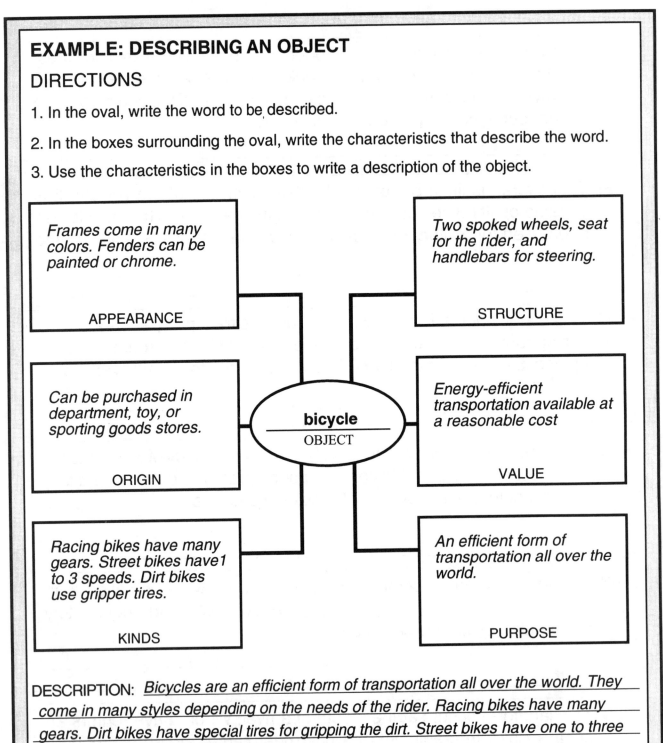

EXAMPLE: DESCRIBING AN OBJECT

DIRECTIONS

1. In the oval, write the word to be described.

2. In the boxes surrounding the oval, write the characteristics that describe the word.

3. Use the characteristics in the boxes to write a description of the object.

Frames come in many colors. Fenders can be painted or chrome.

APPEARANCE

Two spoked wheels, seat for the rider, and handlebars for steering.

STRUCTURE

Can be purchased in department, toy, or sporting goods stores.

ORIGIN

bicycle
OBJECT

Energy-efficient transportation available at a reasonable cost

VALUE

Racing bikes have many gears. Street bikes have 1 to 3 speeds. Dirt bikes use gripper tires.

KINDS

An efficient form of transportation all over the world.

PURPOSE

DESCRIPTION: *Bicycles are an efficient form of transportation all over the world. They come in many styles depending on the needs of the rider. Racing bikes have many gears. Dirt bikes have special tires for gripping the dirt. Street bikes have one to three gears. Bikes can be painted to suit the owner.*

WRITING DESCRIPTIONS

DIRECTIONS: Follow the directions given. Use the diagram at the bottom of the page to help you write a description of beans.

F-59

DIRECTIONS

1. Look at the word to be described.

2. In the boxes surrounding the oval, write the characteristics that describe the word.

3. Use the characteristics in the boxes to write a description of the object.

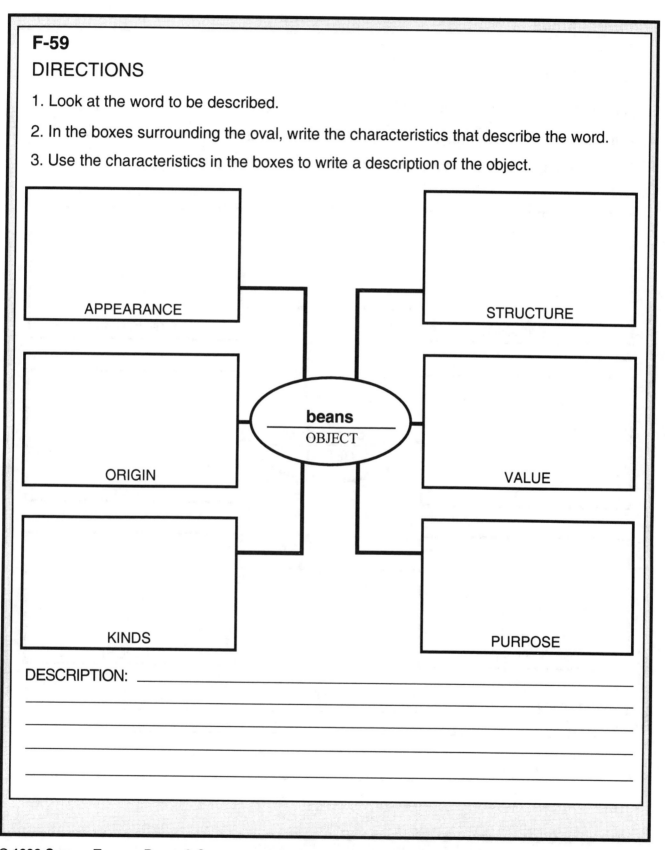

APPEARANCE

STRUCTURE

ORIGIN

beans
OBJECT

VALUE

KINDS

PURPOSE

DESCRIPTION: _____

_____

_____

_____

_____

WRITING DESCRIPTIONS

DIRECTIONS: Follow the directions given. Use the diagram below to help you write a descriptions of a computer.

F-60
DIRECTIONS

1. Look at the word to be described.

2. In the boxes surrounding the oval, write the characteristics that describe the word.

3. Use the characteristics in the boxes to write a description of the object.

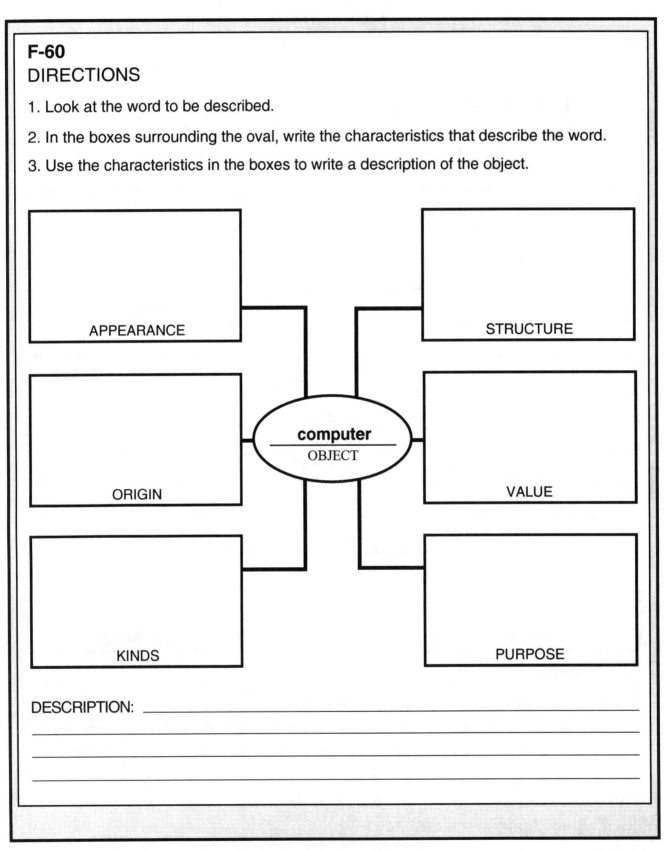

APPEARANCE

STRUCTURE

ORIGIN

VALUE

computer
OBJECT

KINDS

PURPOSE

DESCRIPTION: _____

_____

_____

_____

WRITING DESCRIPTIONS

DIRECTIONS: Follow the directions given. Use the diagram below to help you write description of a school.

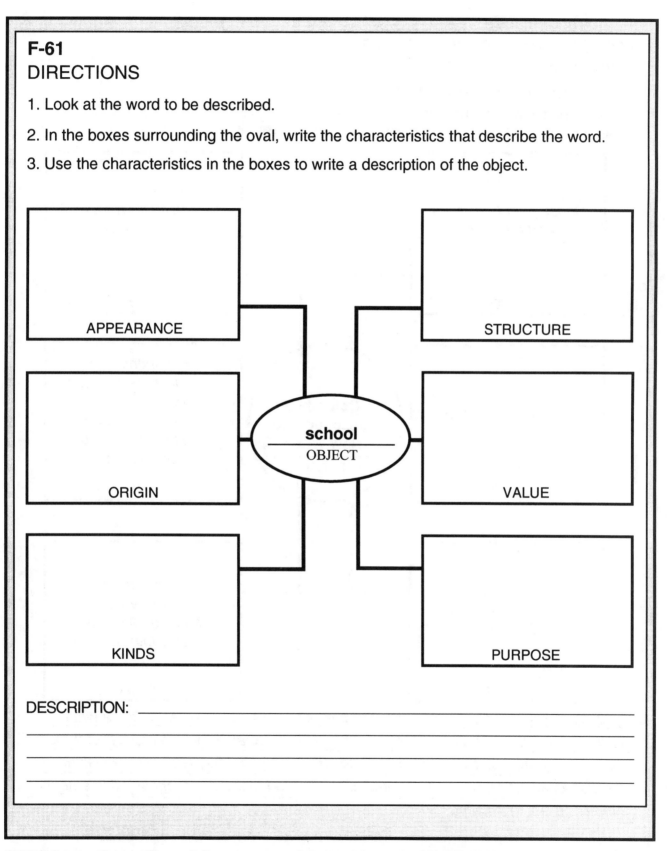

F-61

DIRECTIONS

1. Look at the word to be described.

2. In the boxes surrounding the oval, write the characteristics that describe the word.

3. Use the characteristics in the boxes to write a description of the object.

APPEARANCE

STRUCTURE

ORIGIN

school

OBJECT

VALUE

KINDS

PURPOSE

DESCRIPTION: _____

_____

_____

_____

WRITING DESCRIPTIONS

DIRECTIONS: Follow the directions given in the example.

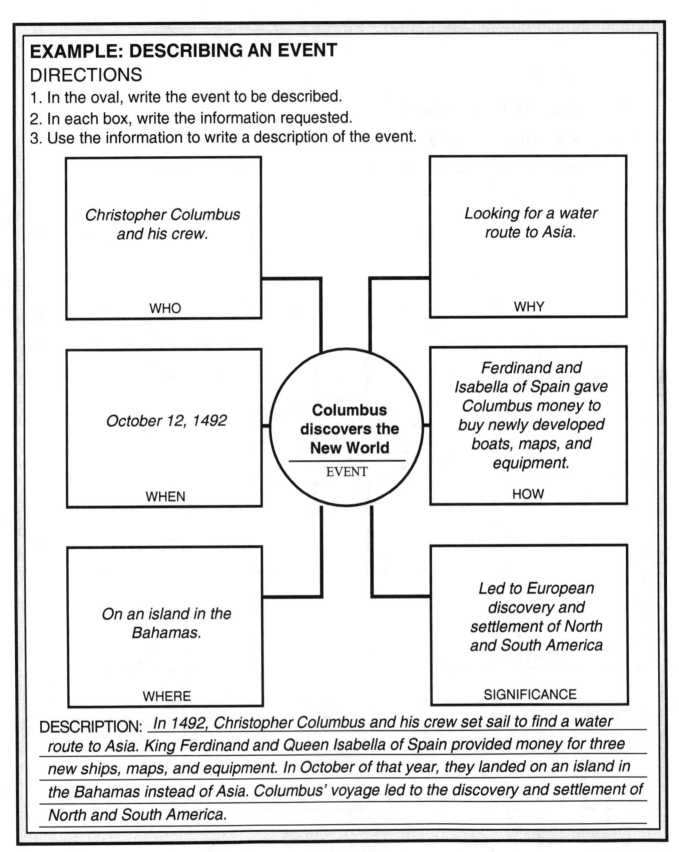

EXAMPLE: DESCRIBING AN EVENT
DIRECTIONS
1. In the oval, write the event to be described.
2. In each box, write the information requested.
3. Use the information to write a description of the event.

Christopher Columbus and his crew.

WHO

Looking for a water route to Asia.

WHY

October 12, 1492

WHEN

Columbus discovers the New World

EVENT

Ferdinand and Isabella of Spain gave Columbus money to buy newly developed boats, maps, and equipment.

HOW

On an island in the Bahamas.

WHERE

Led to European discovery and settlement of North and South America

SIGNIFICANCE

DESCRIPTION: *In 1492, Christopher Columbus and his crew set sail to find a water route to Asia. King Ferdinand and Queen Isabella of Spain provided money for three new ships, maps, and equipment. In October of that year, they landed on an island in the Bahamas instead of Asia. Columbus' voyage led to the discovery and settlement of North and South America.*

WRITING DESCRIPTIONS

DIRECTIONS: Use the diagram at the bottom of the page to help you write a description of the voyage of the *Mayflower*.

F-62

DIRECTIONS

1. In the oval, write the event to be described.
2. In each box, write the information requested.
3. Use the information to write a description of the event.

WHO

WHY

WHEN

Voyage of the Mayflower

EVENT

HOW

WHERE

SIGNIFICANCE

DESCRIPTION: _____

_____

_____

_____

_____

WRITING DESCRIPTIONS

DIRECTIONS: Use the diagram below to help you write a description of the signing of the Declaration of Independence.

F-63

DIRECTIONS

1. In the oval, write the event to be described.
2. In each box, write the information requested.
3. Use the information to write a description of the event.

WHO

WHY

WHEN

The Signing of
the Declaration
of Independence

EVENT

HOW

WHERE

SIGNIFICANCE

DESCRIPTION: _____

_____

_____

_____

WRITING DESCRIPTIONS

DIRECTIONS: Use the diagram below to help you write a description of the Civil War in the United States.

F-64

DIRECTIONS

1. In the oval, write the event to be described.
2. In each box, write the information requested.
3. Use the information to write a description of the event.

WHO

WHY

WHEN

The United States is divided by Civil War

EVENT

HOW

WHERE

SIGNIFICANCE

DESCRIPTION: _____

_____

_____

_____

WRITING DESCRIPTIONS

DIRECTIONS: Select an interesting and important object in your home, school, or neighborhood. Use the three diagrams to record details and information about the object that would help you describe it to someone who had never seen it. Then use all three diagrams to write your description in the box at the bottom of the next page.

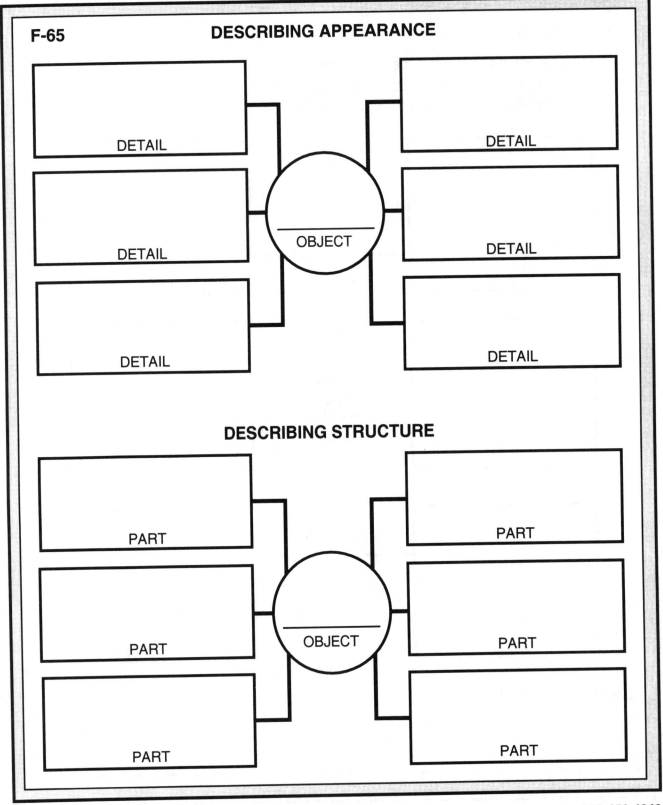

F-65

DESCRIBING APPEARANCE

DETAIL

DETAIL

DETAIL

OBJECT

DETAIL

DETAIL

DETAIL

DESCRIBING STRUCTURE

PART

PART

PART

OBJECT

PART

PART

PART

WRITING DESCRIPTIONS

DIRECTIONS: This is the second page of this lesson. Use this diagram and the two diagrams on the previous page to write your description in the box at the bottom of the page.

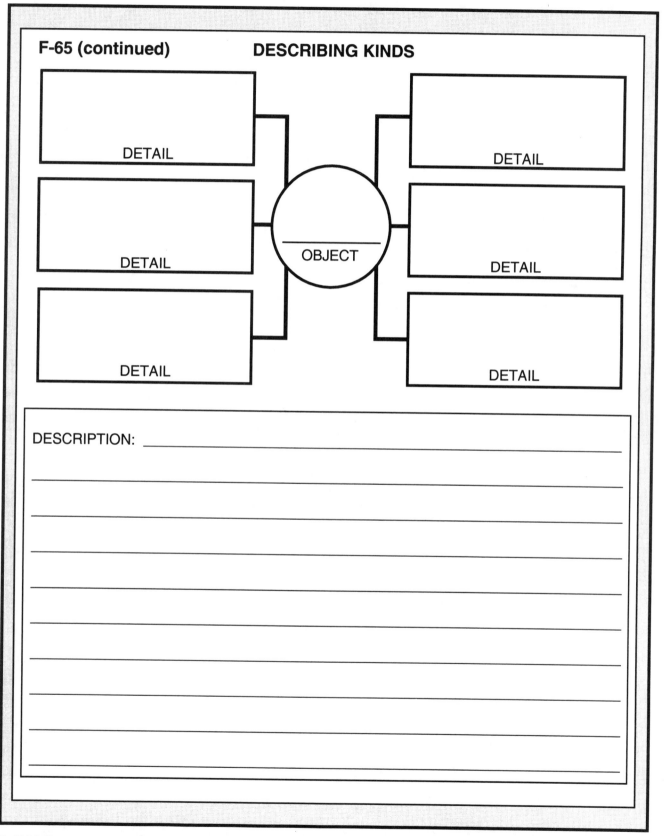

F-65 (continued)   **DESCRIBING KINDS**

DETAIL

DETAIL

DETAIL

OBJECT

DETAIL

DETAIL

DETAIL

DESCRIPTION: _____

_____

_____

_____

_____

_____

_____

_____

_____

CHAPTER SEVEN

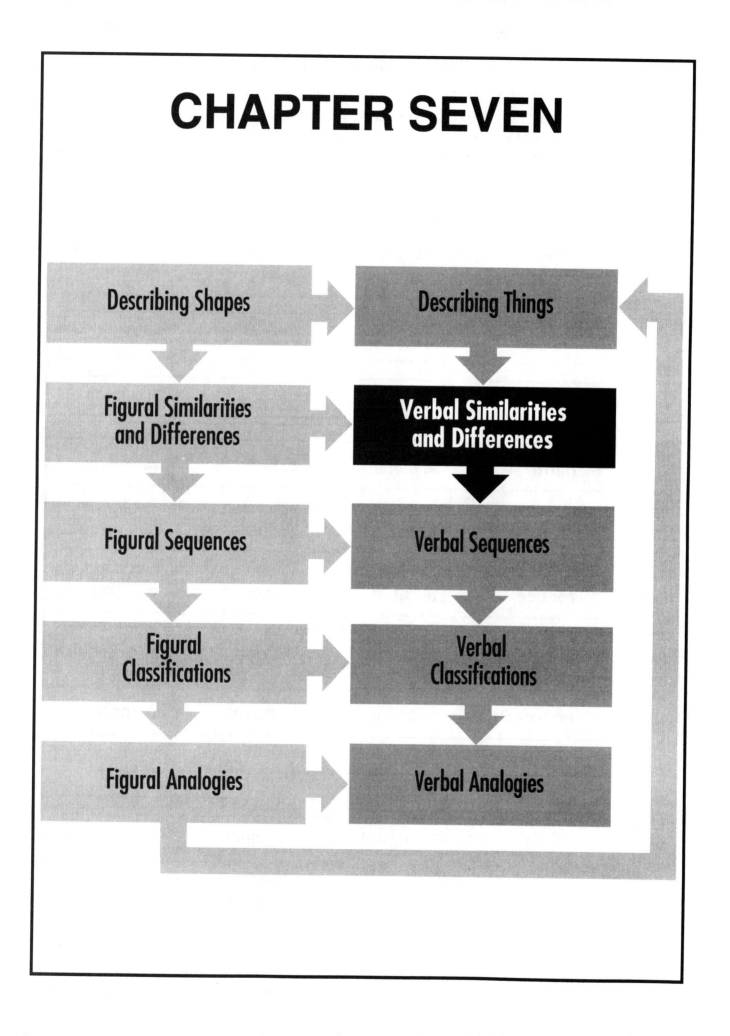

Describing Shapes

Describing Things

Figural Similarities and Differences

Verbal Similarities and Differences

Figural Sequences

Verbal Sequences

Figural Classifications

Verbal Classifications

Figural Analogies

Verbal Analogies

OPPOSITES—SELECT

DIRECTIONS: Each line contains four verbs. Read the first verb and think about what it means. One of the next three verbs will mean the opposite of the first verb. Underline the one that is the opposite of the first verb.

G-1	**play**	**a.** amuse	**b.** entertain	**c.** work
G-2	**allow**	**a.** deny	**b.** let	**c.** permit
G-3	**mend**	**a.** break	**b.** correct	**c.** patch
G-4	**save**	**a.** collect	**b.** store	**c.** spend
G-5	**harm**	**a.** damage	**b.** hurt	**c.** benefit
G-6	**doubt**	**a.** believe	**b.** challenge	**c.** question
G-7	**reduce**	**a.** cut	**b.** diminish	**c.** increase
G-8	**conclude**	**a.** close	**b.** finish	**c.** open
G-9	**approach**	**a.** arrive	**b.** leave	**c.** reach
G-10	**escape**	**a.** depart	**b.** flee	**c.** return
G-11	**reject**	**a.** accept	**b.** dismiss	**c.** overlook
G-12	**overlook**	**a.** miss	**b.** ignore	**c.** choose

OPPOSITES—SELECT

DIRECTIONS: Each line contains four adjectives. Read the first adjective and think about what it means. One of the next three adjectives will mean the opposite of the first adjective. Underline the one that is the opposite of the first adjective.

G-13	**neat**	**a.** clean	**b.** messy	**c.** orderly
G-14	**tight**	**a.** close	**b.** firm	**c.** loose
G-15	**rude**	**a.** discourteous	**b.** polite	**c.** vulgar
G-16	**timid**	**a.** bashful	**b.** bold	**c.** shy
G-17	**familiar**	**a.** common	**b.** known	**c.** strange
G-18	**plain**	**a.** fancy	**b.** ordinary	**c.** simple
G-19	**public**	**a.** free	**b.** open	**c.** private
G-20	**sharp**	**a.** alert	**b.** bright	**c.** slow
G-21	**honest**	**a.** unethical	**b.** lawful	**c.** truthful
G-22	**diverse**	**a.** different	**b.** identical	**c.** varied
G-23	**lively**	**a.** alert	**b.** bright	**c.** sluggish
G-24	**worthless**	**a.** useless	**b.** trivial	**c.** valuable

OPPOSITES—SELECT

DIRECTIONS: Each line contains four adverbs. Read the first adverb and think about what it means. One of the next three adverbs will mean the opposite of the first adverb. Underline the one that is the opposite of the first adverb.

G-25	**accidentally**	a. randomly	b. incidentally	c. purposefully
G-26	**afterward**	a. before	b. later	c. next
G-27	**barely**	a. amply	b. hardly	c. scarcely
G-28	**maybe**	a. perhaps	b. possibly	c. surely
G-29	**deeply**	a. intensely	b. hardly	c. greatly
G-30	**concisely**	a. accurately	b. briefly	c. wordily
G-31	**gradually**	a. slowly	b. eventually	c. suddenly
G-32	**capably**	a. incompetently	b. exceptionally	c. superbly
G-33	**eternally**	a. always	b. forever	c. seldom
G-34	**onward**	a. ahead	b. backward	c. forward
G-35	**mightily**	a. forcefully	b. strongly	c. weakly
G-36	**rarely**	a. infrequently	b. often	c. seldom

OPPOSITES—SUPPLY

DIRECTIONS: Each line contains a verb. Read the verb and think about what it means. Think of another verb (or verbs) that means the opposite of the given verb. Write the verb(s) in the box.

G-37	add

G-38	reject

G-39	excite

G-40	decrease

G-41	multiply

G-42	approve

G-43	capture

G-44	melt

G-45	deny

G-46	emphasize

G-47	depart

G-48	separate

OPPOSITES—SUPPLY

DIRECTIONS: Each line contains a noun. Read the noun and think about what it means. Think of another noun (or nouns) that means the opposite of the given noun. Write the noun(s) in the box.

G-49	**dawn**
G-50	**sorrow**
G-51	**debt**
G-52	**question**
G-53	**youth**
G-54	**plenty**
G-55	**success**
G-56	**native**
G-57	**interior**
G-58	**basement**
G-59	**introduction**
G-60	**shortage**

OPPOSITES—SUPPLY

DIRECTIONS: Each line contains an adjective. Read the adjective and think about what it means. Think of another adjective (or adjectives) that means the opposite of the given adjective. Write the adjectives(s) in the box.

G-61   still

G-62   ancient

G-63   positive

G-64   ordinary

G-65   glad

G-66   excellent

G-67   partial

G-68   past

G-69   difficult

G-70   popular

G-71   impatient

G-72   valuable

SIMILARITIES—SELECT

DIRECTIONS: Each line contains four verbs. Read the first verb and think about what it means. One of the next three verbs means almost the same thing. Underline the one that is most like the first verb in meaning.

G-73	**break**	**a.** crack	**b.** mend	**c.** repair
G-74	**lead**	**a.** attempt	**b.** direct	**c.** follow
G-75	**seem**	**a.** appear	**b.** have	**c.** need
G-76	**begin**	**a.** make	**b.** start	**c.** try
G-77	**jog**	**a.** hike	**b.** pace	**c.** run
G-78	**manage**	**a.** control	**b.** start	**c.** stop
G-79	**continue**	**a.** expect	**b.** prevent	**c.** proceed
G-80	**desire**	**a.** have	**b.** try	**c.** want
G-81	**clear**	**a.** plant	**b.** remove	**c.** set
G-82	**care**	**a.** ignore	**b.** neglect	**c.** tend
G-83	**produce**	**a.** break	**b.** manufacture	**c.** reduce
G-84	**survive**	**a.** die	**b.** perish	**c.** recover

SIMILARITIES—SELECT

DIRECTIONS: Each line contains four adjectives. Read the first adjective and think about what it means. One of the next three adjectives means almost the same thing. Underline the one that is most like the first adjective in meaning.

G-85	**active**	**a.** busy	**b.** quiet	**c.** still
G-86	**tired**	**a.** calm	**b.** rested	**c.** weary
G-87	**curious**	**a.** familiar	**b.** peculiar	**c.** similar
G-88	**personal**	**a.** open	**b.** private	**c.** public
G-89	**initial**	**a.** first	**b.** last	**c.** middle
G-90	**former**	**a.** current	**b.** earlier	**c.** present
G-91	**novel**	**a.** different	**b.** familiar	**c.** old
G-92	**earnest**	**a.** serious	**b.** casual	**c.** careless
G-93	**temporary**	**a.** continuous	**b.** brief	**c.** permanent
G-94	**favorable**	**a.** critical	**b.** friendly	**c.** negative
G-95	**clever**	**a.** average	**b.** dull	**c.** sharp
G-96	**mobile**	**a.** fixed	**b.** movable	**c.** stationary

SIMILARITIES—SELECT

DIRECTIONS: Each line contains four adjectives. Sometimes the same word can have several different meanings. Read the first adjective in each row and think about what it means. Underline the one that is most like the first adjective in meaning.

G-97	**dull**	**a.** boring	**b.** exciting	**c.** loud
G-98	**dull**	**a.** blunt	**b.** even	**c.** sharp

G-99	**hard**	**a.** difficult	**b.** simple	**c.** smooth
G-100	**hard**	**a.** easy	**b.** firm	**c.** loose
G-101	**hard**	**a.** fantastic	**b.** idealistic	**c.** realistic

G-102	**clear**	**a.** bright	**b.** gloomy	**c.** hazy
G-103	**clear**	**a.** blurred	**b.** certain	**c.** vague
G-104	**clear**	**a.** bare	**b.** clogged	**c.** occupied

G-105	**fine**	**a.** awful	**b.** excellent	**c.** poor
G-106	**fine**	**a.** coarse	**b.** rough	**c.** delicate
G-107	**fine**	**a.** broad	**b.** thin	**c.** wide
G-108	**fine**	**a.** clear	**b.** cloudy	**c.** gloomy

SIMILARITIES—SELECT

DIRECTIONS: Each line contains four verbs. Sometimes the same word can have several different meanings. Read the first verb in each row and think about what it means. Underline another verb that is most like the first one in meaning.

G-109	**raise**	**a.** lower	**b.** lift	**c.** slide
G-110	**raise**	**a.** increase	**b.** reduce	**c.** use
G-111	**raise**	**a.** destroy	**b.** grow	**c.** maintain

G-112	**cut**	**a.** peel	**b.** slice	**c.** tear
G-113	**cut**	**a.** hire	**b.** increase	**c.** reduce
G-114	**cut**	**a.** comb	**b.** dry	**c.** shave
G-115	**cut**	**a.** concentrate	**b.** dilute	**c.** thicken

G-116	**fail**	**a.** cure	**b.** decline	**c.** heal
G-117	**fail**	**a.** flunk	**b.** pass	**c.** win
G-118	**fail**	**a.** dwindle	**b.** grow	**c.** supply

G-119	**drop**	**a.** fall	**b.** rise	**c.** soar
G-120	**drop**	**a.** decline	**b.** grow	**c.** hold

SIMILARITIES—SUPPLY

DIRECTIONS: Each line contains a verb. Read the verb and think about what it means. Think of another verb (or verbs) that means almost the same. Write the verb(s) in the box.

G-121   **capture**

G-122   **select**

G-123   **ruin**

G-124   **require**

G-125   **complete**

G-126   **consider**

G-127   **contain**

G-128   **shut**

G-129   **create**

G-130   **proceed**

G-131   **nourish**

G-132   **strike**

SIMILARITIES—SUPPLY

DIRECTIONS: Each line contains an adjective. Read the adjective and think about what it means. Think of another adjective (or adjectives) that means almost the same. Write the adjective(s) in the box.

G-133	**whole**

G-134	**most**

G-135	**extra**

G-136	**single**

G-137	**annual**

G-138	**brilliant**

G-139	**cautious**

G-140	**artificial**

G-141	**polite**

G-142	**minor**

G-143	**substantial**

G-144	**handy**

SIMILARITIES—SUPPLY

DIRECTIONS: Each line contains a noun. Read the noun and think about what it means. Think of a noun (or nouns) that means almost the same. Write the noun(s) in the box.

G-145	**instructor**
G-146	**opportunity**
G-147	**explanation**
G-148	**power**
G-149	**delight**
G-150	**achievement**
G-151	**boundary**
G-152	**career**
G-153	**section**
G-154	**announcement**
G-155	**device**
G-156	**supplement**

HOW ALIKE?—SELECT

DIRECTIONS: Each line contains two words related to social studies. Think about the ways the two words are alike. Underline the sentence(s) that is true of both words.

G-157 postage stamps
coins

a. Both can be collected as a hobby.
b. Both are produced by the government.
c. Both have a monetary value printed on them.

G-158 king
president

a. Both are elected.
b. Both are national leaders.
c. Both participate in national ceremonies.

G-159 goods
services

a. Both are objects.
b. Both can be purchased.
c. Both require workers.

G-160 globe
map

a. Both are drawings of all or part of the earth.
b. Both are flat.
c. Both can be used to estimate distances between places.

G-161 lake
ocean

a. Both are bodies of water.
b. Both can be located on maps.
c. Both contain drinkable water.

G-162 checks
money

a. Both can be obtained at a bank.
b. Both can be used to buy things.
c. Both need to be endorsed.

HOW ALIKE?—SELECT

DIRECTIONS: Each line contains two words related to communication. Think about the ways the two words are alike. Underline the sentence(s) that is true of both words.

G-163 magazine
newspaper

   a. Both are usually published daily.
   b. Both have editors.
   c. Both can have reporters.

G-164 radio
telephone

   a. Both deliver sounds.
   b. Both can be dialed or tuned.
   c. Both broadcast programs.

G-165 fax
letter

   a. Both are delivered by the postal service.
   b. Both require special sending and receiving equipment.
   c. Both convey information.

G-166 debate
political speech

   a. Both present opposing points of view.
   b. Both involve speaking.
   c. Both concern the speakers' opinions.

G-167 television news
historical documentary

   a. Both are based on fact.
   b. Both discuss current issues.
   c. Both are informative.

G-168 conversation
lecture

   a. Both convey information.
   b. Both involve speaking.
   c. Both are spoken by teachers or visiting experts.

HOW ALIKE?—SELECT

DIRECTIONS: Each line contains two words related to science. Think about the ways the two words are alike. Underline the sentence(s) that is true of both words.

G-169 noise
sound

a. Both are caused by vibrations.
b. Both can be heard.
c. Both are never pleasant

G-170 root
stem

a. Both are parts of a plant.
b. Both are above ground.
c. Some kinds of each can be eaten.

G-171 lever
pulley

a. Both are simple machines.
b. Both need ropes or strings.
c. Both can make work easier.

G-172 frog
snake

a. Both have backbones.
b. Both are reptiles.
c. Both are amphibians.

G-173 corn
wheat

a. Both are grasses.
b. Both are grains.
c. Both can be eaten.

G-174 ice
cloud

a. Both are solid.
b. Both are forms of water.
c. Both take up space.

HOW ALIKE?—SELECT

DIRECTIONS: Each line contains two words related to art or music. Think about the ways the two words are alike. Underline the sentence(s) that is true of both words.

G-175 painting
photograph

a. Both are pictures.
b. Both can be sold in art galleries.
c. Both must represent real objects.

G-176 piano
xylophone

a. Both are musical instruments.
b. Both have keys.
c. Both are played by hitting with a stick.

G-177 marching band
orchestra

a. Both have horn players.
b. Both have violin players.
c. Both produce music.

G-178 artist
composer

a. Both are talented people.
b. Both are involved in the arts.
c. Both write music.

G-179 paints
musical instruments

a. Both are used by musicians.
b. Both can be used by talented people.
c. Both can be held in the hand.

G-180 canvas
music staff paper

a. Both can be used to produce a creative work.
b. Both have paint applied to them.
c. Both are used to write music.

HOW ALIKE AND HOW DIFFERENT?

DIRECTIONS: Each line contains two words related to social studies. Describe how the words are alike and how they are different.

G-181 neighborhood community	HOW ALIKE?
	HOW DIFFERENT?

G-182 mayor governor	HOW ALIKE?
	HOW DIFFERENT?

G-183 country continent	HOW ALIKE?
	HOW DIFFERENT?

G-184 weather climate	HOW ALIKE?
	HOW DIFFERENT?

G-185 dictatorship democracy	HOW ALIKE?
	HOW DIFFERENT?

HOW ALIKE AND HOW DIFFERENT?

DIRECTIONS: Each line contains two words related to science. Describe how the words are alike and how they are different.

| **G-186**
light
sound | HOW ALIKE? |
| | HOW DIFFERENT? |

| **G-187**
amphibian
reptile | HOW ALIKE? |
| | HOW DIFFERENT? |

| **G-188**
fruit
seed | HOW ALIKE? |
| | HOW DIFFERENT? |

| **G-189**
machine
work | HOW ALIKE? |
| | HOW DIFFERENT? |

| **G-190**
planet
star | HOW ALIKE? |
| | HOW DIFFERENT? |

HOW ALIKE AND HOW DIFFERENT?

DIRECTIONS: Each line contains two words related to mathematics. Describe how the words are alike and how they are different.

G-191 square rectangle	HOW ALIKE?
	HOW DIFFERENT?

G-192 rectangle parallelogram	HOW ALIKE?
	HOW DIFFERENT?

G-193 parallelogram rhombus	HOW ALIKE?
	HOW DIFFERENT?

G-194 parallelogram trapezoid	HOW ALIKE?
	HOW DIFFERENT?

G-195 square rhombus	HOW ALIKE?
	HOW DIFFERENT?

WORD WEB—SELECT AND SUPPLY

DIRECTIONS: Sometimes common words have more than one meaning. In each blank box below, write a word from the choice box that has almost the same meaning as the synonym next to the blank.

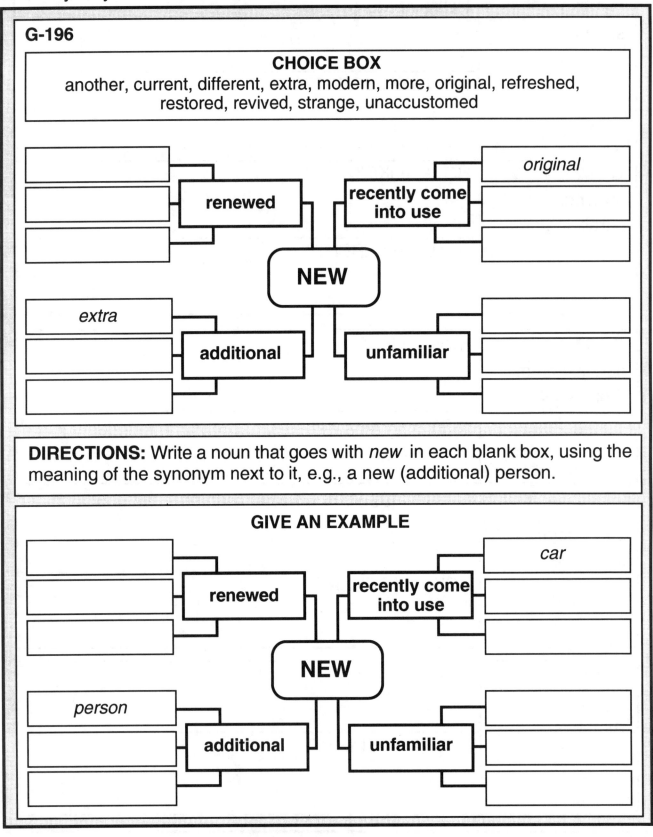

G-196

CHOICE BOX
another, current, different, extra, modern, more, original, refreshed, restored, revived, strange, unaccustomed

original

renewed

recently come into use

NEW

extra

additional

unfamiliar

DIRECTIONS: Write a noun that goes with *new* in each blank box, using the meaning of the synonym next to it, e.g., a new (additional) person.

GIVE AN EXAMPLE

car

renewed

recently come into use

NEW

person

additional

unfamiliar

WORD WEB—SELECT AND SUPPLY

DIRECTIONS: Sometimes common words have more than one meaning. In each blank box below, write a word from the choice box that has almost the same meaning as the synonym next to the blank.

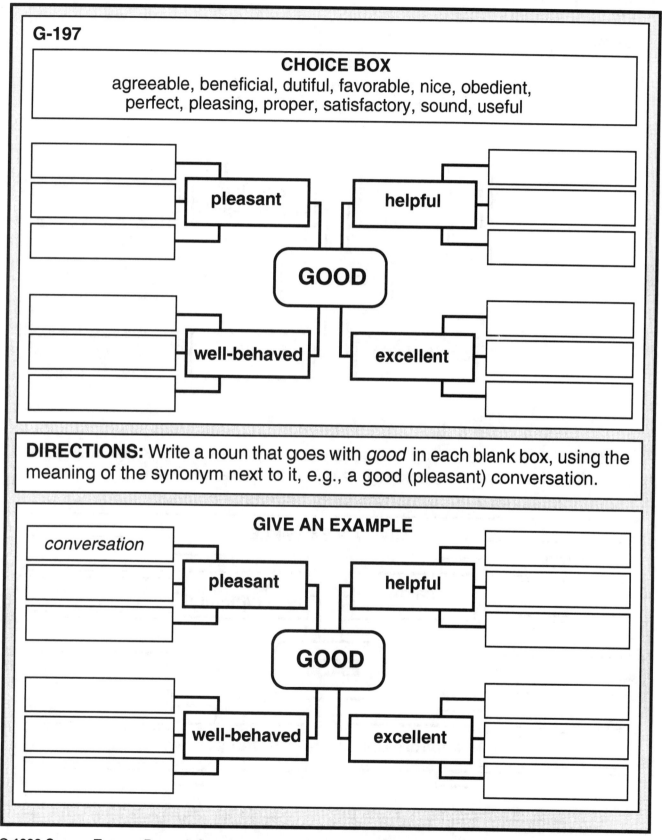

G-197

CHOICE BOX
agreeable, beneficial, dutiful, favorable, nice, obedient,
perfect, pleasing, proper, satisfactory, sound, useful

pleasant

helpful

GOOD

well-behaved

excellent

DIRECTIONS: Write a noun that goes with *good* in each blank box, using the meaning of the synonym next to it, e.g., a good (pleasant) conversation.

GIVE AN EXAMPLE

conversation

pleasant

helpful

GOOD

well-behaved

excellent

WORD WEB—SELECT AND SUPPLY

DIRECTIONS: Sometimes common words have more than one meaning. In each blank box below, write a word from the choice box that has almost the same meaning as the synonym next to the blank.

G-198

CHOICE BOX
comfy, cozy, effortless, good-natured, obliging, placid, serene, simple, smooth, sociable, soft, tranquil

calm

causing little difficulty

EASY

comfortable

friendly

DIRECTIONS: Write a noun that goes with *easy* in each blank box, using the meaning of the synonym next to it, e.g., an easy (calm) feeling.

GIVE AN EXAMPLE

feeling

calm

causing little difficulty

EASY

comfortable

friendly

WORD WEB—SELECT AND SUPPLY

DIRECTIONS: Sometimes common words have more than one meaning. In each blank box below, write a word from the choice box that has almost the same meaning as the synonym next to the blank.

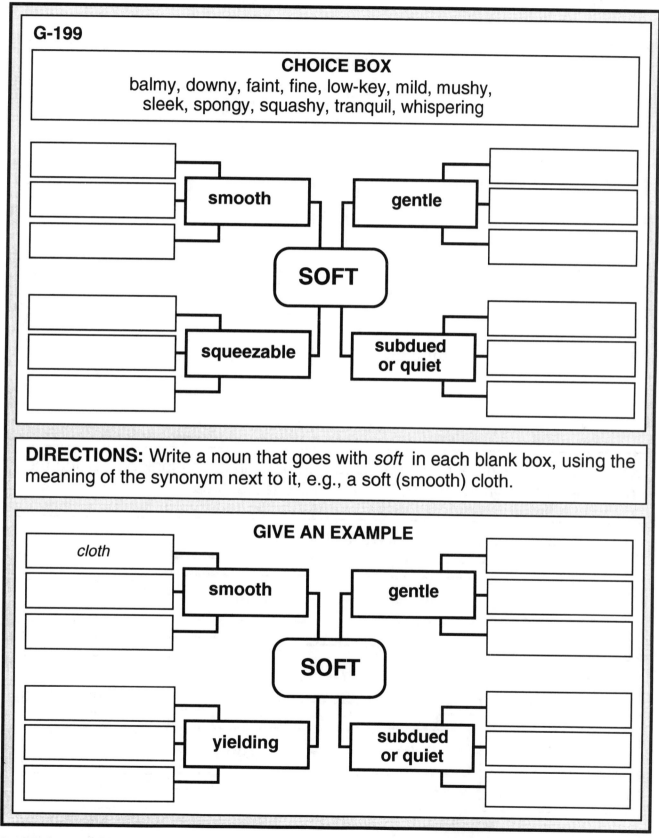

G-199

CHOICE BOX
balmy, downy, faint, fine, low-key, mild, mushy,
sleek, spongy, squashy, tranquil, whispering

smooth

gentle

SOFT

squeezable

subdued
or quiet

DIRECTIONS: Write a noun that goes with *soft* in each blank box, using the meaning of the synonym next to it, e.g., a soft (smooth) cloth.

GIVE AN EXAMPLE

cloth

smooth

gentle

SOFT

yielding

subdued
or quiet

WORD WEB—SELECT AND SUPPLY

DIRECTIONS: Sometimes common words have more than one meaning. In each blank box below, write a word from the choice box that has almost the same meaning as the synonym next to the blank.

G-200

CHOICE BOX
compressed, factual, genuine, heavy, intense,
packed, real, rugged, serious, solid, tough, violent

actual

firm

HARD

difficult

strong

DIRECTIONS: Write a noun that goes with *hard* in each blank box, using the meaning of the synonym next to it, e.g., hard (actual) data.

GIVE AN EXAMPLE

data

actual

firm

HARD

difficult

strong

WORD WEB—SELECT AND SUPPLY

DIRECTIONS: Sometimes common words have more than one meaning. In each blank box below, write a word from the choice box that has almost the same meaning as the synonym next to the blank.

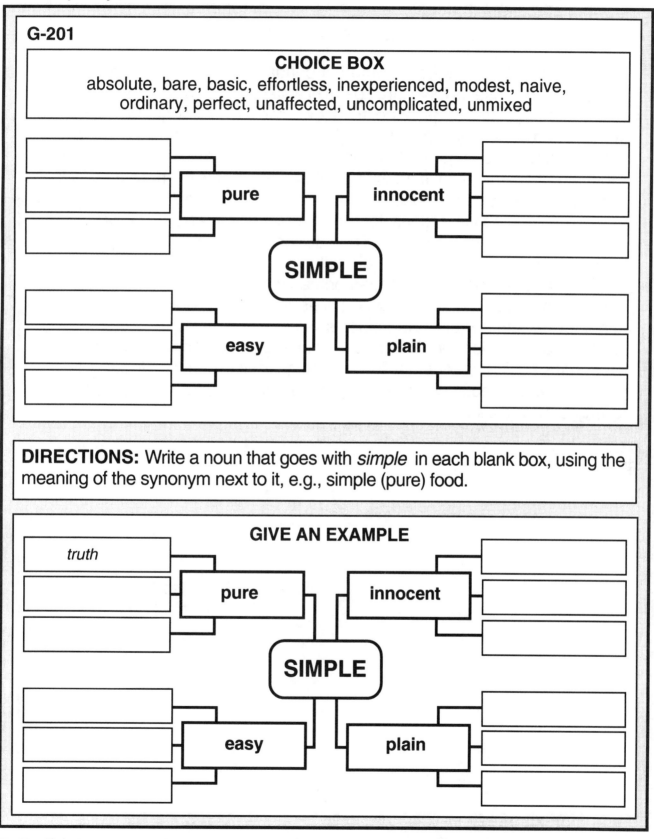

G-201

CHOICE BOX
absolute, bare, basic, effortless, inexperienced, modest, naive, ordinary, perfect, unaffected, uncomplicated, unmixed

pure

innocent

SIMPLE

easy

plain

DIRECTIONS: Write a noun that goes with *simple* in each blank box, using the meaning of the synonym next to it, e.g., simple (pure) food.

GIVE AN EXAMPLE

truth

pure

innocent

SIMPLE

easy

plain

COMPARE AND CONTRAST—GRAPHIC ORGANIZER

DIRECTIONS: Read the following information about spiders and insects. Use this information to compare and contrast spiders and insects in the graphic organizer on the next page.

INSECTS AND SPIDERS

Insects and spiders have jointed appendages, segmented bodies, and exoskeletons. Insects have three pairs of walking legs and spiders have four pairs. Their jointed legs bend to allow quick movement. Insects have segmented bodies with three parts: the head, the thorax, and the abdomen. Spiders have two major body parts, the cephalothorax and the abdomen. Both types of animal have an exoskeleton. This is an external skeleton that protects the body and is molted as the animal grows. Insects have antennae. Antennae are sense organs found on the head that can detect odors. Spiders do not have antennae. They do, however, have spinnerets which produce the fine silk used for their webs.

Spiders are predators that feed primarily on other insects. Spiders can swallow only liquids, so digestive juices are pumped onto the prey, it is digested externally, and the spider swallows the resulting liquid. Insects obtain food by a variety of methods, including biting, lapping, and sucking. Butterflies suck nectar from a flower through their proboscis (feeding tube). Honeybees lap nectar with their tongues. Beetles, wasps, and ants use their powerful biting jaws.

COMPARE AND CONTRAST—GRAPHIC ORGANIZER

DIRECTIONS: Use the graphic organizer below to compare and contrast insects and spiders.

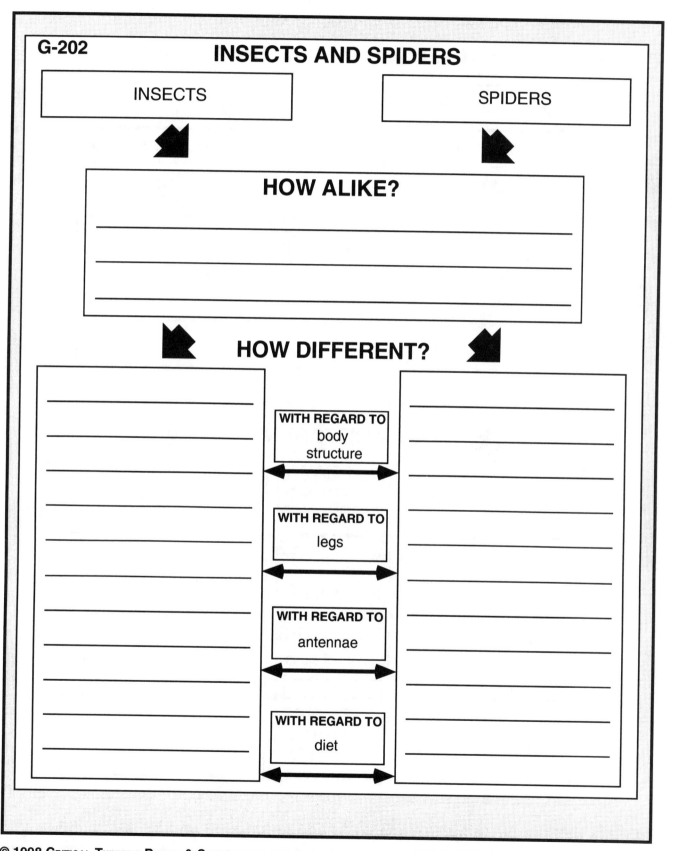

COMPARE AND CONTRAST—GRAPHIC ORGANIZER

DIRECTIONS: Use the graphic organizer below to compare and contrast a parallelogram and an isosceles trapezoid.

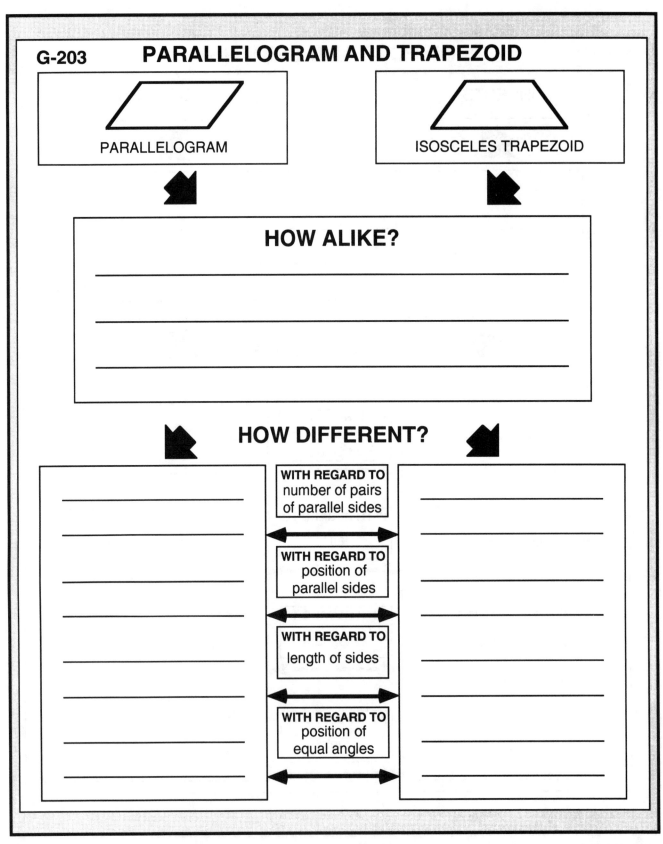

G-203 **PARALLELOGRAM AND TRAPEZOID**

PARALLELOGRAM

ISOSCELES TRAPEZOID

HOW ALIKE?

HOW DIFFERENT?

WITH REGARD TO number of pairs of parallel sides

WITH REGARD TO position of parallel sides

WITH REGARD TO length of sides

WITH REGARD TO position of equal angles

COMPARE AND CONTRAST—GRAPHIC ORGANIZER

DIRECTIONS: Use the graphic organizer below to compare and contrast democracy and dictatorship.

CHAPTER EIGHT

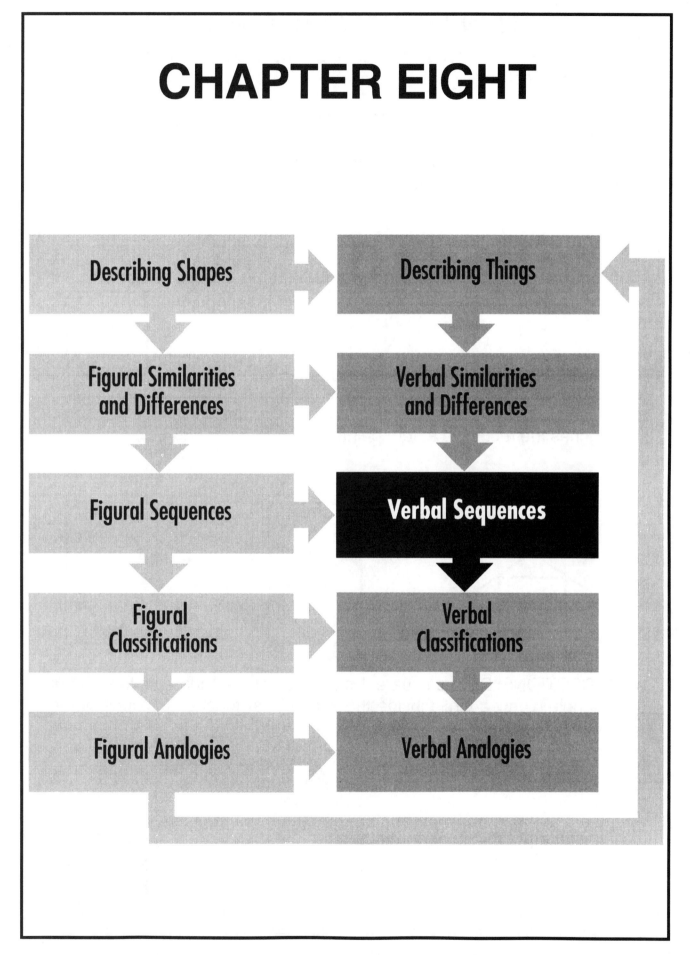

Describing Shapes

Describing Things

Figural Similarities and Differences

Verbal Similarities and Differences

Figural Sequences

Verbal Sequences

Figural Classifications

Verbal Classifications

Figural Analogies

Verbal Analogies

FOLLOWING DIRECTIONS—SELECT

DIRECTIONS: For each set of directions below, circle the figure that correctly represents the directions.

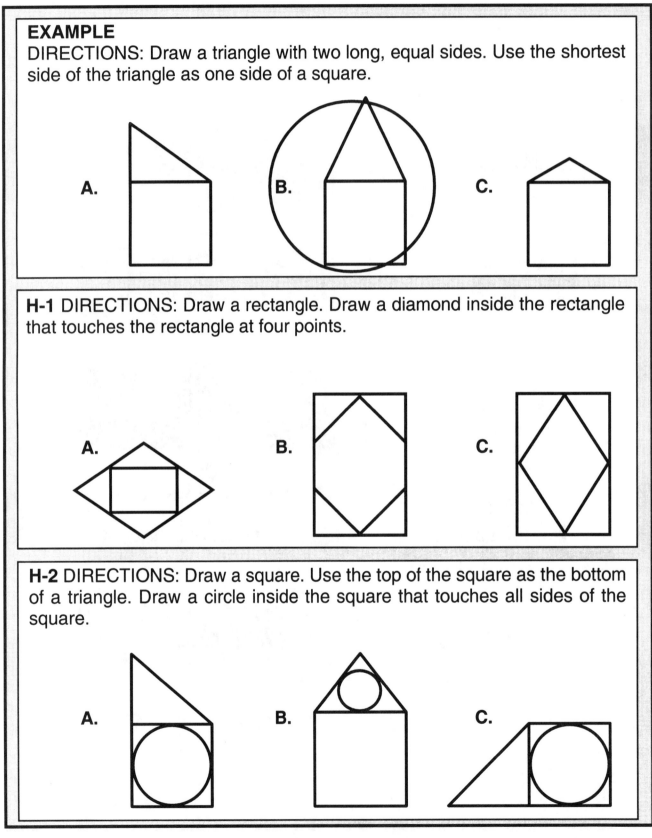

EXAMPLE
DIRECTIONS: Draw a triangle with two long, equal sides. Use the shortest side of the triangle as one side of a square.

A.   B.   C.

H-1 DIRECTIONS: Draw a rectangle. Draw a diamond inside the rectangle that touches the rectangle at four points.

A.   B.   C.

H-2 DIRECTIONS: Draw a square. Use the top of the square as the bottom of a triangle. Draw a circle inside the square that touches all sides of the square.

A.   B.   C.

FOLLOWING DIRECTIONS—SELECT

DIRECTIONS: For each set of directions below, circle the figure that correctly represents the directions.

H-3 DIRECTIONS: Draw a right triangle with the base and height the same length. Draw a rectangle using the height of the triangle as the long side of the rectangle. Inside the triangle, draw a circle that touches all sides of the triangle.

H-4 DIRECTIONS: Draw two squares, one above the other. Draw a triangle inside the upper square. Draw a circle inside the lower square.

H-5 DIRECTIONS: Draw a square. Divide the square into two equal parts by drawing a line from the upper left corner to the lower right corner. Draw a rectangle using the bottom of the square as the top of the rectangle.

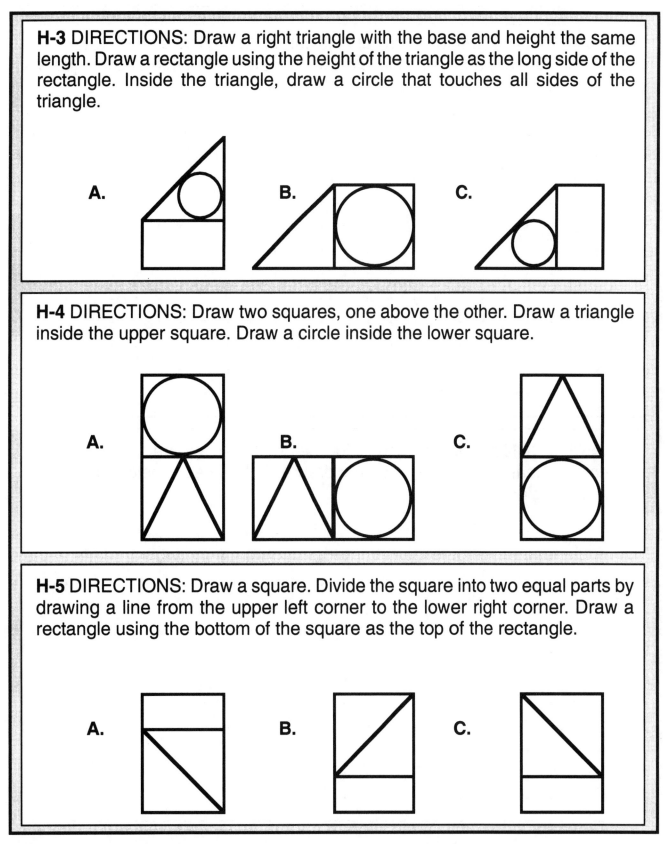

FOLLOWING DIRECTIONS—SUPPLY

DIRECTIONS: For each set of directions below, draw a figure that correctly represents the directions.

H-6 DIRECTIONS: Using the grid of dots below, draw a circle near the center of the grid. Directly above the circle draw a square. To the right of the square draw a triangle.

H-7 DIRECTIONS: Using the grid of dots below, draw a square near the lower left corner. Near the upper right corner draw a circle. Directly below the circle draw a triangle.

FOLLOWING DIRECTIONS—SUPPLY

DIRECTIONS: For each set of directions below, draw a figure that correctly represents the directions.

H-8 DIRECTIONS: Using the grid of dots below, draw a circle near the center of the grid. To the right of the circle, draw a triangle that is taller than the circle. To the left of the circle, draw a square that is shorter than the circle.

H-9 DIRECTIONS: Using the grid of dots below, draw a large rectangle. Inside the rectangle, draw a white circle and a black square. The square should be to the right of the circle.

FOLLOWING DIRECTIONS—SUPPLY

INSTRUCTIONS: Each problem should be drawn on a whole sheet of paper. Follow the directions exactly.

H-10 DIRECTIONS

a. Find the midpoint of the left side of the paper and draw a small square (the midpoint is halfway down the paper).

b. Find the midpoint of the right side of the paper and draw a small square.

c. Draw a line across the paper that touches each square but does not go into either square.

H-11 DIRECTIONS

a. Write an "X" in each of the four corners of the paper.

b. Draw an arrow from the top left corner to the bottom left corner.

c. Draw an arrow from the bottom left corner to the bottom right corner.

d. What large letter did you form?

H-12 DIRECTIONS

a. Draw a line from the middle of the top of the paper to the middle of the bottom of the paper.

b. Draw a line from the middle of the left edge of the paper to the middle of the right edge of the paper.

c. Using the point where the lines cross as the center of a circle, draw the biggest circle you can.

H-13 DIRECTIONS

a. Draw a line up and down the paper and keep the line about an inch from the left edge of the paper.

b. Draw a line across the page and keep it about an inch below the top of the paper.

c. Darken the square that is formed in the upper left corner.

WRITING DIRECTIONS

INSTRUCTIONS: Look at the figure on the left very carefully. Write directions for drawing the figure so that a classmate could draw the figure without seeing it.

H-14

_____

_____

_____

_____

_____

_____

_____

_____

_____

_____

_____

_____

H-15

_____

_____

_____

_____

_____

_____

_____

_____

_____

_____

_____

_____

WRITING DIRECTIONS

INSTRUCTIONS: Look at the figure on the left very carefully. Write directions for drawing the figure so that a classmate could draw the figure without seeing it.

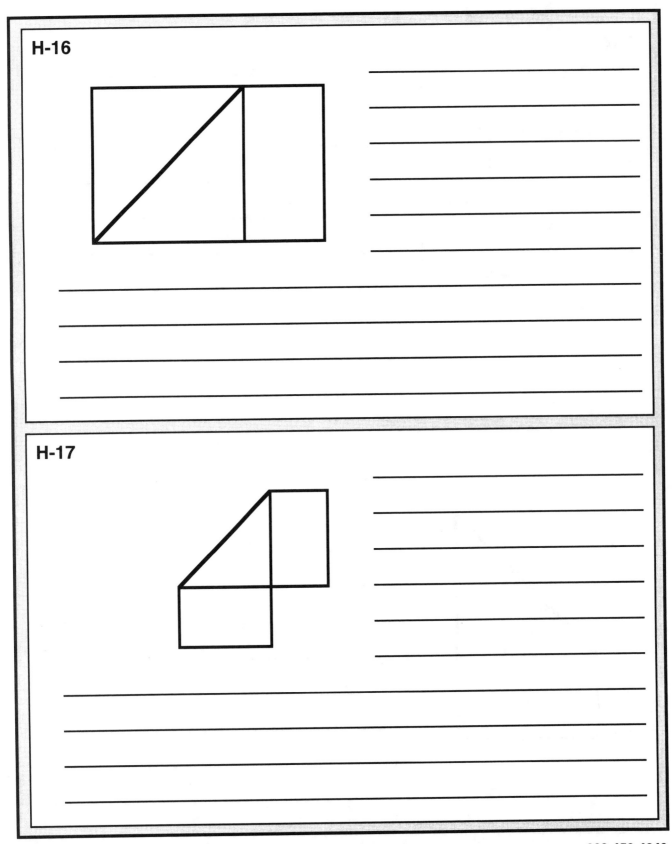

H-16

H-17

RECOGNIZING DIRECTION—A

DIRECTIONS: Imagine that you are standing in the circle, facing the direction of the arrow. The square is straight ahead. Fill in the blanks below to describe the shapes that are to your left, to your right, or behind you.

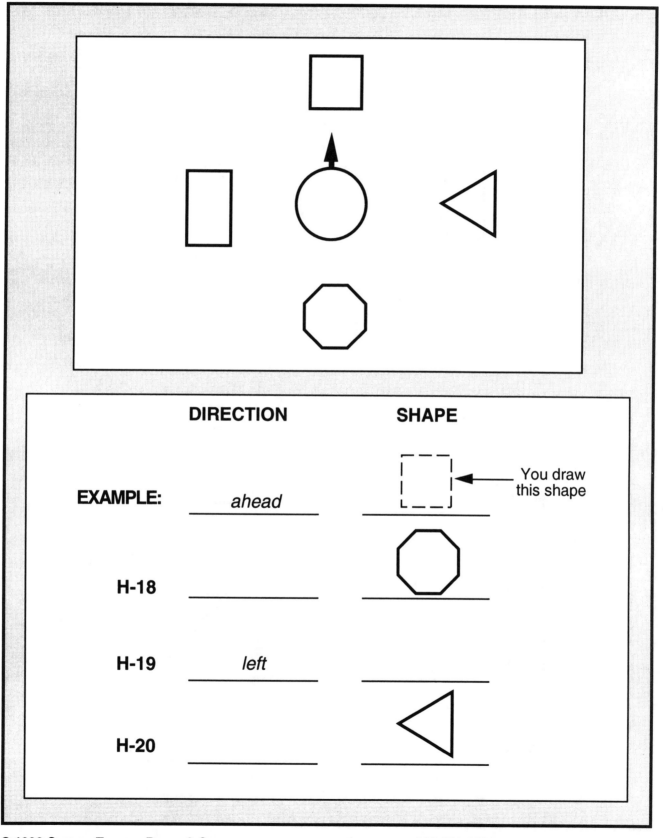

	DIRECTION	SHAPE	
EXAMPLE:	*ahead*		← You draw this shape
H-18			
H-19	*left*		
H-20			

RECOGNIZING DIRECTION—A

DIRECTIONS: Imagine that you are standing in the circle, facing the direction of the arrow. The hexagon is straight ahead. Fill in the blanks below to describe the shapes that are to your left, to your right, or behind you.

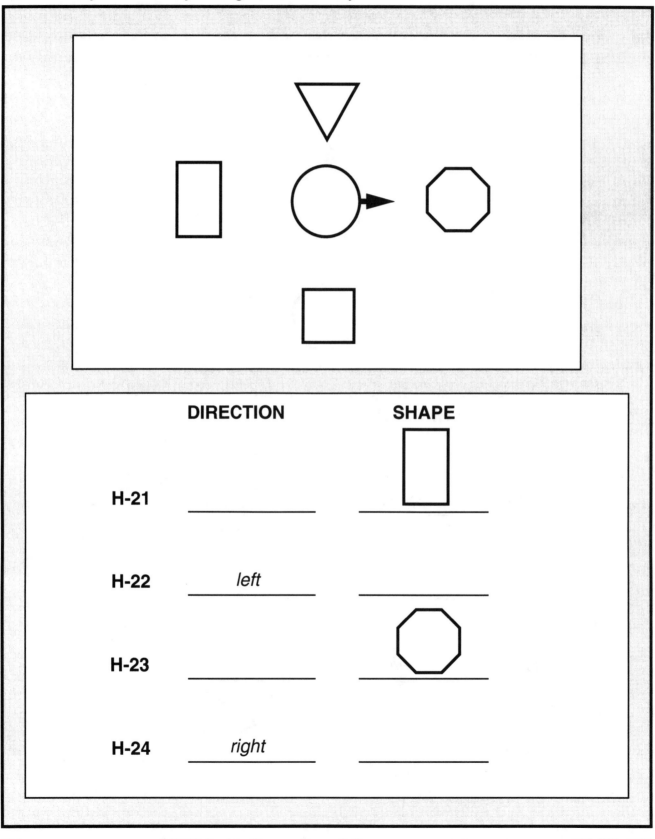

	DIRECTION	SHAPE
H-21	_____	rectangle
H-22	*left*	_____
H-23	_____	octagon
H-24	*right*	_____

RECOGNIZING DIRECTION—B

DIRECTIONS: Imagine that you are standing in the circle below, facing north (N), west (W), south (S), or east (E). Draw the shape you are facing or the shape on your right. For example, if you are facing north (N), as shown in the example, then the rectangle is straight ahead and the triangle is on your right. Trace the triangle in the blank in the first row. Next, imagine that you are facing west (W); draw the missing shape in the blank in the second row.

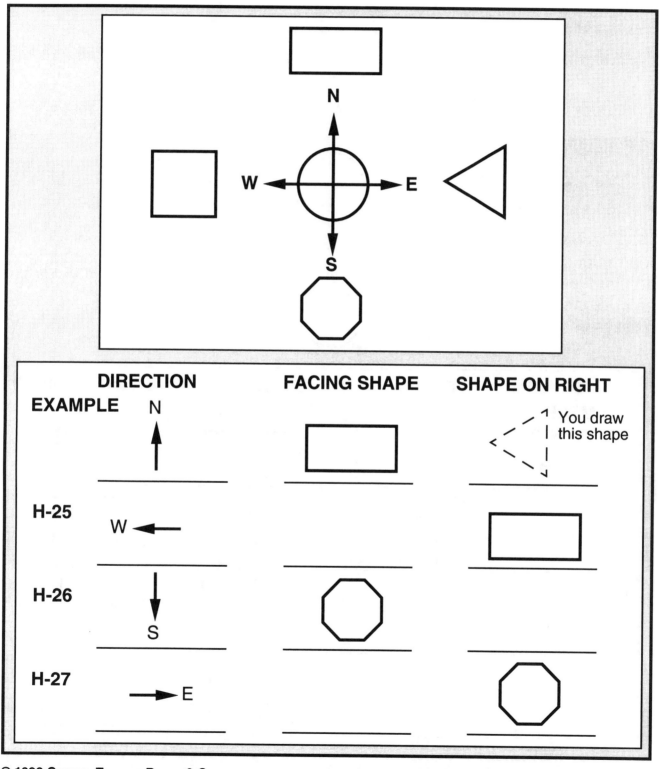

RECOGNIZING DIRECTION—B

DIRECTIONS: Imagine that you are standing in the circle below, facing either north (N), west (W), south (S), or east (E). By knowing the positions of two or more shapes, determine the direction you are facing and draw any missing shapes. For example, if the rectangle is on your right and the octagon is on your left, then you will be facing the square. (Draw the square.) If you are facing the square, you are facing west. (Draw the letter and arrow.)

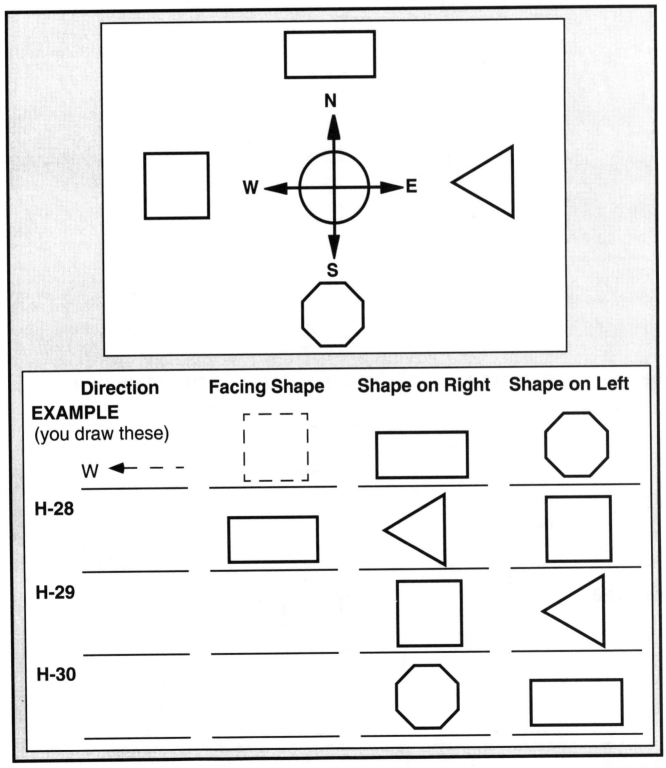

© 1998 CRITICAL THINKING BOOKS & SOFTWARE • WWW.CRITICALTHINKING.COM • 800-458-4849

RECOGNIZING DIRECTION—B

DIRECTIONS: Imagine that you are standing in the circle below, facing either north (N), west (W), south (S), or east (E). By knowing the positions of two or more shapes, determine the direction you are facing. Draw the missing shapes and directions.

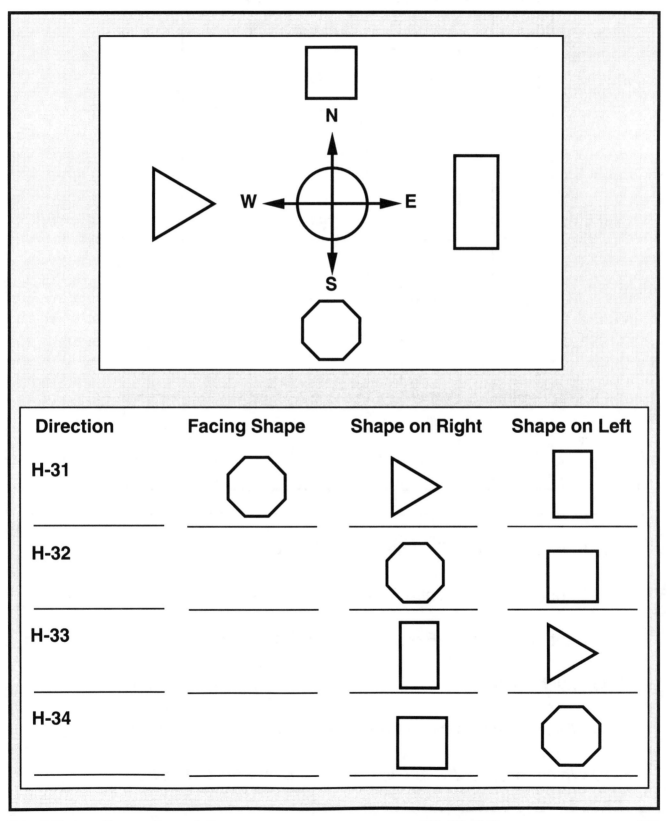

DESCRIBING LOCATIONS

DIRECTIONS: Locate the parts of Midville described in the exercises. Read the instructions for each exercise and mark the map accordingly.

H-35 Print a "P" where Second Avenue and C Street cross.

H-36 Print a "Q" where Third Avenue and A Street cross.

H-37 Print an "R" where First Avenue and D Street cross.

H-38 Which letter (P, Q, or R) is closest to West Park? Answer: _____

H-39 Which letter is in the northern part of Midville?   Answer: _____

H-40 Which Street or Avenue is closest to East Park? Answer: _____

DESCRIBING LOCATIONS

DIRECTIONS: Locate the parts of Midville described in the exercises. Read the instructions for each exercise and answer the questions.

H-41 You are facing West Park. Third Avenue is one block behind you. C Street is one block to your right. You are located where _____ Street meets___ _____ Avenue.

What street or avenue is one block to your left?   Answer: _____

How far are you from North Park?   Answer: _____ blocks.

H-42 You have moved and are now facing South. C Street is one block behind you. Third Avenue is now two blocks to your left. You are now located where _____ Street meets _____ Avenue.

What street or avenue is one block ahead of you? Answer: _____

How far are you from East Park?   Answer: _____ blocks.

DESCRIBING DIRECTIONS

DIRECTIONS: Locate the parts of Midville described in the exercises. Read the instructions for each exercise and answer the questions.

EXAMPLE: If you start at Third Avenue and D Street and travel three blocks south, you will be at the corner of Third Avenue and A Street. (Follow the arrows from Start to Finish.)

H-43 If you start at Fourth Avenue and C Street and travel three blocks west, where will you be?

Answer: Where _____ Street meets _____ Avenue.

H-44 If you start at Second Avenue and D Street and travel in a straight line to Fourth Avenue and D Street, how far have you traveled?

Answer: _____ blocks.

In what direction did you travel? Answer: _____

DESCRIBING DIRECTIONS

DIRECTIONS: Locate the parts of Midville described in the exercises. Read the instructions for each exercise and answer the questions.

H-45 Describe the path shown by the arrows between points X and Y.

Go _____ blocks to the _____ and _____ blocks to the_____ .
   (number)   (direction)   (number)   (direction)

H-46 Draw and describe another path having one turn which will go from point X to point Y.

Go _____ blocks to the _____ and _____ blocks to the_____ .
   (number)   (direction)   (number)   (direction)

How many total blocks are traveled in each path? Answer: Each path is _____ blocks long.
   (number)

DESCRIBING DIRECTIONS

DIRECTIONS: Locate the parts of Midville described in the exercises. Read the instructions for each exercise and answer the questions.

H-47 Describe the path shown by the arrows between points P and Q.

Go _____ blocks to the _____ and _____ blocks to the _____.
      (number)   (direction)   (number)   (direction)

H-48 Draw and describe another path having one turn which will go from point P to point Q.

Go _____ blocks to the _____ and _____ blocks to the _____.
      (number)   (direction)   (number)   (direction)

How many total blocks are traveled in each path?

Answer: Each path is _____ blocks long.
                      (number)

DESCRIBING DIRECTIONS

DIRECTIONS: Locate the parts of Midville described in the exercises. Read the instructions for each exercise and answer the questions.

H-49 Use a dotted line (. . . . .) to draw a path from point R to point S that is four blocks long and has two turns. Describe the path.

Go _____ blocks to the _____ and _____ blocks to the _____
    (number)   (direction)   (number)   (direction)

and _____ blocks to the _____.
    (number)   (direction)

H-50 Use a dashed line (– – –) to draw another path from point R to point S that is four blocks long and has two turns. Describe the path.

Go _____ blocks to the _____ and _____ blocks to the _____
    (number)   (direction)   (number)   (direction)

and _____ blocks to the _____.
    (number)   (direction)

TIME SEQUENCE—SELECT

DIRECTIONS: The first two words in each group suggest an order of occurrence. On the blank, write the word from the column on the right that will continue the time sequence.

H-51 leave, travel, _____

arrive
depart
drive

H-52 earn, save, _____

gain
receive
spend

H-53 plan, build, _____

construct
design
occupy

H-54 cause, event, _____

chance
reason
result

H-55 early, prompt, _____

late
now
soon

H-56 measure, mark, _____

cut
line
rule

H-57 sleep, waken, _____

rise
slumber
stir

TIME SEQUENCE—RANK

DIRECTIONS: On the lines below, rewrite each group of words in order of occurrence from earliest to latest.

H-58 clean, cook, eat

_____, _____, _____

H-59 dial, hang up, talk

_____, _____, _____

H-60 buy, shop, use

_____, _____, _____

H-61 attack, battle, defeat

_____, _____, _____

H-62 lesson, performance, practice

_____, _____, _____

H-63 continue, finish, start

_____, _____, _____

H-64 dry, rinse, wash

_____, _____, _____

TIME SEQUENCE—SUPPLY

DIRECTIONS: The words or phrases in each group suggest an order of occurrence. Think of a word that will continue the time sequence and write it in the blank. You may need to use a dictionary.

H-65 born, live, _____

H-66 plow, plant, _____

H-67 begin, continue, _____

H-68 past, present, _____

H-69 dawn, morning, _____

H-70 hurt, treat, _____

H-71 inhale, hold breath, _____

H-72 read catalog, select product, _____

H-73 enroll, attend, _____

DEGREE OF MEANING—SELECT

DIRECTIONS: The words in each group suggest a sequence of rank, degree, size, or order. In the blank, write the word from the column on the right that will come next in the sequence.

H-74 chilly, frosty, _____

brisk
cool
freezing

H-75 ahead, beside, _____

behind
beneath
between

H-76 hint, ask, _____

demand
request
suggest

H-77 sad, depressed, _____

hopeless
sorry
unhappy

H-78 scarce, adequate, _____

enough
few
plenty

H-79 satisfactory, admirable, _____

average
ordinary
excellent

H-80 mist, light rain, _____

downpour
drizzle
fog

DEGREE OF MEANING—SELECT

DIRECTIONS: The words in each group suggest a sequence of rank, degree, size, or order. In the blank, write the word from the column on the right that will come next in the sequence.

H-81 gentle, firm, _____

harsh
mild
tender

H-82 exact, similar, _____

alike
different
identical

H-83 asleep, calm, active, _____

excited
quiet
resting

H-84 incomplete, poor, _____

careless
average
worthless

H-85 shy, fearful, _____

bashful
coy
terrified

H-86 fatigued, weary, _____

drained
exhausted
tired

H-87 bothered, displeased, _____

annoyed
disappointed
disgusted

DEGREE OF MEANING—RANK

DIRECTIONS: On the lines below, rewrite each group of words in order from least or smallest to greatest or largest in degree, rank, size, or order.

H-88 delighted, pleased, thrilled

_____, _____, _____

H-89 danger, safety, threat

_____, _____, _____

H-90 doze, nap, sleep

_____, _____, _____

H-91 bright, dark, dim

_____, _____, _____

H-92 desert, jungle, prairie

_____, _____, _____

H-93 lake, ocean, pond

_____, _____, _____

H-94 continent, country, state

_____, _____, _____

DEGREE OF MEANING—RANK

DIRECTIONS: On the lines below, rewrite each group of words in order from lowest or smallest to highest or largest in degree, rank, size, or order.

H-95 class, pupil, school

_____, _____, _____

H-96 painful, sore, tender

_____, _____, _____

H-97 burst, full, swell

_____, _____, _____

H-98 empty, overflowing, full

_____, _____, _____

H-99 full, hungry, starving

_____, _____, _____

H-100 gallon, pint, quart

_____, _____, _____

H-101 foot, inch, yard

_____, _____, _____

DEGREE OF MEANING—SUPPLY

DIRECTIONS: The words in each group suggest a sequence of degree, rank, size, or order. Think of a word that will continue the sequence and write it in the blank. You may need to use a dictionary.

H-102 mayor, governor, _____

H-103 front, side, _____

H-104 few, many, _____

H-105 far, farther, _____

H-106 more, some, _____

H-107 word, sentence, _____

H-108 same, similar, _____

H-109 good, better, _____

H-110 cool, warm, _____

DEGREE OF MEANING—SUPPLY

DIRECTIONS: On the lines below, rewrite each group of words in order from lowest or smallest to highest or largest in degree, rank, size, or order.

H-111 short, average, _____

H-112 dark, dawn, _____

H-113 day, week, _____

H-114 caterpillar, cocoon, _____

H-115 scene, act, _____

H-116 home, neighborhood, _____

H-117 foal, colt, _____

H-118 duet, trio, _____

H-119 tenor, baritone _____

TRANSITIVITY—COMPARISON

DIRECTIONS: In these sentences, animals or objects are being compared according to some characteristic they have in common. Read the sentences and use the diagrams to figure out the order. Then list the items in order.

H-120   The adult fox terrier is about four inches taller than the West Highland terrier (Westie). The Airedale is the largest dog in the terrier breed. List the terriers in descending order beginning with the largest.

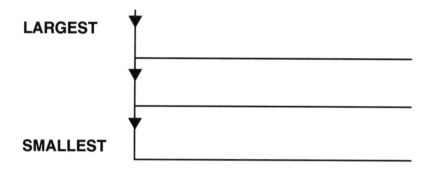

H-121   A bus is faster than a bicycle. Subway trains are faster than buses but slower than monorail trains. List the vehicles in descending order beginning with the fastest.

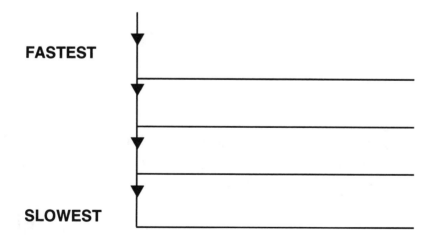

TRANSITIVITY—COMPARISON

DIRECTIONS: In these sentences, people or objects are being compared according to some characteristic they have in common (age, size, or position). Read the sentences and use the diagrams to figure out the order. List the items in order.

H-122   Mary is older than Gloria. Gloria is younger than Elizabeth. Michelle is older than Elizabeth but younger than Mary. Write the four names in order, starting with the name of the oldest person.

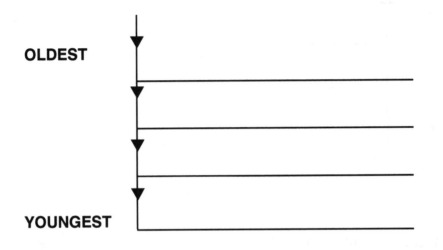

H-123   Three houses are in a row. One is modern, one is colonial, and one is Victorian. The colonial house is north of the modern house and south of the Victorian house. List the houses in order from north to south.

NORTH _____, _____, _____, **SOUTH**

H-124   Christine, Eric, Jesse, John, and Taryn are in line at the movie. Taryn is in front of Eric but behind John. Christine is behind Eric but in front of Jesse. List the children in order from front to rear.

FRONT   **REAR**

_____, _____, _____, _____, _____

TRANSITIVITY—COMPARISON

DIRECTIONS: In these sentences, events are being compared according to their occurrence. Arrange the events in order of occurrence from earliest to latest.

H-125   John Quincy Adams, the sixth president of the United States, was the son of John Adams, the second president. John Adams became president after two terms as vice president during the presidency of George Washington. Thomas Jefferson followed John Adams as president.

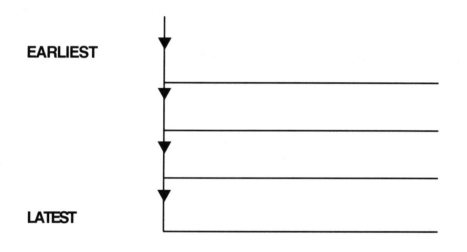

EARLIEST

LATEST

H-126   The oldest permanent European settlement in the United States is St. Augustine, Florida. Plymouth, Massachusetts, was settled thirteen years after the Jamestown, Virginia colony. List these historic cities in the order they were settled.

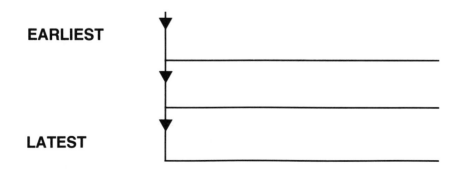

EARLIEST

LATEST

TRANSITIVITY—COMPARISON

DIRECTIONS: In these sentences, events are being compared according to their occurrence. Arrange the events in order of occurrence from earliest to latest.

H-127 Number these sentences in order of occurrence from the earliest to the latest. Use the time line to keep track of the time order.

_____ a. Between eighteen months and two years, a baby begins to speak in sentences.

_____ b. One of a newborn baby's first skills is grasping objects or toys.

_____ c. The infant begins to crawl when it is about six months old.

_____ d. Soon after a baby's first birthday, the child begins to use words.

EVENTS IN INFANT'S LIFE

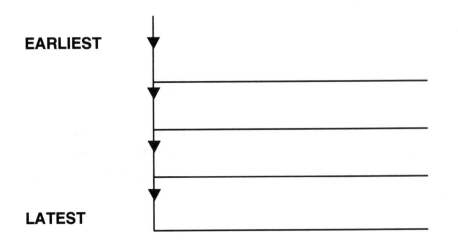

EARLIEST

LATEST

TRANSITIVITY—COMPARISON

DIRECTIONS: In these sentences, events are being compared according to their occurrence. Arrange the events in order of occurrence from earliest to latest.

H-128   Number these sentences in order of occurrence from the earliest to the latest. Use the time line to keep track of the time order.

_____   a. Bob Keeshan played Captain Kangaroo on the *Captain Kangaroo Show*.

_____   b. Before playing Captain Kangaroo, Bob Keeshan played Clarabelle the Clown on the *Howdy Doody Show*.

_____   c. After the success of *Sesame Street*, Children's Television Workshop developed *The Electric Company*.

_____   d. Recognizing the educational benefits of the *Captain Kangaroo Show*, Children's Television Workshop produced *Sesame Street* to emphasize learning concepts for young children.

List these children's television shows from the earliest to the latest.

CHILDREN'S TELEVISION SHOWS

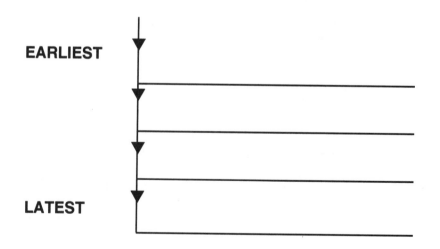

EARLIEST

LATEST

COMMON SEQUENCES

DIRECTIONS: Many things you do must be done in order. List the phrases in the order they should occur.

H-129 **Steps in Taking a Photograph**

Click the shutter
Focus the camera
Have film processed
Load film into camera
Purchase film

1. _____
2. _____
3. _____
4. _____
5. _____

H-130 **Steps in Making a Long Distance Call**

Dial area code
Dial one (1)
Dial seven-digit number
Hang up
Lift receiver
Talk

1. _____
2. _____
3. _____
4. _____
5. _____
6. _____

COMMON SEQUENCES

DIRECTIONS: Many things you do must be done in order. List the phrases in the order they should occur.

H-131   Steps in Planning a Candy Sale

Buy the materials to make candy
Cook the candy
Decide on the type of candy you will make
Find a recipe for the candy
Package the candy
Sell the candy

1. _____
2. _____
3. _____
4. _____
5. _____
6. _____

H-132   Steps in Adopting a Dog

Ask your parents if you can have a dog
Go to the animal shelter with your family
Pay for the license and adoption fee
Pick out the dog
Take the dog home
Talk with your family about the kind of dog that is best for the family

1. _____
2. _____
3. _____
4. _____
5. _____
6. _____

TRANSITIVITY—FAMILY TREE

Family tree diagrams are used to show relationships between generations in a family. By using symbols, the diagram helps you organize relationships between

husband and wife

parent and child

sister and brother

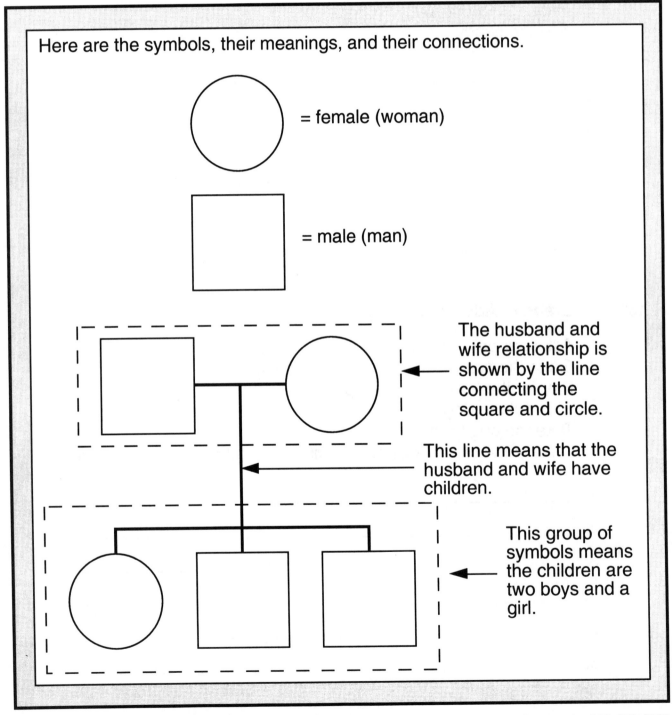

Here are the symbols, their meanings, and their connections.

= female (woman)

= male (man)

The husband and wife relationship is shown by the line connecting the square and circle.

This line means that the husband and wife have children.

This group of symbols means the children are two boys and a girl.

 © 1998 CRITICAL THINKING BOOKS & SOFTWARE • WWW.CRITICALTHINKING.COM • 800-458-4849

TRANSITIVITY—FAMILY TREE

DIRECTIONS: In the family tree diagram below, circles represent females and squares represent males. Use the clues fo fill in the diagram.

CLUES

Juan and Rosita have the same names as their grandparents. Marie has the same name as her mother.

One of Jose's daughters has the same name as Jose's mother.

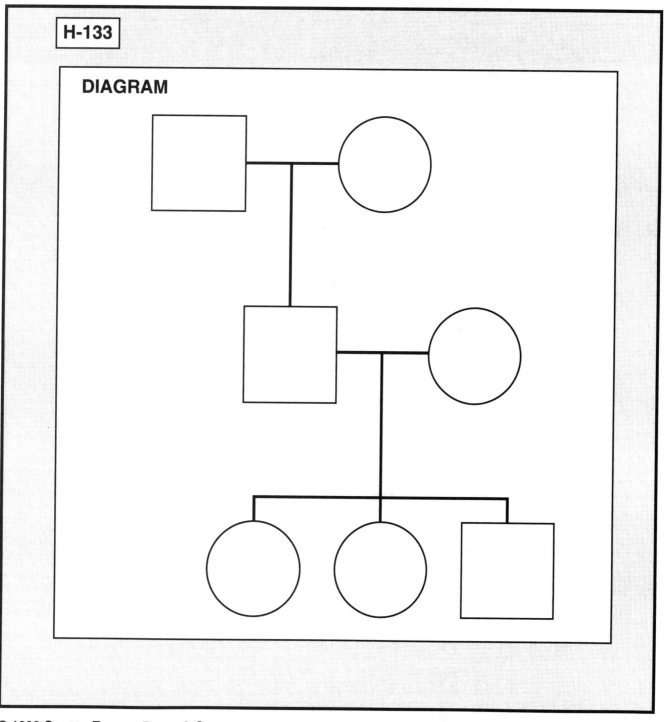

H-133

DIAGRAM

TRANSITIVITY—FAMILY TREE

DIRECTIONS: In the family tree diagram below, circles represent females and squares represent males. Use the clues fo fill in the diagram.

CLUES

Jim is the father of Bill and Mary.

Jane is Mary's sister.

Helen is Mary's mother.

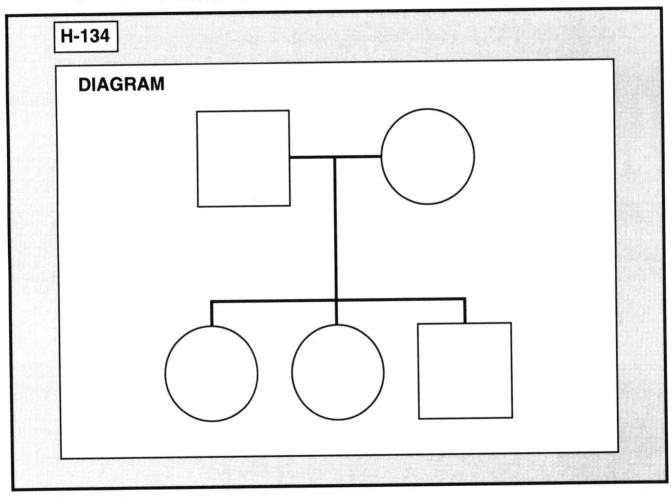

H-134

DIAGRAM

QUESTIONS

1. What is the name of Jim's wife? _____

2. What is the name of Jane's brother? _____

3. What is the name of Bill's mother? _____

4. What is the name of Jane's father? _____

TRANSITIVITY—FAMILY TREE

DIRECTIONS: In the family tree diagram below, circles represent females and squares represent males. Use the clues fo fill in the diagram.

CLUES

Michael and Irene Cooper have two children.
The children are named for Michael's father and Irene's mother.
The grandparents are Frank and Ruth Brown, and John and Bonnie Cooper.

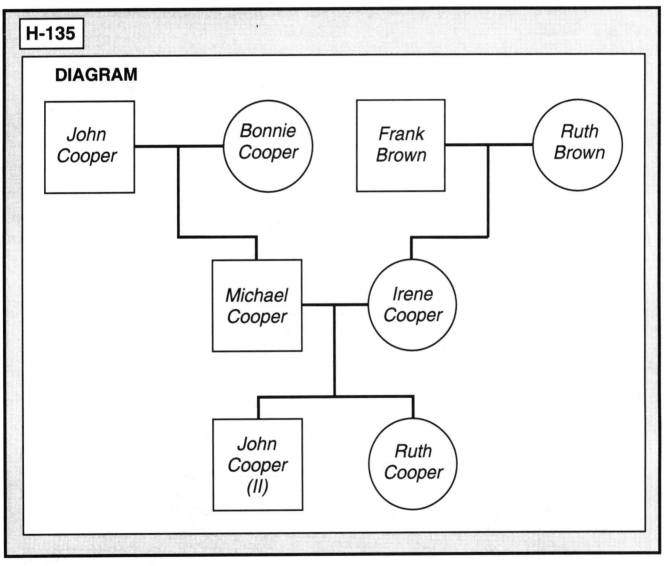

H-135

DIAGRAM

QUESTIONS

1. What was Irene's name before she got married?

_____

2. What are the names of Michael and Irene's children?

_____

YOUR FAMILY TREE

DIRECTIONS: Write the first and last names of a member of your family in each square or circle. If all your sisters and brothers won't fit on the row beside your name, add their names to the row below.

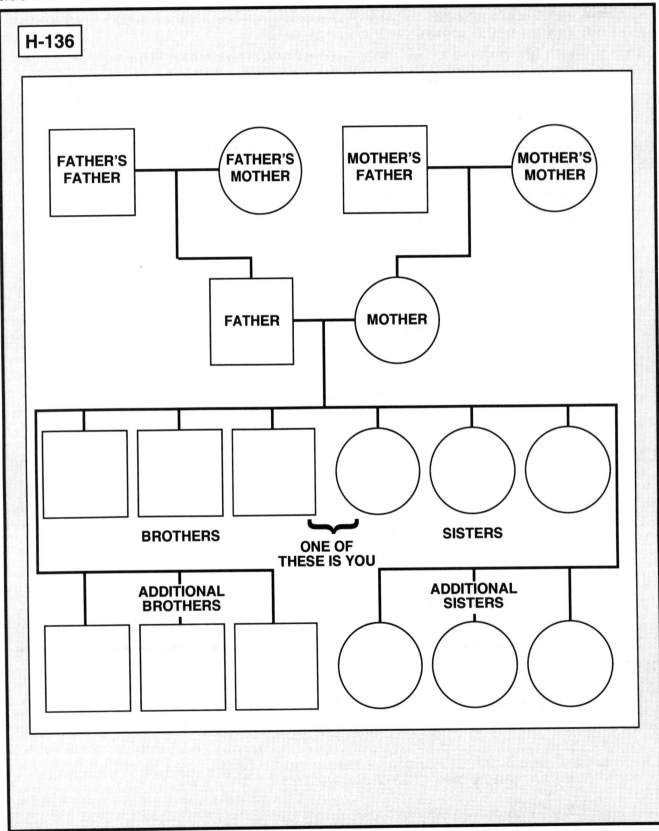

DEDUCTIVE REASONING—INSTRUCTIONS

A *Mind Benders* ® problem asks you to match items with their characteristics. Making a matrix helps you work the problem. Here is a Mind Bender® involving three people and their pets.

EXAMPLE

Michael, Sarah, and Tina own a cat, a goldfish, or a parakeet. From the clues below, match the pet owner's names with the pets.

a. Tina is allergic to animal fur.

b. Michael's pet does not use kitty litter or live in a cage.

STEP 1 From the clue "Tina is allergic to animal fur," you can figure out that Tina does not own the cat. Find the row marked *T* for Tina and write "NO" in the column marked *C* for cat.

	C	G	P
M			
S			
T	NO		

STEP 2 The second clue, "Michael's pet does not use kitty litter or live in a cage," tells you that Michael does not own a cat or a bird. Find the row marked *M* for Michael and write "NO" in both the *C* column for cat and the *P* column for parakeet.

	C	G	P
M	NO		NO
S			
T	NO		

STEP 3 You know that each person owns a pet. Since neither Michael nor Tina owns the cat, Sarah must be the cat owner. Write "YES" in the *S* row for Sarah and the *C* column for cat.

	C	G	P
M	NO		NO
S	YES		
T	NO		

DEDUCTIVE REASONING—INSTRUCTIONS

STEP 4   Since Sarah owns the cat, Sarah does not own the goldfish or the parakeet. Write "NO" in the *S* row in both the *G* column for goldfish and the *P* column for parakeet.

	C	G	P
M	NO		NO
S	YES	NO	NO
T	NO		

STEP 5   By the same kind of reasoning, you see that the only vacancy in the *M* row is in the *G* column (for goldfish). From this, you figure out (deduce) that Michael is the goldfish owner. Write a "YES" in this position.

	C	G	P
M	NO	YES	NO
S	YES	NO	NO
T	NO		

STEP 6   Since Michael owns the goldfish, then neither Sarah nor Tina own the goldfish. You have already figured out (deduced) that Sarah doesn't own the goldfish. Now you know that Tina doesn't either. Mark "NO" in the *T* row and the *G* column.

	C	G	P
M	NO	YES	NO
S	YES	NO	NO
T	NO	NO	

STEP 7   The only vacancy remaining on the chart is in the T row and the P column. You now know that Tina is the parakeet owner. You are now ready to fill in the answers:

Sarah is the cat owner.

Michael is the goldfish owner.

Tina is the parakeet owner.

DEDUCTIVE REASONING

H-137 In looking up her family tree, Mrs. Bradford found that members of her family had been born in Bourne, Dartmouth, and Salem. Her ancestors' names were Abraham, James, and Nathaniel. From the clues below match the names with the places of birth.

a. Nathaniel was older than James.

b. Abraham's mother and father came from Europe and settled in Salem just before he was born.

c. The youngest Bradford was born in Dartmouth.

	Abraham	James	Nathaniel
Bourne			
Dartmouth			
Salem			

Abraham was born in

_____.

James was born in

_____.

Nathaniel was born in

_____.

H-138 Onju, Pedro, and Richard are all in different grades at school. The children are either in the thrid, fourth, or fifth grade. From the clues below, match the children with their grade.

a. Pedro and Onju are not in the third grade.

b. Onju is in a higher grade than Pedro.

	3rd	4th	5th
Onju			
Pedro			
Richard			

Onju is in _____ grade.

Pedro is in _____ grade.

Richard is in _____ grade.

DEDUCTIVE REASONING

H-139   A mouse, a rabbit, and a tiger are called Cicero, Ego, or Fred. From the clues below, match the name with the animal.

    a. Ego is larger than a mouse.

    b. Cicero is older than the rabbit but younger than the tiger.

    c. Fred is older than Cicero.

	Mouse	Rabbit	Tiger
Cicero			
Ego			
Fred			

Cicero is the _____.

Ego is the _____.

Fred is the _____.

H-140   David, Hector, and Maria are on different teams. They are either of the baseball team, the football team, or the swimming team. From the clues below, match the students with their teams.

    a. Maria can't swim.

    b. David is better at swimming than Hector.

    c. Hector is the quarterback on his team.

	Baseball	Football	Swimming
D			
H			
M			

David is on the _____ team.

Hector is on the _____ team.

Maria is on the _____ team.

DEDUCTIVE REASONING

H-141   Anita, Beth, and Juan are a cook, a nurse, and a typist. From the clues below, match each person with their job.

a. Juan cannot type.

b. Anita is neither the nurse nor the typist.

	Cook	Nurse	Typist
A			
B			
J			

Anita is the _____.

Beth is the _____.

Juan is the _____.

H-142   Mr. Allen, Mr. Franklin, Ms. Smith, and Mrs. Townsend teach either first grade, second grade, third grade, or art. From the clues below match each teacher with his or her class.

a. Mr. Allen does not teach reading or arithmetic.

b. Ms. Smith teaches a lower grade than Mrs. Townsend, but a higher grade than Mr. Franklin.

	1st	2nd	3rd	Art
A				
F				
S				
T				

Mr. Allen is the _____ teacher.

Mr. Franklin is the _____ teacher.

Ms. Smith is the _____ teacher.

Mrs. Townsend is the _____ teacher.

DEDUCTIVE REASONING

H-143 George, Nancy, and Shannon are an astronaut, a computer programmer, and a mathematics teacher. From the clues below, match the people with their professions.

a. George is not the astronaut or the computer programmer.

b. Nancy is not the astronaut.

	George	Nancy	Shannon
A			
CP			
MT			

George is the _____.

Nancy is the _____.

Shannon is the _____.

H-144 Three racing car drivers named Graham, Mario, and Pancho entered cars in a 24-hour race and each won a prize. From the clues below, determine who drove each car and what prize was won by each driver.

a. The coupe won a higher prize than Mario's car.

b. Mario did not drive the Spyder.

c. A hatchback won a prize.

d. Graham's car won first prize.

e. The Spyder came in second.

	Coupe	Hatch-back	Spyder
Graham			
Mario			
Pancho			

Place	Car	Driver
First		
Second		
Third		

DEDUCTIVE REASONING

H-145   Bob, Chris, Nancy, and Pat have different colored bikes. The bikes are red, blue, green, and white. From the clues below, match the bikes with the owners.

a. Bob and Chris have ten-speed bikes.

b. Chris's friend has a blue bike.

c. Nancy has a three-speed and is a friend of the owner of the white bike.

d. Nancy sometimes rides her brother's blue ten-speed bike.

e. Pat does not like his friend's green bike.

f. The red bike has one speed.

	Bob	Chris	Nancy	Pat
Red				
Blue				
Green				
White				

	Axe	Hammer	Pliers	Saw
Bill				
Jane				
Kim				
Tom				

Diagram for problem **H-146** below.

H-146   Bill, Jane, Kim, and Tom brought an axe, a hammer, a pair of pliers, or a saw to build a project at school. From the clues below, match the students with the tools. (Use the diagram above on the right)

a. Neither Bill nor the girl with the pliers brought the hammer.

b. Jane couldn't find a cutting tool.

c. Kim brought her mom's hammer.

d. Bill lost his axe before the project started.

263

DEDUCTIVE REASONING

H-147   In science class, students learn the eating habits of several types of animals. Some animals eat meat and others eat plants. Some animals eat both plants and animals. Some animals eat plankton. For her science project, Marisa picked four animals of different sizes and studied their eating habits. From the clues below, match the eating habits with the sizes of the four animals. The animal sizes can be described as small, medium, large, and very large.

a. The large animal is neither a meat eater nor a plankton eater.

b. The medium-sized animal is larger than the plankton eater.

c. The meat eater is larger than the plant eater.

d. The plant eater is not large.

	Meat	Plant	Meat & Plant	Plankton
Small				
Medium				
Large				
Very Large				

FOLLOWING YES–NO RULES—A

DIRECTIONS: Darken the correct circles along the path from START to FINISH by following the YES–NO rule.

RULE BOX
YES—color is the same   NO—color is not the same

EXAMPLE

H-148

FOLLOWING YES–NO RULES—A

DIRECTIONS: Darken the correct circles along the path from START to FINISH by following the YES–NO rule.

RULE BOX
YES—color is the same   NO—color is not the same

H-149

H-150

FOLLOWING YES–NO RULES—B

DIRECTIONS: Follow the arrows from START to FINISH. In the box near each arrow write "YES" or "NO" according to the YES–NO rule.

RULE BOX

YES—color is the same   NO—color is not the same

H-151

H-152

FOLLOWING YES–NO RULES—B

DIRECTIONS: Follow the arrows from START to FINISH. In the box near each arrow write "YES" or "NO" according to the YES–NO rule.

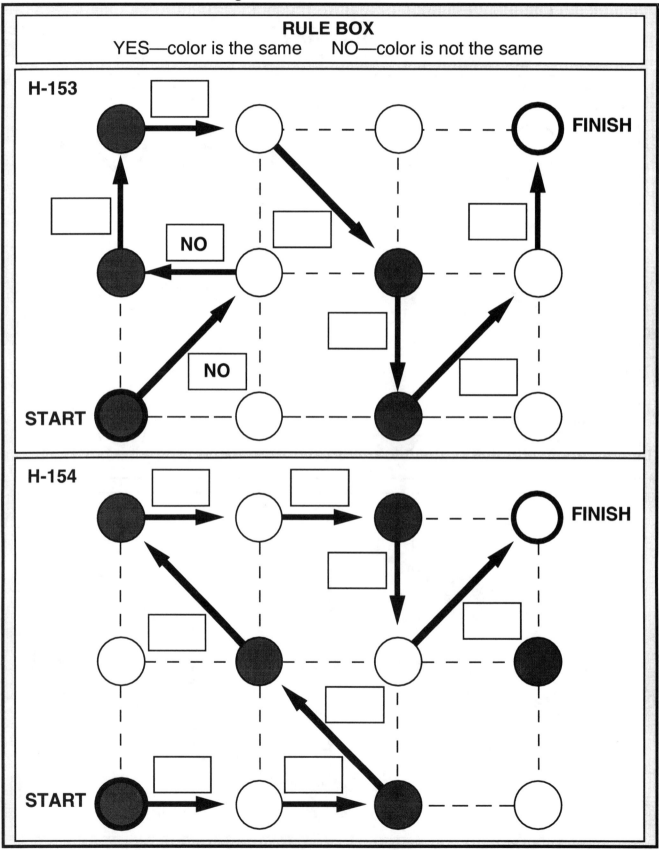

WRITING YES–NO RULES

DIRECTIONS: In each exercise below, there are three paths from START to FINISH. One path is dotted ○ ○ ○, one path is solid ——, and one path is dashed – – –. Supply the rule for each path.

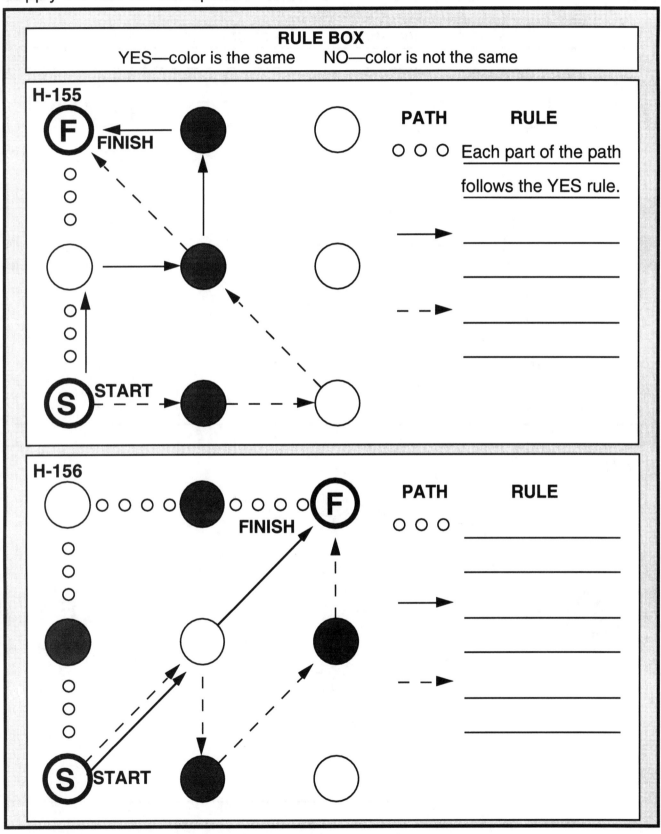

RULE BOX

YES—color is the same   NO—color is not the same

H-155

PATH	RULE
○ ○ ○	Each part of the path follows the YES rule.
→	_____
- - →	_____

H-156

PATH	RULE
○ ○ ○	_____
→	_____
- - →	_____

FOLLOWING YES–NO RULES—SUPPLY

DIRECTIONS: Two blank grids are provided for you to make up your own YES-NO exercises. Trade your exercises with a classmate.

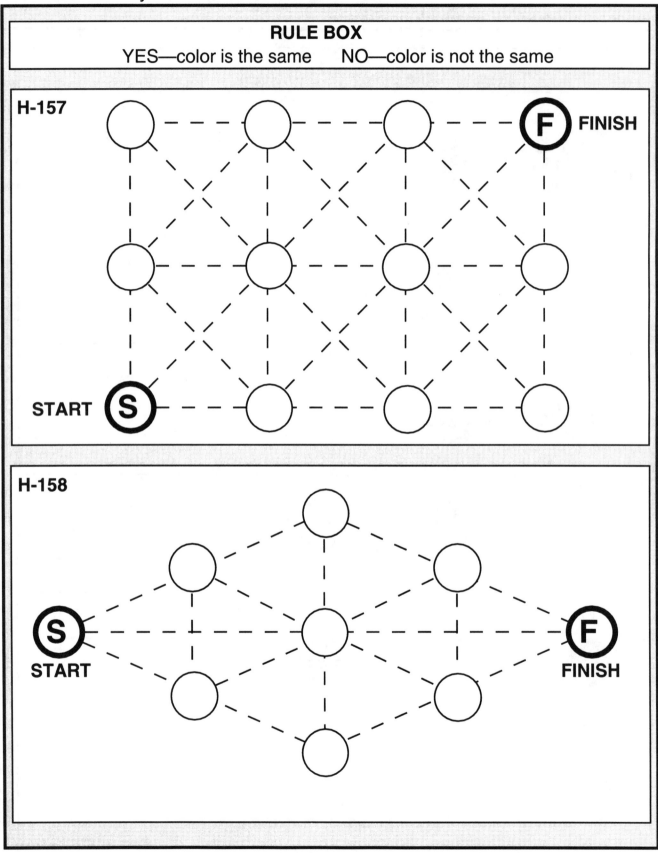

RULE BOX

YES—color is the same   NO—color is not the same

H-157

FINISH

START

H-158

START

FINISH

COMPLETING TRUE–FALSE TABLES

DIRECTIONS: After reading the example, complete the TRUE–FALSE table below.

This group of shapes will be used to produce TRUE–FALSE tables

EXAMPLE of a completed TRUE–FALSE table

	IT IS STRIPED	IT IS CHECKED	IT IS SQUARE
(striped square)	TRUE	FALSE	TRUE
(checked square)	FALSE	TRUE	TRUE
(checked circle)	FALSE	TRUE	FALSE

H-159   Complete the following table.

	IT IS BLACK	IT IS STRIPED	IT IS CHECKED	IT IS SQUARE
(black square)	TRUE	FALSE	FALSE	TRUE
(striped square)				
(checked square)				
(black circle)				
(striped circle)				
(checked circle)				

COMPLETING TRUE–FALSE TABLES

DIRECTIONS: Complete the TRUE–FALSE tables below.

This group of shapes will be used to produce TRUE–FALSE tables

H-160   Complete the following table.

	IT IS BLACK	IT IS STRIPED	IT IS NOT BLACK
△	FALSE	FALSE	TRUE
⊘			
■			

H-161   Complete the following table.

	IT IS BLACK	IT IS STRIPED	IT IS NOT BLACK	IT IS NOT STRIPED
△	FALSE	FALSE	TRUE	TRUE
⊘		TRUE		
▨	FALSE			
●			FALSE	
■				TRUE
△				TRUE

FOLLOWING IF–THEN RULES

DIRECTIONS: From the group of shapes, circle the shapes that follow the rule.

EXAMPLE
RULE: If the shape is a square, then it is white.

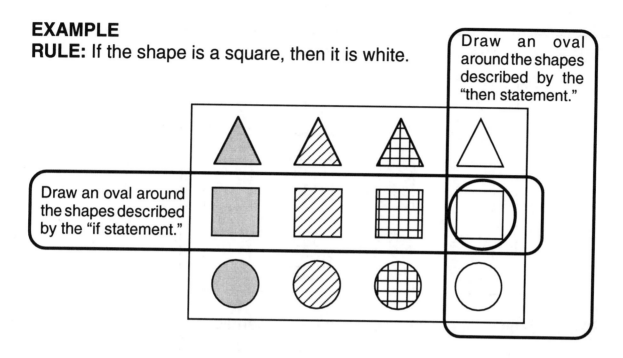

Draw an oval around the shapes described by the "then statement."

Draw an oval around the shapes described by the "if statement."

The phrase "if the shape is a square" means that only squares are being considered by the rule. Draw an oval around the row of squares.

The phrase "then it is white" means that only white shapes follow the rule. Draw an oval around the column of white shapes. There is only one shape, the white square, that follows the rule. Notice that it is enclosed by both the "if-oval" and the "then-oval."

Draw a circle around the white square to show that it follows the rule. It follows the "if" part of the rule because it is a square, it follows the "then" part because it is white.

H-162 RULE: If the shape is a circle, then it is gray.

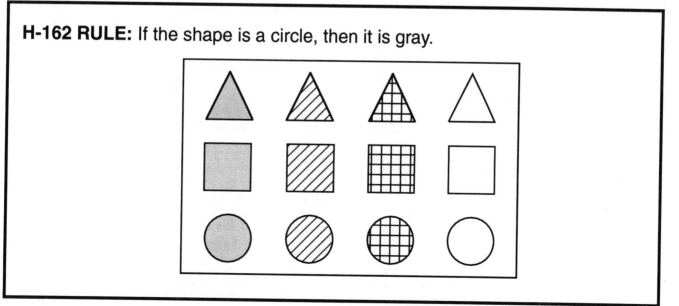

FOLLOWING IF–THEN RULES—A

DIRECTIONS: From the group of shapes, circle the shapes that follow the rule.

H-163 RULE: If the shape is white, then it is a square.

H-164 RULE: If the shape is striped, then it is a triangle.

H-165 RULE: If the shape is checked, then it is a circle.

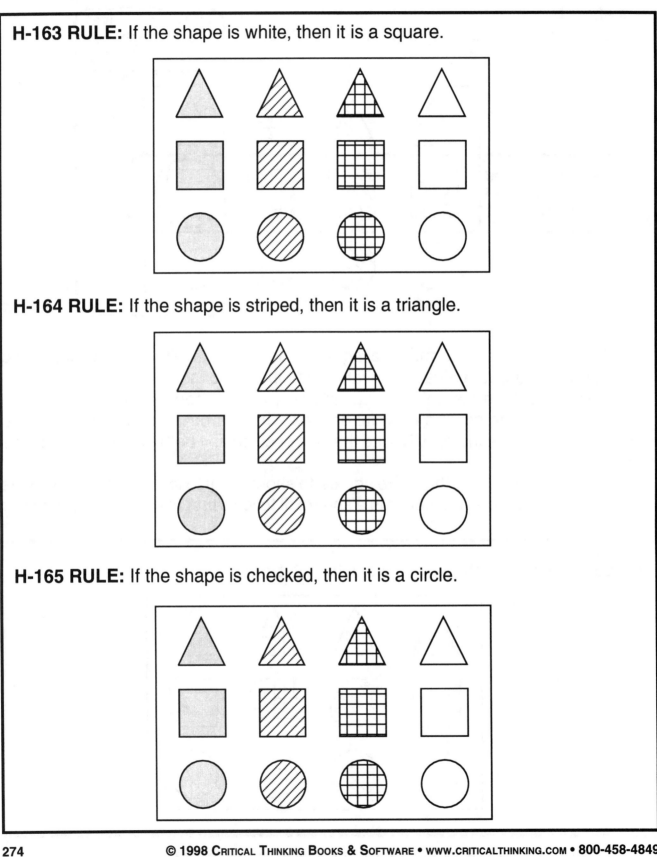

FOLLOWING IF–THEN RULES—A

DIRECTIONS: From the group of shapes, circle the shapes that follow the rule.

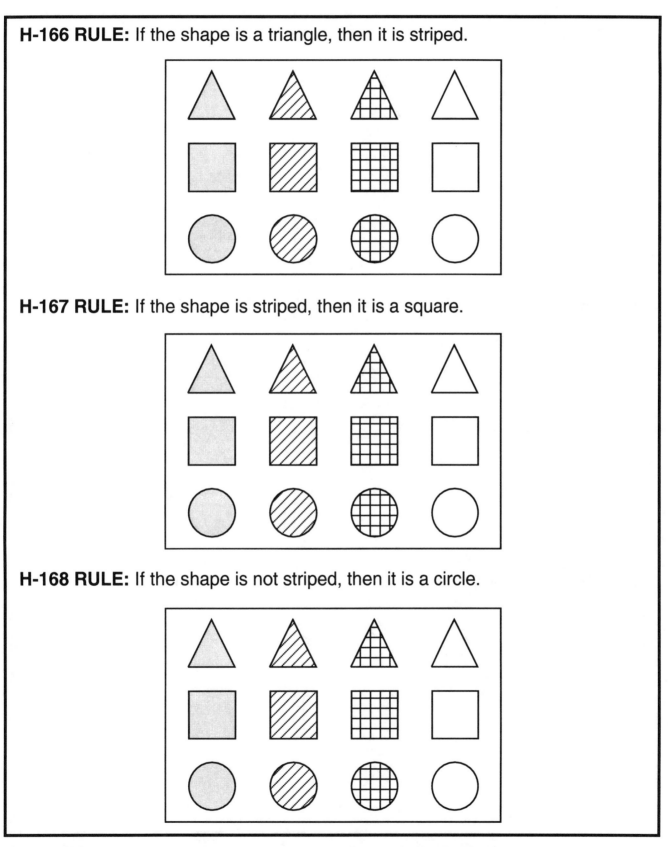

H-166 RULE: If the shape is a triangle, then it is striped.

H-167 RULE: If the shape is striped, then it is a square.

H-168 RULE: If the shape is not striped, then it is a circle.

FOLLOWING IF–THEN RULES—A

DIRECTIONS: From the group of shapes, circle the shapes that follow the rule.

H-169 RULE: If the shape is a square, then it is checked.

H-170 RULE: If the shape is not a square, then it is striped.

H-171 RULE: If the shape is not a square, then it is not white.

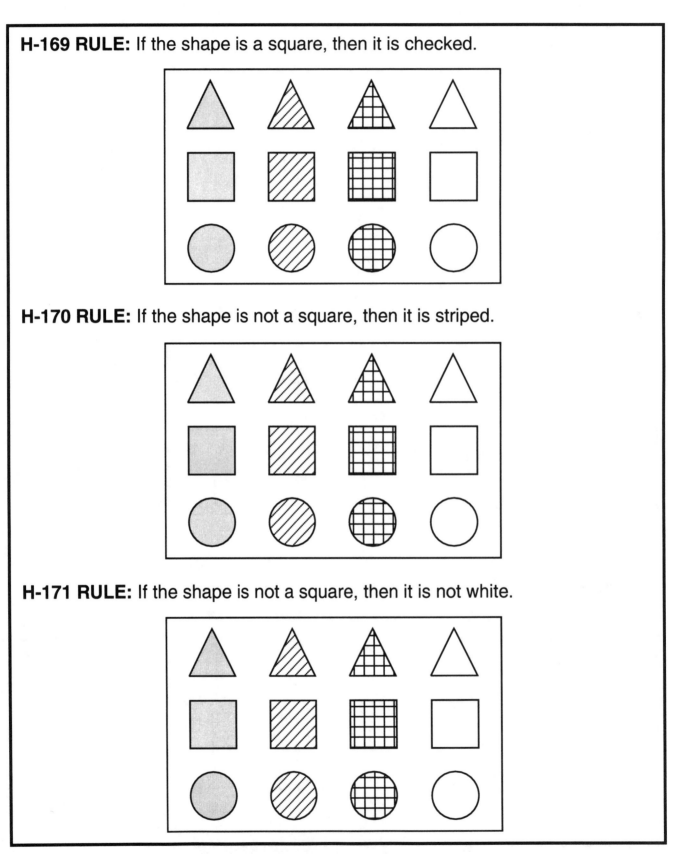

FOLLOWING IF–THEN RULES—B

DIRECTIONS: Decide which groups of shapes (1, 2, 3, 4) fit the rule.

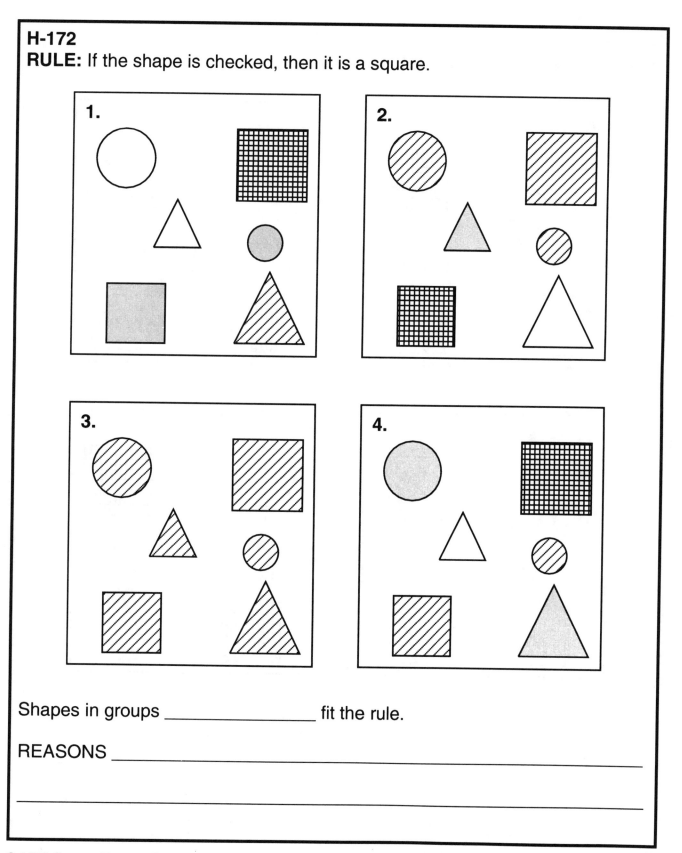

H-172
RULE: If the shape is checked, then it is a square.

Shapes in groups _____ fit the rule.

REASONS _____

_____

FOLLOWING IF–THEN RULES—B

DIRECTIONS: Decide which groups of shapes (1, 2, 3, 4) fit the rule.

H-173
RULE: If the shape is a circle, then it is striped.

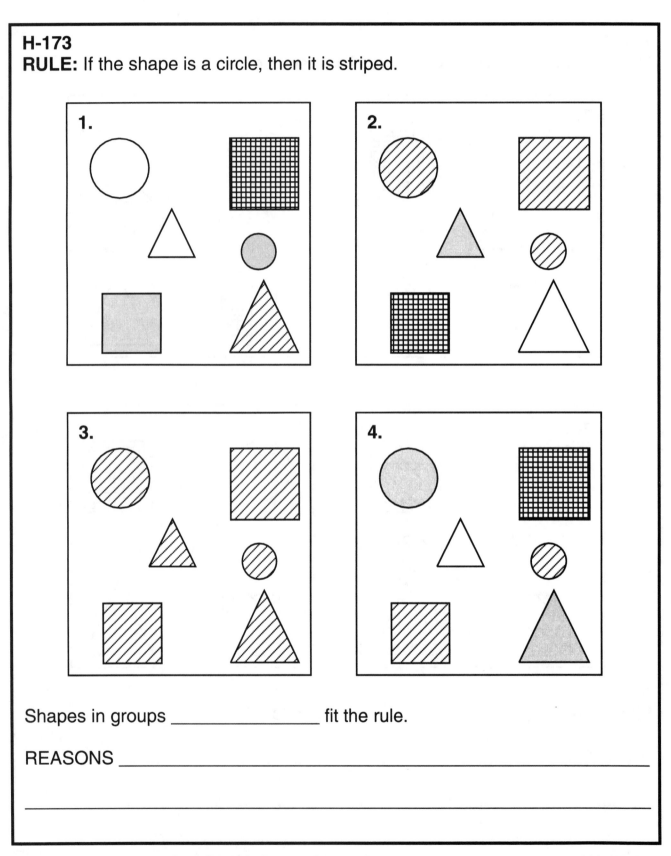

Shapes in groups _____ fit the rule.

REASONS _____

_____

FOLLOWING IF–THEN RULES—B

DIRECTIONS: Mark the shapes so that all of them fit the rule.

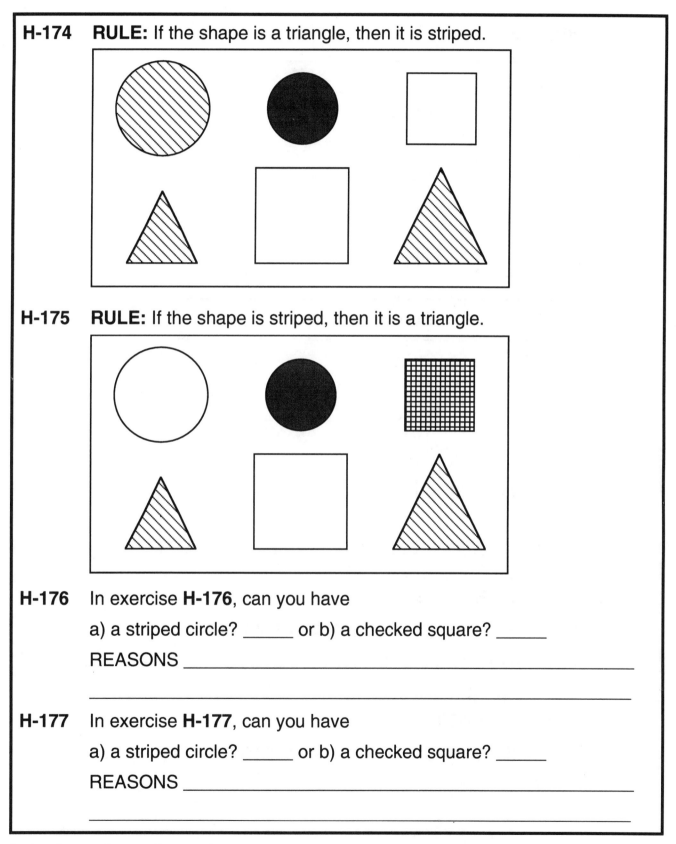

H-174   **RULE:** If the shape is a triangle, then it is striped.

H-175   **RULE:** If the shape is striped, then it is a triangle.

H-176   In exercise **H-176**, can you have

a) a striped circle? _____ or b) a checked square? _____

REASONS _____

_____

H-177   In exercise **H-177**, can you have

a) a striped circle? _____ or b) a checked square? _____

REASONS _____

_____

FOLLOWING IF–THEN RULES—B

DIRECTIONS: Mark the shapes so that all of them fit the rule.

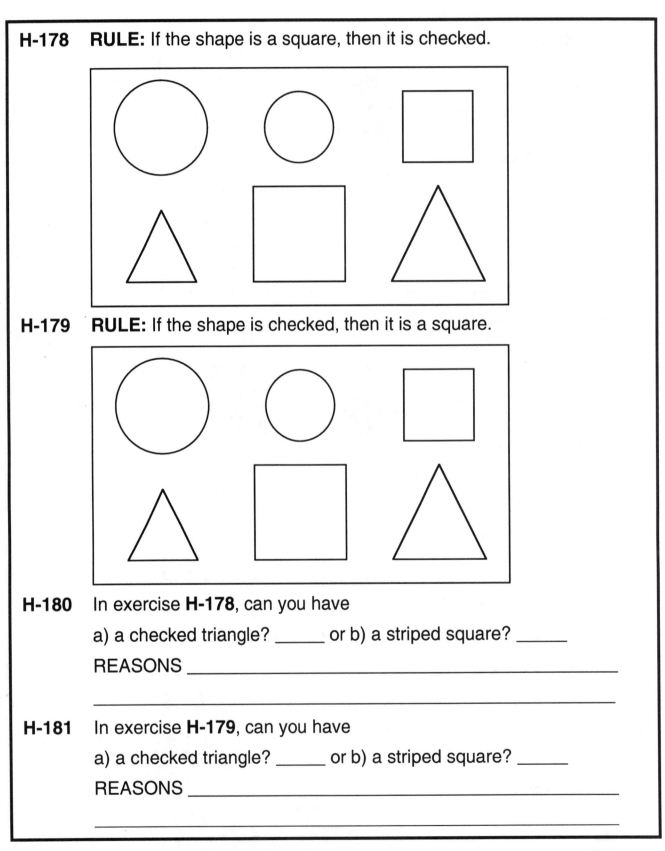

H-178   **RULE:** If the shape is a square, then it is checked.

H-179   **RULE:** If the shape is checked, then it is a square.

H-180   In exercise **H-178**, can you have

a) a checked triangle? _____ or b) a striped square? _____

REASONS _____

_____

H-181   In exercise **H-179**, can you have

a) a checked triangle? _____ or b) a striped square? _____

REASONS _____

_____

GRAPHIC ORGANIZER–CYCLE DIAGRAM

DIRECTIONS: Many sequences in nature repeat. They are called *cycles.* Use the sentences in the choice box to show the food chain cycle. Write each step in the correct box.

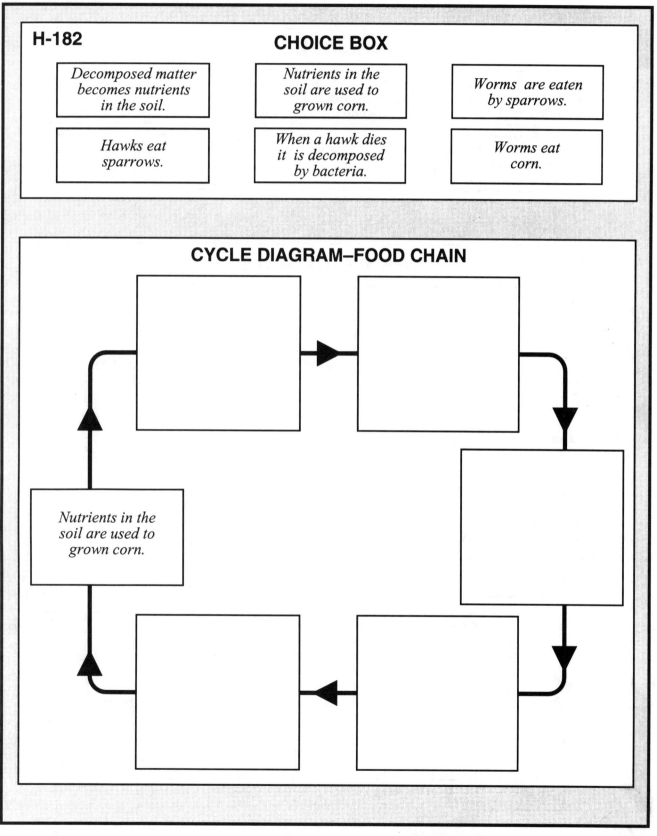

H-182

CHOICE BOX

Decomposed matter becomes nutrients in the soil.	*Nutrients in the soil are used to grown corn.*	*Worms are eaten by sparrows.*
Hawks eat sparrows.	*When a hawk dies it is decomposed by bacteria.*	*Worms eat corn.*

CYCLE DIAGRAM–FOOD CHAIN

Nutrients in the soil are used to grown corn.

GRAPHIC ORGANIZER–CYCLE DIAGRAM

DIRECTIONS: Many sequences in nature repeat. They are called *cycles*. Use the sentences in the choice box to show the water cycle. Write each step in the correct box.

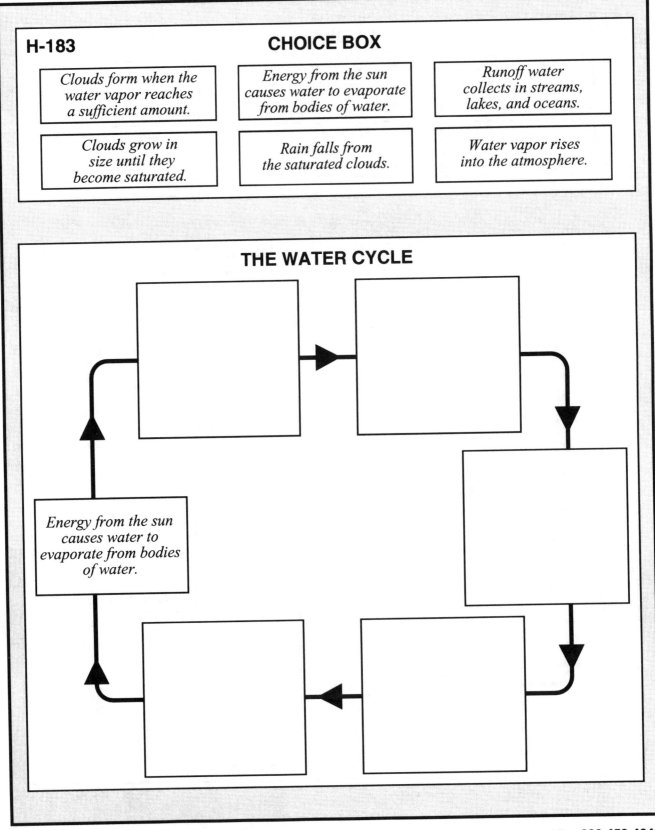

H-183

CHOICE BOX

Clouds form when the water vapor reaches a sufficient amount.

Energy from the sun causes water to evaporate from bodies of water.

Runoff water collects in streams, lakes, and oceans.

Clouds grow in size until they become saturated.

Rain falls from the saturated clouds.

Water vapor rises into the atmosphere.

THE WATER CYCLE

Energy from the sun causes water to evaporate from bodies of water.

GRAPHIC ORGANIZER–CYCLE DIAGRAM

DIRECTIONS: Many sequences in nature repeat. They are called *cycles*. Use the sentences in the choice box to show the water cycle. Write each step in the correct box.

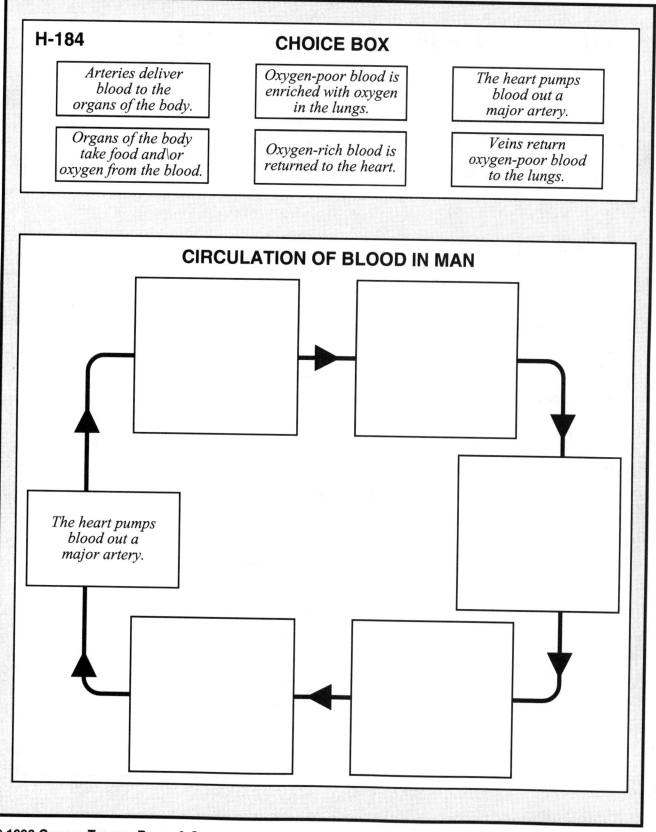

H-184

CHOICE BOX

Arteries deliver blood to the organs of the body.

Oxygen-poor blood is enriched with oxygen in the lungs.

The heart pumps blood out a major artery.

Organs of the body take food and\or oxygen from the blood.

Oxygen-rich blood is returned to the heart.

Veins return oxygen-poor blood to the lungs.

CIRCULATION OF BLOOD IN MAN

The heart pumps blood out a major artery.

GRAPHIC ORGANIZER–TIME LINE

DIRECTIONS: Using the list on the left, mark each president's term of office in its correct chronological order on the time line at the right. Remember to count the spaces.

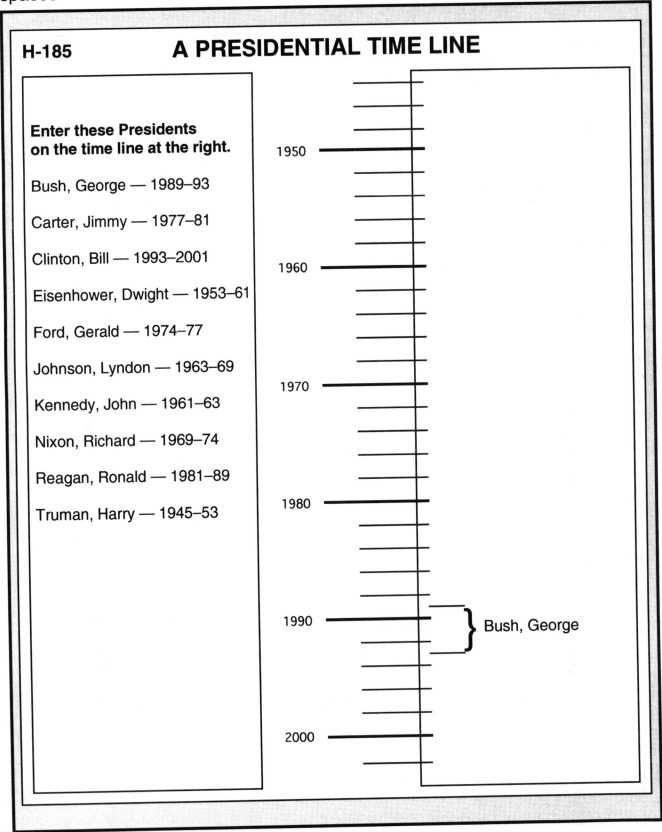

A PRESIDENTIAL TIME LINE

H-185

Enter these Presidents on the time line at the right.

Bush, George — 1989–93

Carter, Jimmy — 1977–81

Clinton, Bill — 1993–2001

Eisenhower, Dwight — 1953–61

Ford, Gerald — 1974–77

Johnson, Lyndon — 1963–69

Kennedy, John — 1961–63

Nixon, Richard — 1969–74

Reagan, Ronald — 1981–89

Truman, Harry — 1945–53

1950

1960

1970

1980

1990 } Bush, George

2000

GRAPHIC ORGANIZER–TIME LINE

DIRECTIONS: Using the list on the left, mark each war in its correct chronological order on the time line at the right. Remember to count the spaces.

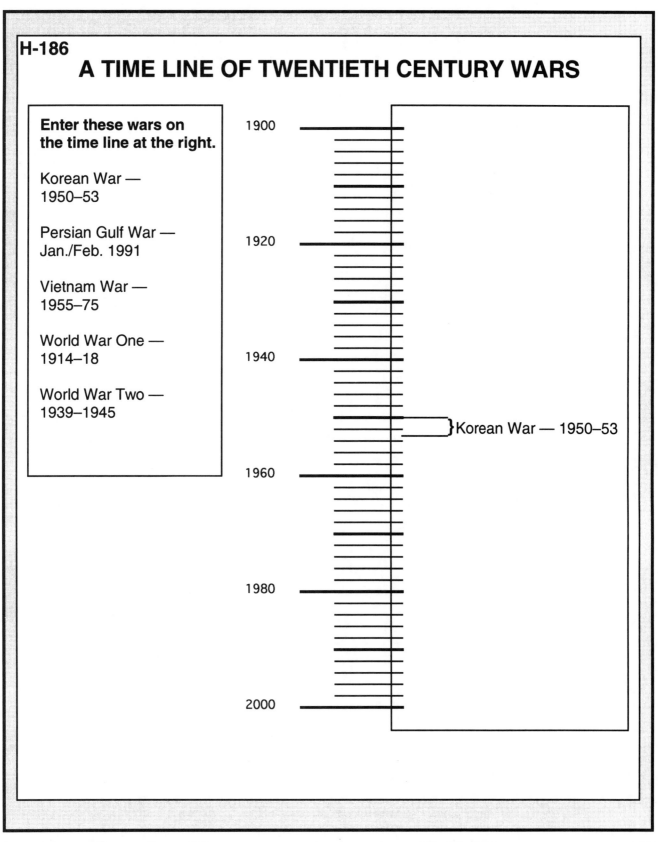

H-186

A TIME LINE OF TWENTIETH CENTURY WARS

Enter these wars on the time line at the right.

Korean War —
1950–53

Persian Gulf War —
Jan./Feb. 1991

Vietnam War —
1955–75

World War One —
1914–18

World War Two —
1939–1945

1900

1920

1940

}Korean War — 1950–53

1960

1980

2000

CHAPTER NINE

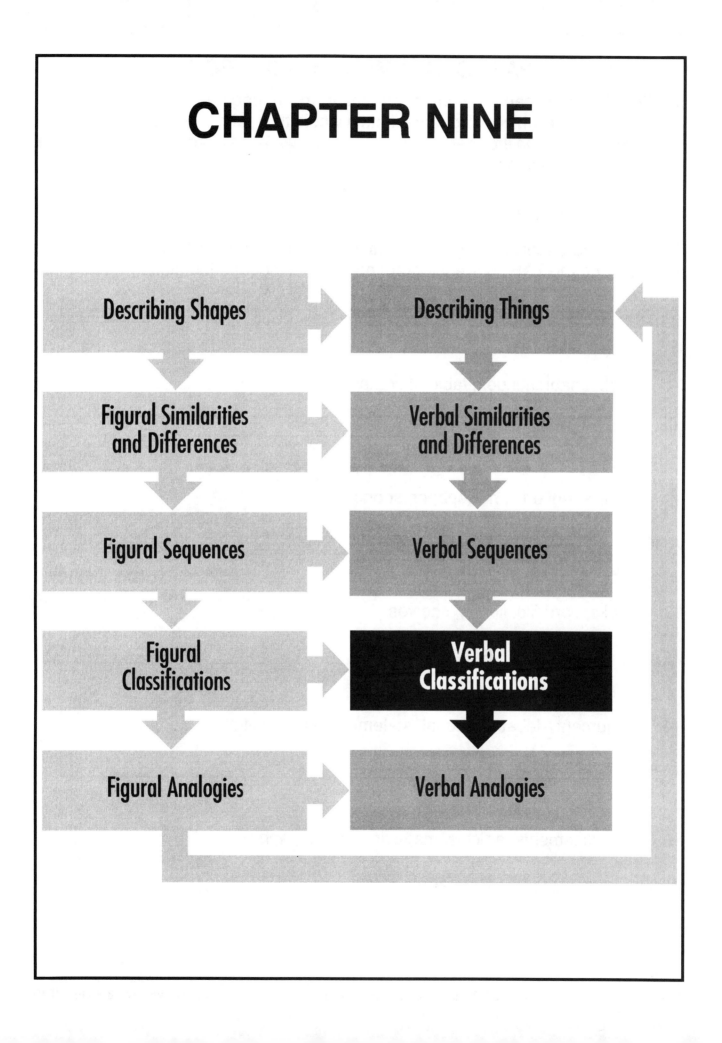

Describing Shapes → Describing Things

Figural Similarities and Differences → Verbal Similarities and Differences

Figural Sequences → Verbal Sequences

Figural Classifications → Verbal Classifications

Figural Analogies → Verbal Analogies

PARTS OF A WHOLE—SELECT

DIRECTIONS: On each line are four words from language arts lessons. Read the words and decide which word represents a whole thing and which words are parts of the whole thing. On the lines below each group, write the word that represents the whole thing then list the words that are its parts.

EXAMPLE: closing, greeting, letter, signature

The words represent parts of a letter that you might write to a friend. The WHOLE is the letter and the PARTS are the greeting, the closing, and the signature.

WHOLE ____*letter*____ PARTS ____*greeting*____, ____*closing*____, ____*signature*____

I-1   book, chapter, index, table of contents

WHOLE _____ PARTS _____, _____, _____

I-2   comics, editorial, newspaper, sports

WHOLE _____ PARTS _____, _____, _____

I-3   books, card file, library, shelves

WHOLE _____ PARTS _____, _____, _____

I-4   argument, debate, rebuttal, statement of proposition

WHOLE _____ PARTS _____, _____, _____

I-5   advertisements, articles, magazine, photographs

WHOLE _____ PARTS _____, _____, _____

PARTS OF A WHOLE—SELECT

DIRECTIONS: On each line are four words from social studies lessons. Read the words and decide which word represents a whole thing and which words are parts of the whole thing. On the lines below each group, write the word that represents the whole thing then list the words that are its parts.

I-6   alleys, block, buildings, streets

WHOLE _____ PARTS _____, _____, _____

I-7   churches, homes, neighborhood, schools

WHOLE _____ PARTS _____, _____, _____

I-8   city, downtown, neighborhood, suburb

WHOLE _____ PARTS _____, _____, _____

I-9   cities, county, rural areas, towns

WHOLE _____ PARTS _____, _____, _____

I-10   cities, counties, state, townships

WHOLE _____ PARTS _____, _____, _____

I-11   forests, mountains, nation, rivers

WHOLE _____ PARTS _____, _____, _____

I-12   continents, atmosphere, Earth, oceans

WHOLE _____ PARTS _____, _____, _____

PARTS OF A WHOLE—SELECT

DIRECTIONS: On each line are four words from science lessons. Read the words and decide which word represents a whole thing and which words are parts of the whole thing. On the lines below each group first write the word that represents the whole thing and then list the words that are parts of the whole thing.

I-13 leaves, plant, root, stem

WHOLE _____ PARTS _____, _____, _____

I-14 backbone, brain, heart, mammal

WHOLE _____ PARTS _____, _____, _____

I-15 blossom, bulb, stem, tulip

WHOLE _____ PARTS _____, _____, _____

I-16 fruit, pulp, seeds, skin

WHOLE _____ PARTS _____, _____, _____

I-17 antennae, insect, jointed legs, segmented abdomen

WHOLE _____ PARTS _____, _____, _____

I-18 backbone, fish, gills, scales

WHOLE _____ PARTS _____, _____, _____

I-19 beak, bird, feathers, wings

WHOLE _____ PARTS _____, _____, _____

CLASS AND MEMBERS—SELECT

DIRECTIONS: On each line are four words from language arts lessons. Read the words and decide which word represents the class to which the other words belong. On the lines below each group, write the word that represents the class then list the words that are members of that class.

I-20 drama, fiction, novel, short story

CLASS_____ MEMBERS _____, _____, _____

I-21 autobiographies, diaries, journals, personal histories

CLASS_____ MEMBERS _____, _____, _____

I-22 a, an, articles, the

CLASS_____ MEMBERS _____, _____, _____

I-23 exclamations, questions, sentences, statements

CLASS_____ MEMBERS _____, _____, _____

I-24 figures of speech, metaphors, personification, similes

CLASS_____ MEMBERS _____, _____, _____

I-25 adjectives, adverbs, nouns, parts of speech

CLASS_____ MEMBERS _____, _____, _____

I-26 almanac, atlas, dictionary, reference book

CLASS_____ MEMBERS _____, _____, _____

CLASS AND MEMBERS—SELECT

DIRECTIONS: On each line are four words from social studies lessons. Read the words and decide which word represents the class to which the other words belong. On the lines below each group, write the word that represents the class then list the words that are members of that class.

I-27 appliances, clothing, food, goods

CLASS _____ MEMBERS _____, _____, _____

I-28 kings, leaders, presidents, prime ministers

CLASS _____ MEMBERS _____, _____, _____

I-29 city, federal, government, state

CLASS _____ MEMBERS _____, _____, _____

I-30 economics, geography, history, social sciences

CLASS _____ MEMBERS _____, _____, _____

I-31 elementary, high, middle, school

CLASS _____ MEMBERS _____, _____, _____

I-32 cleaning, repairing, protecting, service

CLASS _____ MEMBERS _____, _____, _____

I-33 democracy, government, monarchy, republic

CLASS _____ MEMBERS _____, _____, _____

CLASS AND MEMBERS—SELECT

DIRECTIONS: On each line are four words from science lessons. Read the words and decide which word represents the class to which the other words belong. On the lines below each group, write the word that represents the class then list the words that are members of that class.

I-34   corn, grain, oats, wheat

CLASS _____ MEMBERS _____, _____, _____

I-35   ape, mammal, man, whale

CLASS _____ MEMBERS _____, _____, _____

I-36   daisy, flower, rose, tulip

CLASS _____ MEMBERS _____, _____, _____

I-37   apple, banana, fruit, pear

CLASS _____ MEMBERS _____, _____, _____

I-38   beetle, fly, grasshopper, insect

CLASS _____ MEMBERS _____, _____, _____

I-39   fish, guppy, perch, trout

CLASS _____ MEMBERS _____, _____, _____

I-40   bird, heron, penguin, sandpiper

CLASS _____ MEMBERS _____, _____, _____

SENTENCES CONTAINING CLASSES AND SUBCLASSES

DIRECTIONS: In each sentence there are three words that name members of a class. Underline these words. Inside each box, write the words in order from most general class to the most specific class. The general class (1) will contain the less general class (2) and the most specific class (3). Write the most general class on line (1), the less general class on line (2), and the most specific class on line (3).

EXAMPLE The <u>orange</u> is a popular <u>citrus fruit</u>. "Fruit" is the most general class and belongs on line 1. "Citrus" is a kind of fruit and belongs on line 2. "Orange" is a kind of citrus fruit and belongs on line 3.

I-41 When asked to select a vegetable, Jan selected lima beans.

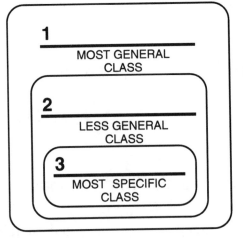

I-42 Yolanda went to the pastry shop to buy a cherry pie.

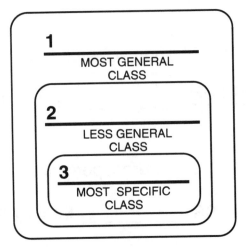

SENTENCES CONTAINING CLASSES AND SUBCLASSES

DIRECTIONS: In each sentence, underline three words that name members of a class. In each box, write the words in order from the most general class on line 1 to the most specific class on line 3.

I-43   Maria reads many kinds of books, but mysteries are her favorite kind of fiction.

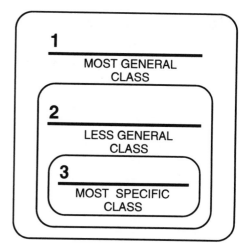

I-44   Raymond owns a camper-van recreational vehicle.

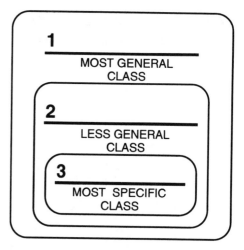

I-45   Mr. Baker went to the lumberyard and bought some pine boards.

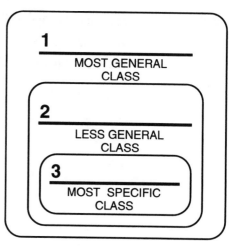

SENTENCES CONTAINING CLASSES AND SUBCLASSES

DIRECTIONS: In each sentence, underline three words that name members of a class. In each box, write the words in order from the most general class on line 1 to the most specific class on line 3.

I-46   A ladybug was the only beetle that Josh could find for his insect collection.

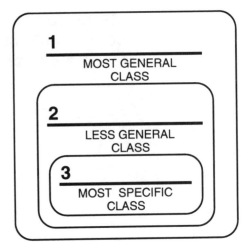

I-47   Mrs. Elledge used weed killer on her dandelion plants.

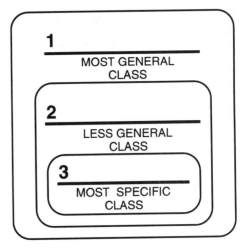

I-48   Some people think the black widow spider is an insect, but actually it is an arachnid.

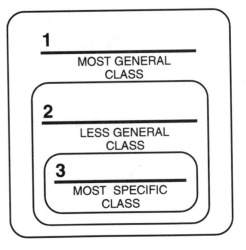

SENTENCES CONTAINING CLASSES AND SUBCLASSES

DIRECTIONS: In each sentence, underline three words that name members of a class. In each box, write the words in order from the most general class on line 1 to the most specific class on line 3.

I-49 The worker honeybee is the insect that produces honey.

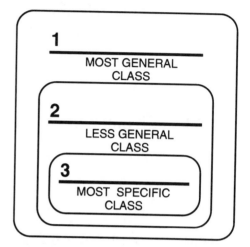

I-50 The Galapagos tortoise is a large reptile that lives on the land.

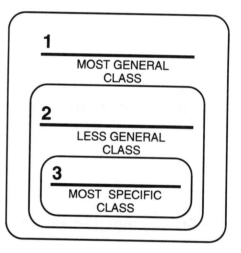

I-51 The heron is a beautiful wading bird found in the South.

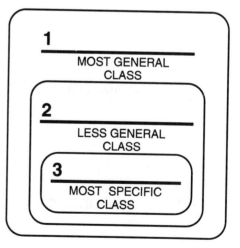

HOW ARE THESE WORDS ALIKE?–SELECT

DIRECTIONS: Circle the letter in front of the answer that **best** describes the class of words.

I-52   alarm, horn, siren

      a. bell
      b. safety
      c. warning

I-53   blotch, smear, stain

      a. blemish
      b. rip
      c. tear

I-54   different, odd, peculiar

      a. little
      b. strange
      c. weak

I-55   dollar, peso, pound

      a. coin
      b. money
      c. penny

I-56   aim, design, intend

      a. draw
      b. finish
      c. plan

I-57   grab, grasp, grip

      a. hit
      b. hold
      c. try

I-58   caution, slow, yield

      a. intersection
      b. stop light
      c. warning

HOW ARE THESE WORDS ALIKE?–SELECT

DIRECTIONS: Circle the letter in front of the answer that **best** describes the class of words.

I-59　border, hem, rim

a. center
b. edge
c. part

I-60　even, level, planed

a. rough
b. slant
c. smooth

I-61　fable, fairy tale, myth

a. fact
b. fiction
c. history

I-62　clock, ruler, thermometer

a. electrical devices
b. measuring devices
c. mechanical devices

I-63　fork, knife, spoon

a. drawing tools
b. kitchen tools
c. woodworking tools

I-64　chisel, drill, saw

a. drawing tools
b. kitchen tools
c. woodworking tools

I-65　compass, ruler, protractor

a. drawing tools
b. kitchen tools
c. woodworking tools

HOW ARE THESE WORDS ALIKE?—SELECT

DIRECTIONS: Each exercise contains three words that belong to a common class. From the choice box, select the class that **best** describes each group of words and write it on the line. The words in the choice box may be used more than once.

CHOICE BOX
high, line, show

I-66   path, road, route,   _____

I-67   direct, guide, lead,   _____

I-68   big, soaring, tall,   _____

I-69   produce, put on, stage,   _____

I-70   business, job, work,   _____

I-71   film, movie, motion picture,   _____

I-72   piercing, sharp, shrill,   _____

I-73   disclose, discover, present,   _____

I-74   column, rank, row,   _____

I-75   costly, dear, expensive,   _____

I-76   indicate, read, register,   _____

I-77   display, offer, supply,   _____

HOW ARE THESE WORDS ALIKE?–SELECT

DIRECTIONS: Each exercise contains three words that belong to a common class. From the choice box, select the class that **best** describes each group of words and write it on the line. The words in the choice box may be used more than once.

CHOICE BOX
band, change, fair, spring

I-78   average, ordinary, plain, _____

I-79   hop, leap, jump, _____

I-80   swap, switch, trade, _____

I-81   favorable, honest, just, _____

I-82   club, team, troop, _____

I-83   brook, season, wire coil, _____

I-84   group, musicians, orchestra, _____

I-85   shift, turn, vary, _____

I-86   clear, light, sunny, _____

I-87   belt, strip, stripe, _____

I-88   coins, substitute, variety, _____

I-89   display, entertainment, festival, _____

HOW ARE THESE WORDS ALIKE?–SELECT

DIRECTIONS: Each exercise contains three words that belong to a common class. From the choice box, select the class that **best** describes each group of words and write it on the line. The words in the choice box may be used more than once.

CHOICE BOX
flow, kind, party, pass

I-90   go, proceed, travel,   _____

I-91   band, crew, group,   _____

I-92   pour, spout, stream,   _____

I-93   beat, outdo, top,   _____

I-94   friendly, pleasant, tender,   _____

I-95   proceed, rise, spring,   _____

I-96   give, hand, reach,   _____

I-97   club, side, union,   _____

I-98   a throw, ticket, valley,   _____

I-99   current, flood, tide,   _____

I-100   class, sort, type,   _____

HOW ARE THESE NOUNS ALIKE?—EXPLAIN

DIRECTIONS: Each group of three nouns has a similar meaning. Explain how the nouns in each group are alike.

EXAMPLE: chalk, plaster, sugar

> *These materials are all white powders*.

I-101 claws, horns, tusks

_____

I-102 court, diamond, rink

_____

I-103 glare, gleam, ray

_____

I-104 cure, medication, remedy

_____

I-105 hush, quiet, still

_____

I-106 adornment, ornament, ribbon

_____

HOW ARE THESE VERBS ALIKE?—EXPLAIN

DIRECTIONS: Each group of three verbs has a similar meaning. Explain how the verbs in each group are alike.

I-107 ask, inquire, quiz

_____

I-108 float, glide, soar

_____

I-109 boil, evaporate, vaporize

_____

I-110 jog, sprint, dash

_____

I-111 mumble, murmur, whisper

_____

I-112 await, expect, hope

_____

I-113 blast, burst, explode

_____

HOW ARE THESE ADJECTIVES ALIKE?—EXPLAIN

DIRECTIONS: Each group of three adjectives has a similar meaning. Explain how the adjectives in each group are alike.

I-114 brave, fearless, gallant

_____

I-115 gentle, kind, tender

_____

I-116 gross, large, massive

_____

I-117 slender, slight, slim

_____

I-118 firm, sure, steady

_____

I-119 forceful, mighty, powerful

_____

I-120 passive, quiet, still

_____

HOW ARE THESE WEATHER WORDS ALIKE?—EXPLAIN

DIRECTIONS: Each group of three words describes a weather condition. Explain how the terms in each group are alike.

I-121   drizzle, shower, sprinkle

_____

I-122   nippy, chilly, cool

_____

I-123   bright, clear, cloudless

_____

I-124   blustery, breezy, gusty

_____

I-125   foggy, hazy, overcast

_____

I-126   damp, muggy, sticky

_____

I-127   cloudburst, downpour, thunderstorm

_____

EXPLAIN THE EXCEPTION

DIRECTIONS: Each group of four words contains one member that is an exception to the class. Explain how the similar words are alike and how the exception is different.

EXAMPLE: candle, eye, lamp, star

Candle, lamp, and star are similar because they give off light. Eye is the exception to the class "things that give off light." The eye receives light but does not give off light.

I-128 cloud, rain, snow, umbrella

_____

_____

_____

I-129 cabbage, corn, lettuce, spinach

_____

_____

_____

I-130 relax, rest, sleep, work

_____

_____

_____

I-131 hear, look, read, see

_____

_____

_____

EXPLAIN THE EXCEPTION

DIRECTIONS: Each group of four words contains one member that is an exception to the class. Explain how the similar words are alike and how the exception is different.

I-132   ice, iron, water, wood

_____

_____

_____

I-133   clams, crabs, minnows, snail

_____

_____

_____

I-134   bacon, beef, eggs, ham

_____

_____

_____

I-135   basket, bottle, can, jar

_____

_____

_____

I-136   button, pocket, snap, zipper

_____

_____

_____

EXPLAIN THE EXCEPTION

DIRECTIONS: Each group of four words contains one member that is an exception to the class. Explain how the similar words are alike and how the exception is different.

I-137   cartoons, newscast, situation comedy, soap opera

_____

_____

_____

I-138   clock, ruler, tape measure, yardstick

_____

_____

_____

I-139   flute, trumpet, tuba, violin

_____

_____

_____

I-140   automobile, bicycle, motorcycle, truck

_____

_____

_____

I-141   bottle, cup, mug, strainer

_____

_____

_____

SORTING INTO CLASSES

DIRECTIONS: Sort the following words into two classes: those which suggest happiness and those which suggest sadness.

I-142	CHOICE BOX	
	cheerless, content, delighted, discouraged, dismal, displeased, dreary, fortunate, groaning, joyous, lucky, miserable, satisfied, sorrowful, successful	
HAPPY		**SAD**

SORTING INTO CLASSES

DIRECTIONS: Sort the following words into the categories of people, places, and things.

I-143	CHOICE BOX	
actor, airport, beach, bicycle, book, captain, computer, crew, doctor, factory, friend, garden, house, newspaper, nurse, office, pilot, school, station, stove, teacher, television, vegetable, zoo		

PEOPLE	PLACES	THINGS

SORTING INTO CLASSES

DIRECTIONS: Sort the following list of words into groups of words that tell who, when, or where.

I-144	CHOICE BOX	
all, always, anybody, anyone, downstairs, downtown, early, everybody, eyeryone, far away, inside, in town, later, long ago, nearby, never, next door, nobody, no one, now, outside, some, somebody, someone, sometimes, sooner, today, tomorrow, upstairs, uptown, yesterday.		
WHO	**WHEN**	**WHERE**

SORTING INTO CLASSES

DIRECTIONS: Sort the following animals into the categories of birds, forest animals, and water animals. Animals may belong in more than one category.

I-145	CHOICE BOX	
beaver, chipmunk, cougar, dolphin, eagle, eel, frog, heron, loon, moose, ostrich, owl, pelican, penguin, porpoise, raccoon, shark, sloth, weasel, whale		
BIRDS	**FOREST ANIMALS**	**WATER ANIMALS**
_____	_____	_____
_____	_____	_____
_____	_____	_____
_____	_____	_____
_____	_____	_____
_____	_____	_____
_____	_____	_____
_____	_____	_____
_____	_____	_____
_____	_____	_____
_____	_____	_____

BRANCHING DIAGRAMS

DIRECTIONS: Use the branching diagram below to classify recreational activities into sports and games. The sports can be divided into team or individual sports. Games may be described as table games or movement games.

I-146	RECREATIONAL ACTIVITIES
	baseball, checkers, chess, football, golf, gymnastics, hockey, hopscotch, jump rope, soccer, skating, skiing, tag

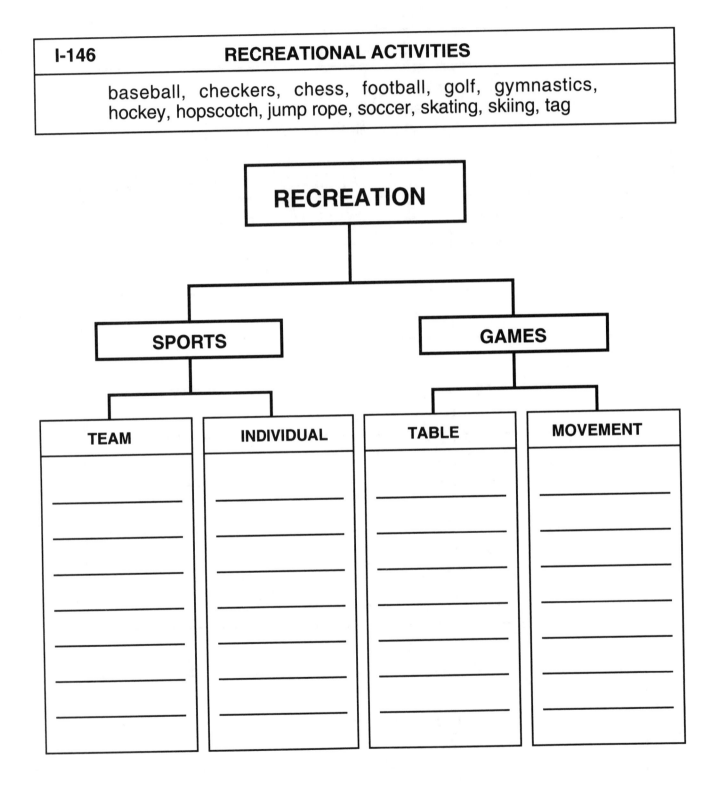

BRANCHING DIAGRAMS

DIRECTIONS: On the next page there is a branching diagram that can be used to classify living things into large subclasses of plants and animals. These subclasses can be further subdivided into smaller groups.

I-147 Use the diagram on the next page to classify the following living things.

ant	elephant	potato
bean	horse	robin
bee	maple	rose
butterfly	minnow	shark
carrot	oak	tulip
cat	ostrich	tuna
chicken	pine	violet

BRANCHING DIAGRAM FOR EXERCISE I-147

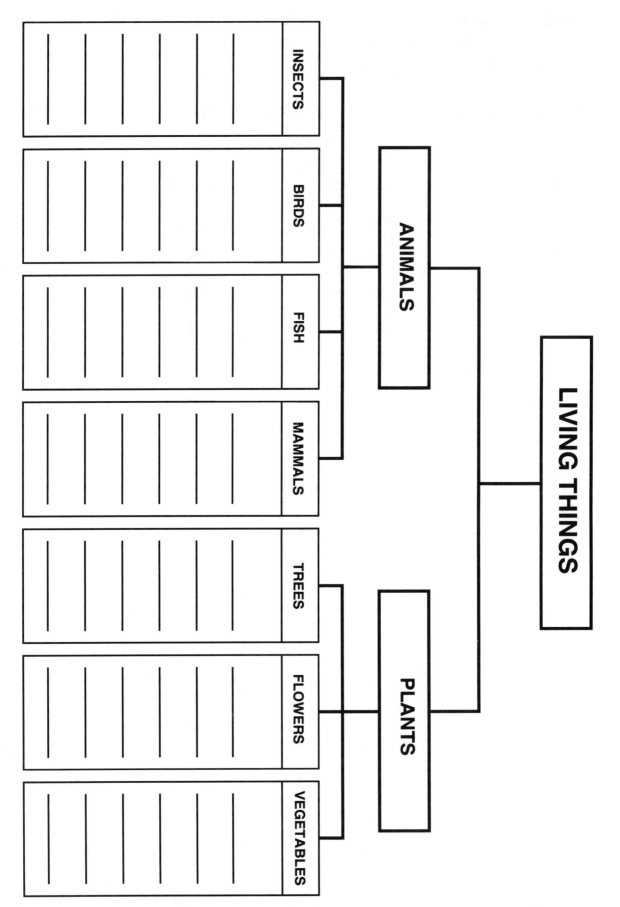

DIAGRAMMING CLASSES—THREE EXAMPLES

EXAMPLE 1: bicycles, trucks, vehicles

The first diagram pictures two distinctly different classes within a common class. The large circle represents vehicles. The smaller circles represent bicycles and trucks.

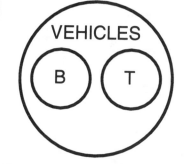

A bicycle is a kind of vehicle, and a truck is a kind of vehicle. However, no truck is a bicycle.

B = bicycles
T = trucks

EXAMPLE 2: truck, van, vehicles

The second diagram pictures a class-subclass relationship. All of the items in one class are members of a larger class.

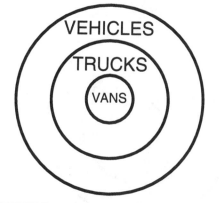

A truck is a kind of vehicle, and a van is a kind of truck. The smaller circle representing trucks is inside the large circle representing vehicles. The smallest circle representing vans is inside the circle representing trucks because all vans are trucks.

EXAMPLE 3: bicycles, mopeds, motorcycles, vehicles

Is there a form of bicycle that is also a form of motorcycle?

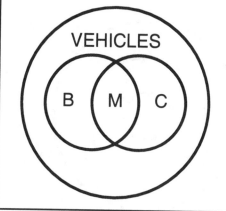

A moped can be operated by peddling like a bicycle. A moped can also be powered by its engine like a motorcycle. This relationship can be shown by an overlapping diagram like this one.

B = bicycles
C = motorcycles
M = mopeds

DIAGRAMMING CLASSES—SELECT

DIRECTIONS: Select the diagram that correctly pictures the way each word group can be classified. Put an "X" through the diagram that cannot be used for this group of words. Label the parts of the correct diagram to show the word relationship.

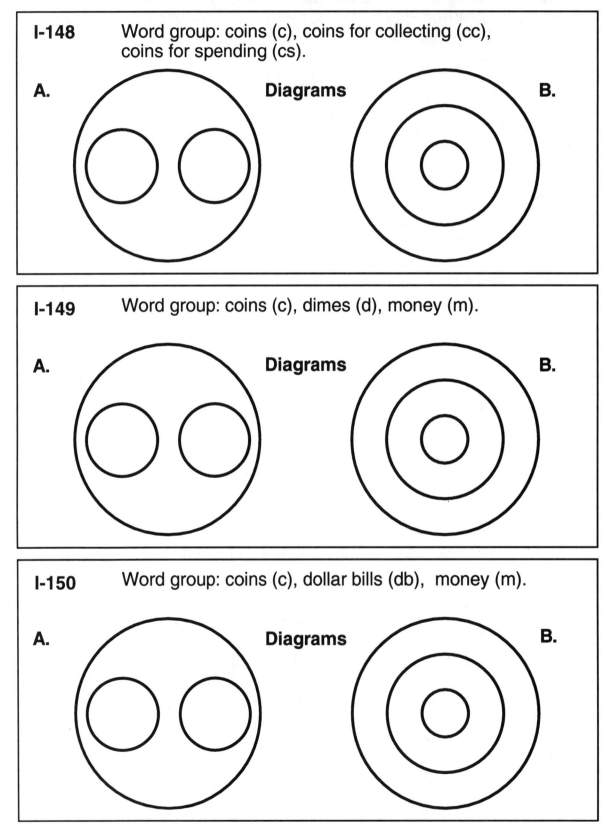

I-148   Word group: coins (c), coins for collecting (cc), coins for spending (cs).

A.   **Diagrams**   **B.**

I-149   Word group: coins (c), dimes (d), money (m).

A.   **Diagrams**   **B.**

I-150   Word group: coins (c), dollar bills (db), money (m).

A.   **Diagrams**   **B.**

DIAGRAMMING CLASSES—SELECT

DIRECTIONS: Draw a line from the group of words to the diagram that pictures the correct relationship. Use the abbreviations in the parentheses to label the diagrams correctly.

WORD GROUPS

I-151

Food (Fo)

Food that grows on vines (Fv)

Fruit (Fr)

Fruit that grows on vines (Frv)

I-152

Food (Fo)

Fruit (Fr)

Oranges (O)

I-153

Food (Fo)

Fruit (Fr)

Vegetables (V)

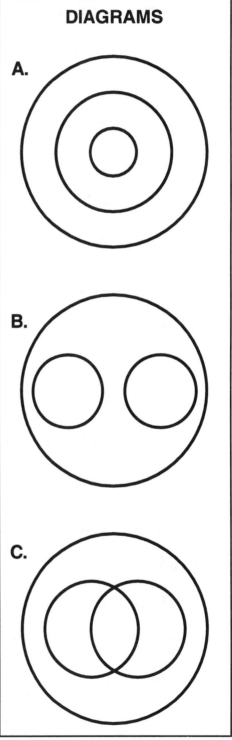

DIAGRAMS

A.

B.

C.

DIAGRAMMING CLASSES—SELECT

DIRECTIONS: Draw a line from the group of words to the diagram that pictures the correct relationship. Use the abbreviations in the parentheses to label the diagrams correctly.

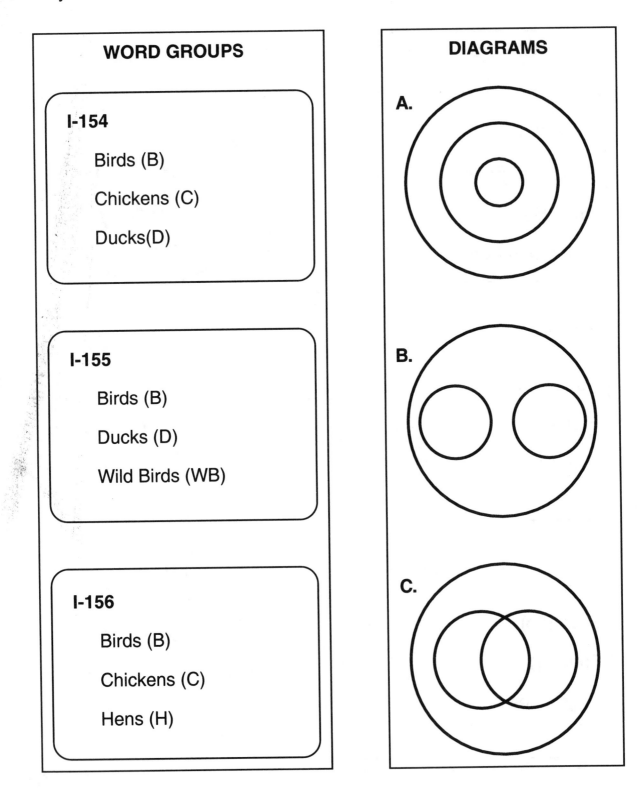

WORD GROUPS

I-154

Birds (B)

Chickens (C)

Ducks (D)

I-155

Birds (B)

Ducks (D)

Wild Birds (WB)

I-156

Birds (B)

Chickens (C)

Hens (H)

DIAGRAMS

A.

B.

C.

DIAGRAMMING CLASSES—SELECT

DIRECTIONS: Draw a line from the group of words to the diagram that pictures the correct relationship. Use the abbreviations in the parentheses to label the diagrams correctly.

WORD GROUPS

I-157

Fathers (F)

Mothers (M)

Parents (P)

I-158

Female Teachers (FT)

Mothers (M)

Women (W)

I-159

Mothers (M)

People (P)

Women (W)

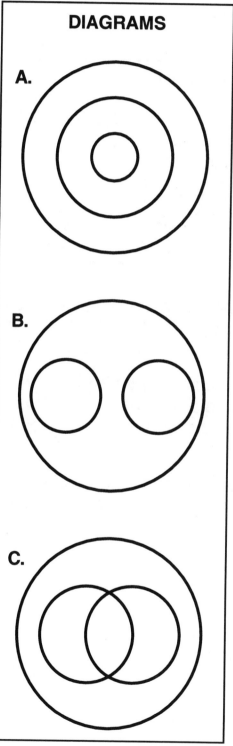

DIAGRAMS

A.

B.

C.

DIAGRAMMING CLASSES—SELECT AND EXPLAIN

DIRECTIONS: In these exercises, you are to describe the relationship between two groups of household items and then pick the diagram that describes this relationship. Use the abbreviations in the parentheses to label the diagram correctly. You may use one of the following phrases to fill in the blank in the sentence describing the classes.

includes, is included in, overlaps, is separate from

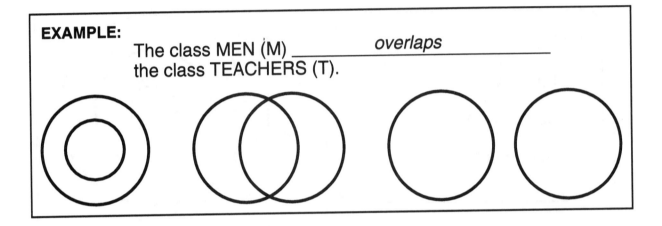

EXAMPLE:

The class MEN (M) _____ *overlaps* _____
the class TEACHERS (T).

Some men are teachers and some teachers are men, thus the class MEN overlaps the class TEACHERS. This means that the second diagram fits. The overlapping part or intersection represents MEN TEACHERS.

If the first diagram is tried with T in the outer circle, it would mean that all men are teachers, which is not true. If the first diagram is tried with M in the outer circle, it would mean that all teachers are men, which is not true. The first diagram does not fit these classes.

If the last diagram is used with M in one circle and T in the other, it would mean that no men are teachers, which is not true. The last diagram does not fit these classes.

DIAGRAMMING CLASSES—SELECT AND EXPLAIN

DIRECTIONS: Describe the relationship between two groups of household items and then pick the diagram that describes this relationship. Use the abbreviations in the parentheses to label the diagram correctly. You may use one of the following phrases to fill in the blank in the sentence describing the classes.

includes, is included in, overlaps, or *is separate from*

EXAMPLE: The class MIRRORS (M) _____*overlaps**_____ the class GLASS OBJECTS (G).

* some mirrors are made of plastic or metal.

I-160 The class WOODEN TABLES (WT) _____ the class FURNITURE (F).

I-161 The class BUILDINGS (B) _____ the class HOUSES (H).

I-162 The class CURTAINS (C) _____ the class WINDOW COVERINGS (W).

DIAGRAMMING CLASSES—SELECT AND EXPLAIN

DIRECTIONS: Describe the relationship between two classes of life science terms and then pick the diagram that describes this relationship. Use the abbreviations in the parentheses to label the diagram correctly. You may use one of the following phrases to fill in the blank in the sentence describing the classes.

includes, is included in, overlaps, or *is separate from*

I-163 The class ANIMALS (A) _____ the class PLANTS (P).

I-164 The class PLANTS (P) _____ the class VEGETABLES (V).

I-165 The class FRUIT (F) _____ the class THINGS THAT GROW ON TREES (T).*some fruit grows on vines

I-166 The class CARROTS (C) _____ the class ROOTS (R).

DIAGRAMMING CLASSES—SELECT AND EXPLAIN

DIRECTIONS: Describe the relationship between two classes of earth science terms and then pick the diagram that describes this relationship. Use the abbreviations in the parentheses to label the diagram correctly. You may use one of the following phrases to fill in the blank in the sentence describing the classes.

includes, is included in, overlaps, or *is separate from*

I-167   The class GASES (G) _____ the class AIR (A).

I-168   The class GASES (G) _____ the class SOLIDS (S).

I-169   The class OCEANS (O) _____ the class BODIES OF WATER (W).

I-170   The class LANDFORMS (L) _____ the class BODIES OF WATER (W).

DIAGRAMMING CLASSES—SELECT AND EXPLAIN

DIRECTIONS: Describe the relationship between two classes of geometry terms and then pick the diagram that describes this relationship. Use the abbreviations in the parentheses to label the diagram correctly. You may use one of the following phrases to fill in the blank in the sentence describing the classes.

includes, is included in, overlaps, or *is separate from*

I-171   The class SQUARES (S) _____ the class QUADRILATERALS (Q).

I-172   The class SQUARES (S) _____ the class CIRCLES (C).

I-173   The class POLYGONS (P) _____ the class HEXAGONS (H).

I-174   The class PARALLEL LINES (P) _____ the class INTERSECTING LINES (I).

OVERLAPPING CLASSES—MATRIX

DIRECTIONS: If words or names can be described by two characteristics, a matrix diagram can be used to show that relationship. Each item must fit in the box that shows the characteristic of the row and the characteristic of the column.

Here is an exercise that illustrates the use of a matrix diagram.

I-175 At Wilson School, it is not possible for students to take both band and chorus, so the boys and girls in Ms. Robinson's class take either band or chorus. Fill in the following matrix diagram showing the music activities of Mrs. Robinson's class.

STUDENT	ACTIVITY
Anne	Chorus
Bruce	Band
Carl	Band
Donna	Band
Harold	Chorus
Ivan	Chorus
Jane	Band
Kathy	Band
Mary	Chorus
Ruth	Chorus

EXAMPLE: Anne is in the chorus.

Anne is a girl and her name belongs in row 2. Anne is in the chorus and her name also belongs in the chorus column—column 2 on the right. Anne's name appears in the matrix as shown below.

		Column 1 **BAND**	Column 2 **CHORUS**
Row 1	**BOYS**		
Row 2	**GIRLS**		*Anne*

OVERLAPPING CLASSES—MATRIX

DIRECTIONS: Sort the following words in the choice box by their material and their use. If an item is commonly made of more than one type of material, list it in more than one row.

I-176	CHOICE BOX
button, brush, bolt, can, cotton, string, clothespin, eraser, aluminum foil, frying pan, glue, ice cream carton, jar, kettle, masking tape, mop, paint scraper, paper cup, pocket, rag, rubber band, safety pin, staple, steel wool, styrofoam sandwich box, tank, toothpaste tube, trash bag, wire, wire brush	

EXAMPLE: nail

A nail is used to fasten boards together. A nail is made of metal. Therefore, a nail can be classified as both a fastener and metal. The word *nail* should be classified in the matrix box in the fastener column and the metal row as shown below.

	FASTENERS	CLEANERS	CONTAINERS
PLASTIC			
METAL			
OTHER			

OVERLAPPING CLASSES—MATRIX

DIRECTIONS: Sort the following words in the choice box by their taste, touch, sound, or appearance. Use the matrix to show whether the word is generally favorable, generally unfavorable, or sometimes favorable. Words may be used in more than one column.

I-177	CHOICE BOX
beautiful, bitter, blinding, bright, cool, deafening, delicious, dull, fine, furry, handsome, icy, loud, musical, noisy, plain, rough, salty, scalding, sharp, soft, soothing, sour, spoiled, sweet, ugly, warm, wet	

EXAMPLE: ripe

Ripe can be used to describe both the appearance and the taste of being ready to eat. Since readiness to eat is favorable, ripe fits into the matrix in the generally favorable row and in both the taste and appearance columns.

	TASTE	TOUCH	SOUND	APPEARANCE
GENERALLY FAVORABLE	*ripe*			*ripe*
GENERALLY UNFAVORABLE				
SOMETIMES FAVORABLE & SOMETIMES UNFAVORABLE				

RELATIONSHIPS—EXPLAIN

DIRECTIONS: Each word in box A is related in the same way to the word on the same line in box B. Describe how the words in box A are related to the words in box B.

I-178

A	B	Relationship
bird	robin	_____
book	novel	
dog	setter	_____
fruit	lemon	
reptile	lizard	_____

I-179

A	B	Relationship
bicycle	handlebar	_____
bird	feather	
chair	arm	_____
river	mouth	
tree	trunk	_____

I-180

A	B	Relationship
beat	rhythm	_____
degree	temperature	
foot	length	_____
month	time	
watt	electricity	_____

I-181

A	B	Relationship
box	lid	_____
building	roof	
hill	crest	_____
mountain	peak	
room	ceiling	_____

RELATIONSHIPS—EXPLAIN

DIRECTIONS: Each word in box A is related in the same way to the word on the same line in box B. Describe how the words in box A are related to the words in box B.

I-182

A	B	Relationship
answer	reply	
ask	question	
peak	top	
pleased	satisfied	
sure	certain	

I-183

A	B	Relationship
breathe	gasp	
diagree	object	
exercise	aerobics	
fasten	buckle	
speak	shout	

I-184

A	B	Relationship
boat	hull	
building	basement	
room	floor	
shoe	sole	
statue	base	

I-185

A	B	Relationship
chef	cooks	
doctor	treats	
navigator	plots	
sentry	guards	
teacher	explains	

RELATIONSHIPS—EXPLAIN

DIRECTIONS: Each word in box A is related in the same way to the word on the same line in box B. Describe how the words in box A are related to the words in box B.

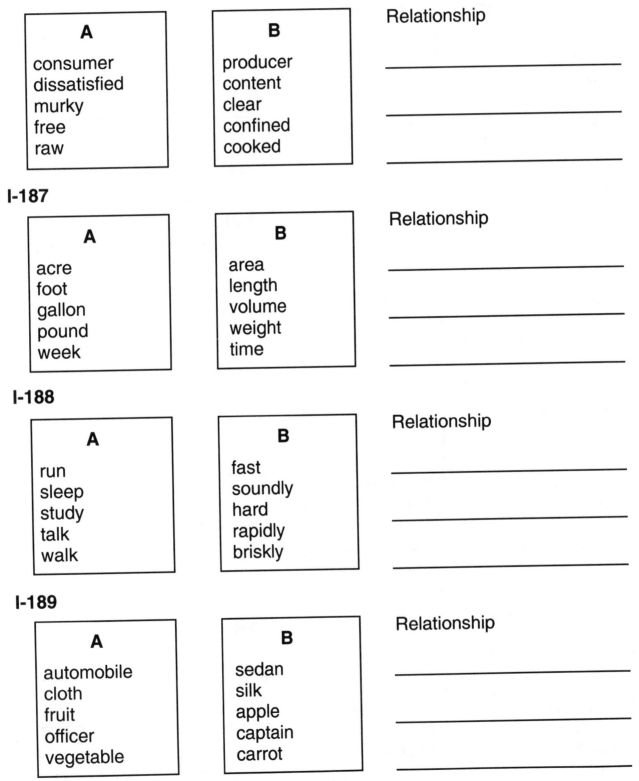

I-186

A	B	Relationship
consumer	producer	_____
dissatisfied	content	
murky	clear	_____
free	confined	
raw	cooked	_____

I-187

A	B	Relationship
acre	area	_____
foot	length	
gallon	volume	_____
pound	weight	
week	time	_____

I-188

A	B	Relationship
run	fast	_____
sleep	soundly	
study	hard	_____
talk	rapidly	
walk	briskly	_____

I-189

A	B	Relationship
automobile	sedan	_____
cloth	silk	
fruit	apple	_____
officer	captain	
vegetable	carrot	_____

CLASSIFYING SHAPES WITH A BULL'S EYE DIAGRAM

DIRECTIONS: Read the definitions of these shapes, complete the diagram below, and draw a conclusion. Hint: Use *all* in your conclusion, as in *"all* fathers are men and *all* men are males."

I-190

SHAPES

DEFINITIONS

This is a **parallelogram**. It is a special quadrilateral with two pairs of parallel sides.

This is a **quadrilateral**. It is a general four-sided figure with no special properties.

This is a **rectangle**. It is a special parallelogram with four square corners.

This is a **square**. It is a special rectangle with four sides that are the same length.

CLASSIFYING SHAPES WITH A BULL'S EYE DIAGRAM

MOST GENERAL CLASS

LESS GENERAL CLASS

MORE SPECIFIC CLASS

MOST SPECIFIC CLASS

CONCLUSION _____

_____

_____

_____

CLASSIFYING SHAPES WITH A MATRIX

DIRECTIONS: Read the definitions of these shapes and complete the matrix below. Put a check mark in the box of every geometry term that applies to each closed, four-sided shape.

I-191 DEFINITIONS

A **parallelogram** is a closed, four-sided shape with two pairs of parallel sides.
A **quadrilateral** is any closed, four-sided shape.
A **rectangle** is a special parallelogram with four square corners (right angles).
A **rhombus** is a special parallelogram with four equal sides.
A **square** is a special rectangle with four sides that are the same length.
A **trapezoid** is a quadrilateral with one pair of parallel sides.

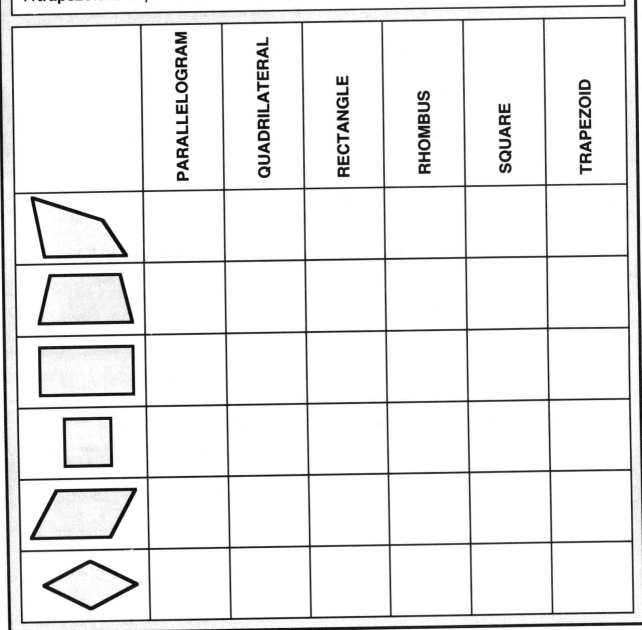

CLASSIFYING SHAPES WITH A BRANCHING DIAGRAM

DIRECTIONS: Name the shapes in the shape box. In each box on the branching diagram, draw the shape that belongs there and write its name.

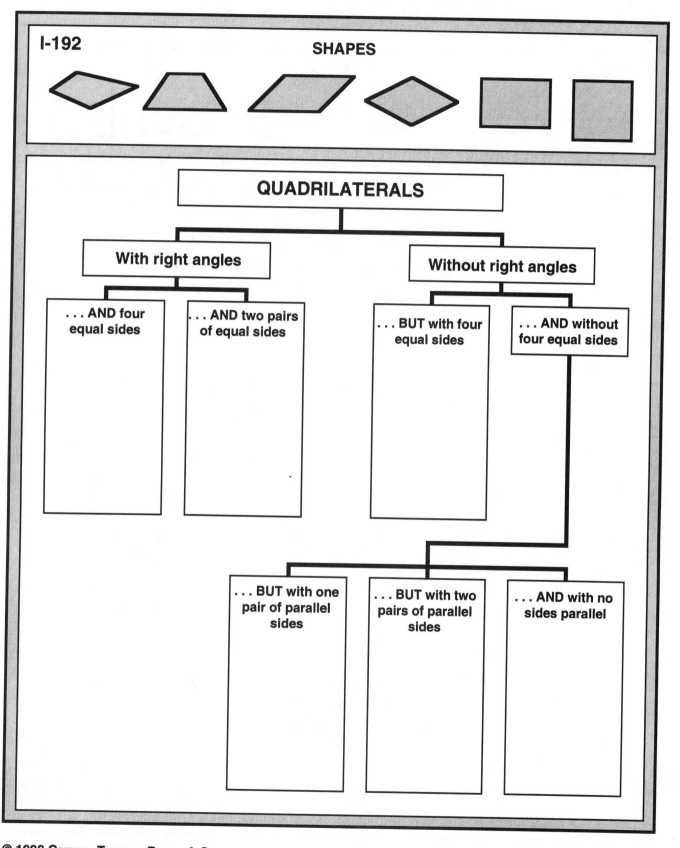

CLASSIFYING SHAPES WITH AN OVERLAPPING CLASSES DIAGRAM

DIRECTIONS: Name the shapes in the shape box. Draw and label each shape in the region of the diagram that best describes it.

CHAPTER TEN

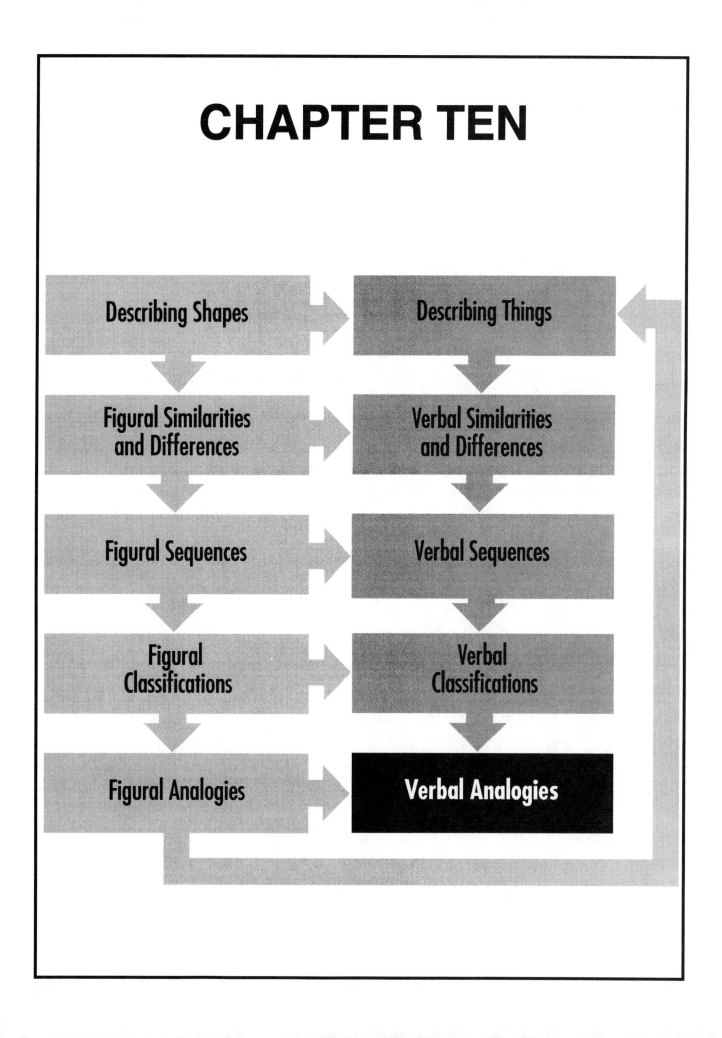

Describing Shapes → Describing Things

Figural Similarities and Differences → Verbal Similarities and Differences

Figural Sequences → Verbal Sequences

Figural Classifications → Verbal Classifications

Figural Analogies → **Verbal Analogies**

ANALOGIES—INSTRUCTIONS

An analogy is a relationship between two word pairs that are related in the same way.

EXAMPLE

father **:** man **::** mother **:** woman

The groups of dots (**:** and **::**) represent words.
In place of the **:** read "is to" or "is related to."
In place of the **::** read "as."
The above analogy should be read

father | **:** | man | **::** | mother | **:** | woman
father | "is to" | man | "as" | mother | "is to" | woman

The relationship between the first pair of words **must be the same** as the relationship between the second pair of words. In the example above, the relationship is "All fathers are men just as all mothers are women."

ANALOGIES—INSTRUCTIONS

Here is an example to help you do analogy exercises.

EXAMPLE

wrist **:** arm **::** ankle **:** _____

a. foot
b. joint
c. leg

1. What is the relationship between wrist and arm?
(The wrist is the joint at the lower end of the arm.)

2. Which word is related to ankle in the same way as arm is related to wrist?

Steps in answering this question:

a. Write the relationship between the first two words as a sentence. Use the words in the order that they appear.

The **wrist** is the joint at the lower end of the **arm**.

b. Write a second sentence below the first using the third word "ankle" and a blank line.

The **wrist** is the joint at the lower end of the **arm**.

The **ankle** is the joint at the lower end of the _____?

c. Look at the possible answers: a. foot, b. joint, c. leg. Try each possibility in the blank and see if it fits.

The **ankle** is the joint at the lower end of the **foot**.
(The ankle is at the upper, not lower, end of the foot.)

The **ankle** is the joint at the lower end of the **joint**.
(Joint describes the relationship, but does not fit in the analogy sentence.)

The **ankle** is the joint at the lower end of the **leg**.
(This is a true sentence and has the **same relationship** as the first sentence.)

ANTONYM OR SYNONYM ANALOGIES—SELECT

DIRECTIONS: In each exercise, decide how the first two words are related. The words are either similar or opposite. Next, look at the third word and then write a word from the list at the right that will complete a similar relationship.

EXAMPLE

fair : just :: right : _____

correct
questionable
wrong

Fair and *just* are similar in meaning. You must pick a word from the list on the right that has about the same meaning as *right*. *Questionable* means neither right nor wrong. *Wrong* is the opposite of *right*. *Correct* has a meaning similar to right and is the answer. Similar words are called *synonyms*; opposite words are called *antonyms*.

J-1   speak : talk   :: listen : _____

discuss
hear
learn

J-2   steal : rob   :: buy : _____

get
purchase
take

J-3   absent : present :: lost : _____

found
here
missing

J-4   learn : study   :: teach : _____

forget
instruct
read

J-5   right : wrong :: true : _____

correct
false
real

ASSOCIATION ANALOGIES—SELECT

DIRECTIONS: In each exercise, decide how the first two words are related. The words will be associated in some way. Next, look at the third word and then write a word from the list at the right that will complete a similar relationship.

EXAMPLE

flour : bread :: fabric : _____

cloth
clothing
material

Flour is associated with breadmaking just as fabric is associated with the making of clothing. *Cloth* and *material* are synonyms for *fabric*. So the best answer is *clothing*.

J-6   knob : door :: key : _____

bolt
hinge
lock

J-7   pie : crust :: clam : _____

crab
shell
oyster

J-8   money : wallet :: liquid : _____

bottle
drink
fluid

J-9 September : autumn :: March : _____

fall
spring
winter

J-10   bank : money :: library : _____

books
buildings
cards

J-11   paw : foot :: fur : _____

animal
beast
hair

J-12   stake : tent :: anchor : _____

boat
dock
pole

"KIND OF" ANALOGIES—SELECT

DIRECTIONS: In each exercise, decide how the first two words are related. The first word represents a "kind of" the second. Next, look at the third word and then write a word from the list at the right that will complete a similar relationship.

EXAMPLE

tea : drink :: pork : _____

beef
meat
salad

Tea is a *kind of* drink. Which of the words on the right answers the question, "Pork is a *kind of* _____?" Pork is not a *kind of* beef and pork is not a *kind of* salad. Pork is a *kind of* meat, so the best answer is *meat*.

J-13 oak : wood :: cotton : _____

cloth
nylon
velvet

J-14 water : liquid :: air : _____

gas
temperature
wind

J-15 nibble : bite :: glimpse : _____

feel
look
taste

J-16 heat : energy :: gasoline : _____

automobile
force
fuel

J-17 marble : stone :: diamond : _____

gold
jewel
money

J-18 map : chart :: photograph : _____

film
painting
picture

J-19 chick : bird :: minnow : _____

animal
fish
tadpole

"PART OF" ANALOGIES—SELECT

DIRECTIONS: In each exercise, decide how the first two words are related. The first word represents a "part of" the second. Next, look at the third word and then write a word from the list at the right that will complete a similar relationship.

EXAMPLE

scales : fish :: bark : _____

dog
skin
tree

Scales are the outer *part of* a fish. Which of the words on the right answers the question, "Bark is the outer *part of* _____?" Dog is not the answer. Dogs bark, but bark is not the outer *part of* a dog. Skin is not the answer. Bark and skin are outer parts, but bark is not the outer *part of* skin. Since bark is the outer *part of* a tree, *tree* is the best answer.

J-20 plant : garden :: tree : _____

branch
forest
pine

J-21 bulb : lamp :: flame : _____

ash
candle
heat

J-22 speech : language :: melody : _____

instrument
music
note

J-23 player : team :: student : _____

class
pupil
teacher

J-24 seat : theater :: cage : _____

animal
bars
zoo

J-25 quarter : game :: season : _____

day
month
year

"USED TO" ANALOGIES—SELECT

DIRECTIONS: In each exercise, decide how the first two words are related. The second word tells what the first word is "used to" do. Next, look at the third word and then write a word from the list at the right that will complete a similar relationship.

EXAMPLE

latch : lock :: knob : _____

bolt
open
swing

A latch is *used to* lock a door. Which of the words on the right answers the question, "Knob is *used to* _____?" *Bolt* is not the answer. A bolt is similar to a latch, but a knob is not *used to* bolt a door. *Swing* is not the answer. A knob is not *used to* swing a door; a hinge is used to swing a door. A knob is *used to* open a door; *open* is the best answer.

J-26 closet : hang :: trunk : _____

clean
dispose
store

J-27 typewriter : write :: calculator : _____

arrange
compute
list

J-28 note : remind :: diary : _____

inform
record
write

J-29 shield : protect :: sword : _____

attack
cover
handle

J-30 pliers : grip :: screwdriver : _____

lock
pound
turn

J-31 sponge : soak up :: towel : _____

dampen
dry
wash

ACTION ANALOGIES—SELECT

DIRECTIONS: In each exercise, decide how the first two words are related. The second word gives an action done by the first word. Next, look at the third word and then write a word from the list at the right that will complete a similar relationship.

EXAMPLE

surgeon : operated :: mechanic : _____

cuts
removes
repairs

An analogy which relates a person to what he or she does, or a thing to what it does is called an action analogy. The main task that a surgeon performs is to "operate" on a patient. The main task that a mechanic performs is to "repair" a broken machine. As part of the repair task, the mechanic may need to cut or remove a part, but neither cutting nor removing is his main task.

J-32 vein : carries :: heart : _____

protects
pumps
stores

J-33 demonstration : shows :: novel : _____

displays
opens
tells

J-34 boxer : fights :: priest : _____

builds
prays
sings

J-35 elastic : stretches :: balloon : _____

deflates
expands
shrinks

J-36 joke : amuses :: lesson : _____

entertains
informs
tests

J-37 conductor : directs :: orchestra : _____

guides
plays
sings

ANTONYM OR SYNONYM ANALOGIES—SELECT

DIRECTIONS: In each exercise, decide how the first two words are related. Next, look at the third word and then write a word from the choice box that will complete a similar relationship. Some words may be used more than once.

CHOICE BOX
few, many, much, one

J-38 pair : twin :: single : _____

J-39 many : several :: some : _____

J-40 number : many :: amount : _____

J-41 sole : only :: several : _____

J-42 few : some :: lone : _____

J-43 few : many :: some : _____

J-44 several : single :: many : _____

J-45 some : several :: few : _____

J-46 few : some :: sole : _____

ASSOCIATION ANALOGIES—SELECT

DIRECTIONS: In each exercise, decide how the first two words are associated. Next, look at the third word and then write a word from the choice box that will complete a similar relationship. Some words may be used more than once.

EXAMPLE: square inch : area :: cubic inch : _____

A square inch is a measurement of area in the same way that a cubic inch is a measurement of volume.

square inch : area :: cubic inch : _____ *volume* _____

CHOICE BOX
area, length, volume, weight

J-47 gallon : volume :: pound : _____

J-48 inch : length :: square inch : _____

J-49 cube : volume :: square : _____

J-50 triangle : area :: pyramid : _____

J-51 sphere : volume :: circle : _____

J-52 acre : area :: gallon : _____

J-53 ton : weight :: cup : _____

J-54 ounce : weight :: cup : _____

J-55 cubic inch : volume :: square inch : _____

ANTONYM OR SYNONYM ANALOGIES—SELECT A PAIR

DIRECTIONS: In each exercise, read the pair of words and decide how they are related. Next, select a pair of words from the choice box that will complete the analogy. The pairs in the choice box may be used more than once.

CHOICE BOX		
all : none	have : possess	send : receive

J-56　　　need : require　　::　_____ : _____

J-57　　　sell : buy　　::　_____ : _____

J-58　　everything : nothing　　::　_____ : _____

J-59　　　make : create　　::　_____ : _____

J-60　　　full : empty　　::　_____ : _____

J-61　　　talk : listen　　::　_____ : _____

J-62　　everyone : no one　　::　_____ : _____

J-63　　　hold : own　　::　_____ : _____

J-64　　　give : get　　::　_____ : _____

ASSOCIATION ANALOGIES—SELECT TWO

DIRECTIONS: In this exercise, two members of an association analogy are supplied. Select two words from the choice box that will complete the analogy. Words in the choice box may be used more than once.

EXAMPLE: garage : _____ :: barn : _____

A garage is associated with the city, while a barn is associated with the country.

```
┌────────────────────────────────────────────────────────────────┐
│                          CHOICE BOX                              │
├────────────────────────────────────────────────────────────────┤
│              city, country, county, nation, state                │
└────────────────────────────────────────────────────────────────┘
```

J-65   mayor : _____ :: governor : _____

J-66   city : _____ :: county : _____

J-67   road : _____ :: avenue : _____

J-68   governor : _____ :: president : _____

J-69   county : _____ :: state : _____

J-70   police chief : _____ :: sheriff : _____

J-71   acre : _____ :: block : _____

J-72   garden : _____ :: farm : _____

ANALOGIES—SELECT TWO

DIRECTIONS: In this exercise, two members of an analogy are supplied. Select two words from the choice box that will complete the analogy. These analogies are of three types—"Used to," "Association," and "Synonyms." Words in the choice box may be used more than once.

CHOICE BOX
hear, read, see, talk

J-73 books   : _____ :: audio tape : _____

J-74 discuss   : _____ ::   listen   : _____

J-75 examine : _____ ::   study   : _____

J-76 inspect   : _____ :: converse : _____

J-77 television : _____ ::   stereo   : _____

J-78 blind   : _____ ::   deaf   : _____

J-79 actors   : _____ ::   editors   : _____

J-80 sounds   : _____ ::   sights   : _____

J-81 observe : _____ ::   chatter   : _____

J-82 telescope : _____ :: telephone : _____

J-83 microphone : _____ :: microscope : _____

ANALOGIES—SELECT TWO

DIRECTIONS: In this exercise, two members of an analogy are supplied. Select two words from the choice box that will complete the analogy. These analogies are of three types—"Action," "Kind of," and "Part of." Words in the choice box may be used more than once.

CHOICE BOX
bear, bird, feathers, fish, fur, robin, scales, tuna

J-84   fur : _____ :: scales : _____

J-85   eagle : feather :: _____ : _____

J-86   bear : mammal :: _____ : _____

J-87   _____ : fish :: _____ : bird

J-88   _____ : flies :: _____ : swims

J-89   lungs : _____ :: gills : _____

J-90   _____ : growls :: _____ : sings

J-91   wing : _____ :: fin : _____

J-92   hair : _____ :: feather : _____

J-93   scales : _____ :: feathers : _____

J-94   tuna : _____ :: robin : _____

ANALOGIES—EXPLAIN

DIRECTIONS: Read these analogies and decide how the words in each pair are related. On the line below each analogy, explain the relationship between the words in each pair.

Here is a list of the kinds of analogies you have practiced. Use the list to help explain these analogies.

ANTONYM	KIND OF	SYNONYM
ASSOCIATION	PART OF	USED TO

EXAMPLE: banana : fruit :: carrot : vegetable

A banana is a kind of fruit just as a carrot is a kind of vegetable.

J-95 bored : excited :: rested : weary

_____

_____

J-96 beef : hamburger :: potatoes : French fries

_____

_____

J-97 compliment : praise :: criticize : blame

_____

_____

J-98 hammer : nail :: bat : ball

_____

_____

ANALOGIES—EXPLAIN

DIRECTIONS: Read these analogies and decide how the words in each pair are related. On the line below each analogy, explain the relationship between the words in each pair.

Here is a list of the kinds of analogies you have practiced. Use the list to help explain these analogies.

ANTONYM	KIND OF	SYNONYM
ASSOCIATION	PART OF	USED TO

J-99 beetle **:** insect **::** snake **:** reptile

_____

_____

J-100 teacher **:** instruction **::** musician **:** entertainment

_____

_____

J-101 stare **:** gaze **::** glance **:** notice

_____

_____

J-102 gusty **:** calm **::** windy **:** still

_____

_____

J-103 pliers **:** grip **::** hammer **:** pound

_____

_____

ANALOGIES—EXPLAIN

DIRECTIONS: Read these analogies and decide how the words in each pair are related. On the line below each analogy, explain the relationship between the words in each pair.

Here is a list of the kinds of analogies you have practiced. Use the list to help explain these analogies.

ANTONYM	KIND OF	SYNONYM
ASSOCIATION	PART OF	USED TO

J-104 wick **:** candle **::** bulb **:** lamp

_____

_____

J-105 budget **:** money **::** schedule **:** time

_____

_____

J-106 even **:** smooth **::** coarse **:** rough

_____

_____

J-107 hook **:** hang **::** anchor **:** hold

_____

_____

J-108 advance **:** retreat **::** forward **:** backward

_____

_____

ANALOGIES—EXPLAIN

DIRECTIONS: Read these analogies and decide how the words in each pair are related. On the line below each analogy, explain the relationship between the words in each pair.

Here is a list of the kinds of analogies you have practiced. Use the list to help explain these analogies.

ANTONYM	KIND OF	SYNONYM
ASSOCIATION	PART OF	USED TO

J-109 dial : radio :: switch : lamp

_____

_____

J-110 cloth : wash :: towel : dry

_____

_____

J-111 fly : sky :: float : water

_____

_____

J-112 ballot : vote :: check : pay

_____

_____

J-113 yam : potato :: lima : bean

_____

_____

ANTONYM OR SYNONYM ANALOGIES—SUPPLY

DIRECTIONS: Look at the first two words. Think about how they are related. The words are either similar or opposite. Next, look at the third word and produce a word from your memory that has a similar relationship as the first two words.

J-114 passenger : traveler :: guest : _____

J-115 valley : peak :: bottom : _____

J-116 twilight : dusk :: autumn : _____

J-117 frequently : often :: shortly : _____

J-118 hunt : search :: locate : _____

J-119 stick : pole :: pit : _____

J-120 close : distant :: near : _____

J-121 insect : bug :: child : _____

J-122 quiet : loud :: silent : _____

J-123 shut : close :: unfasten : _____

J-124 bright : dim :: shiny : _____

J-125 dash : race :: stroll : _____

J-126 sprinkle : rain :: snack : _____

ASSOCIATION ANALOGIES—SUPPLY

DIRECTIONS: Look at the first two words. Think about how they are related. The words will be associated in some way. Next, look at the third word and produce a word from your memory that has a similar relationship as the first two words.

J-127 father : son :: king : _____

J-128 mouse : rat :: pebble : _____

J-129 sheet : bed :: rug : _____

J-130 path : road :: hill : _____

J-131 pink : red :: gray : _____

J-132 seal : pup :: lion : _____

J-133 scared : tremble :: sad : _____

J-134 salesperson : customer :: teacher : _____

J-135 designer : pattern :: architect : _____

J-136 actor : script :: singer : _____

J-137 mother : father :: aunt : _____

J-138 instructor : pupil :: doctor : _____

J-139 cloudburst : rain :: blizzard : _____

"KIND OF" ANALOGIES—SUPPLY

DIRECTIONS: Look at the first two words. Think about how they are related. The first word represents a "kind of" the second. Next, look at the third word and produce a word from your memory that has a similar relationship as the first two words.

J-140 sedan : automobile :: pickup : _____

J-141 refrigerator : appliance :: chair : _____

J-142 jeans : pants :: sneakers : _____

J-143 cherry : berry :: almond : _____

J-144 ice : solid :: water : _____

J-145 hamburger : sandwich :: milk shake : _____

J-146 bean : vegetable :: orange : _____

J-147 granite : rock :: iron : _____

J-148 swan : bird :: ant : _____

J-149 macaroon : cookie :: fudge : _____

J-150 bunk : bed :: rocker : _____

J-151 ten-speed : bicycle :: convertible : _____

J-152 novel : book :: ballad : _____

"PART OF" ANALOGIES—SUPPLY

DIRECTIONS: Look at the first two words. Think about how they are related. The first word represents "part of" the second. Next, look at the third word and produce a word from your memory that has a similar relationship as the first two words.

J-153 tooth : tiger :: tusk : _____

J-154 bone : skeleton :: brick : _____

J-155 leg : pants :: sleeve : _____

J-156 article : newspaper :: chapter : _____

J-157 handle bars : bicycle :: steering wheel : _____

J-158 hip : leg :: shoulder : _____

J-159 intermission : play :: recess : _____

J-160 needle : pine :: blade : _____

J-161 root : plant :: foundation : _____

J-162 tuner : radio :: channel selector : _____

J-163 volume control : stereo :: thermostat : _____

J-164 flaps : airplane :: brakes : _____

J-165 needle : compass :: hands : _____

"USED TO" ANALOGIES—SUPPLY

DIRECTIONS: Look at the first two words. The second word tells what the first word is "used to" do. Next, look at the third word and produce a word from your memory that has a similar relationship as the first two words.

J-166 straw : drink :: fork : _____

J-167 pencil : write :: crayon : _____

J-168 telephone : hear :: telescope : _____

J-169 knife : slice :: scissors : _____

J-170 mop : wash :: broom : _____

J-171 pencil : mark :: ruler : _____

J-172 paperclip : fasten :: shoelace : _____

J-173 finger : touches :: tongue : _____

J-174 glasses : see :: crutches : _____

J-175 food : eat :: juice : _____

J-176 paint : wall :: shingles: _____

J-177 blanket : cover :: basket : _____

J-178 ruler : line :: proctractor : _____

ACTION ANALOGIES—SUPPLY

DIRECTIONS: Look at the first two words. The words are related by some "kind of" action. Next, look at the third word and produce a word from your memory that has a similar relationship as the first two words.

J-179 teacher : teaches :: student : _____

J-180 batter : hits :: fielder : _____

J-181 airplane : flies :: automobile : _____

J-182 latch : locks :: knob : _____

J-183 seamstress : sews :: carpenter : _____

J-184 dynamite : explodes :: candle : _____

J-185 actor : speaks :: author : _____

J-186 pilot : flies :: pianist : _____

J-187 burglar : steals :: customer : _____

J-188 water : boils :: ice : _____

J-189 retailer : sells :: manufacture : _____

J-190 thunder : claps :: lightning : _____

J-191 iron : sinks :: wood : _____

ANALOGIES—SUPPLY

DIRECTIONS: Look at the first two words. Think about how they are related. Next, look at the third word and produce a word from your memory that has a similar relationship as the first two words.

J-192 idle : active :: lazy : _____

J-193 groan : moan :: laugh : _____

J-194 bird : flies :: fish : _____

J-195 mare : stallion :: hen : _____

J-196 arrival : departure :: birth : _____

J-197 hinge : door :: elbow : _____

J-198 woman : blouse :: man : _____

J-199 sand : grain :: rain : _____

J-200 ring : jewelry :: coat : _____

J-201 word : sentence :: letter : _____

J-202 tow : pull :: shove : _____

J-203 flower : seed :: chicken : _____

J-204 flavor : taste :: tone : _____

ANALOGIES—SUPPLY

DIRECTIONS: Look at the first two words. Think about how they are related. Next, look at the third word and produce a word from your memory that has a similar relationship as the first two words.

J-205 fingers : grasp :: teeth : _____

J-206 sight : vision :: touch : _____

J-207 pass : receive :: pitch : _____

J-208 feeble : powerful :: weak : _____

J-209 succeed : win :: fail : _____

J-210 brush : paint :: pencil : _____

J-211 iron : metal :: water : _____

J-212 flock : sheep :: herd : _____

J-213 fake : phony :: actual : _____

J-214 raise : lower :: lift : _____

J-215 steal : rob :: purchase : _____

J-216 valuable : worthless :: expensive : _____

J-217 attorney : lawyer :: physician : _____

ANALOGIES—EXPLAIN AND SUPPLY A PAIR

DIRECTIONS: Read the pair of words and decide how they are related. On the lines below each analogy, explain the relationship between the words. After you have explained the relationship, supply a pair of words that will complete the analogy.

EXAMPLE: gallon : volume :: _____ : _____

The gallon is associated with volume as a measurement of volume. A possible similar association might be pound as a measurement of weight. The analogy would then be:

gallon : volume :: _pound_ : _weight_

J-218   soldier : army : _____ : _____

_____

_____

_____

J-219   dirty : clean : _____ : _____

_____

_____

_____

J-220   oats : grain :: _____ : _____

_____

_____

_____

ANALOGIES—EXPLAIN AND SUPPLY A PAIR

DIRECTIONS: Read the pair of words and decide how they are related. On the lines below each analogy, explain the relationship between the words. After you have explained the relationship, supply a pair of words that will complete the analogy.

J-221   train : track :: _____ : _____

_____

_____

_____

J-222   artist : paints :: _____ : _____

_____

_____

_____

J-223   chief : tribe :: _____ : _____

_____

_____

_____

J-224   quiet : loud :: _____ : _____

_____

_____

_____

ANALOGIES—EXPLAIN AND SUPPLY A PAIR

DIRECTIONS: Read the pair of words and decide how they are related. On the lines below each analogy, explain the relationship between the words. After you have explained the relationship, supply a pair of words that will complete the analogy.

J-225   silly : foolish :: _____ : _____

_____

_____

_____

J-226   lemon : sour :: _____ : _____

_____

_____

_____

J-227   spots : leopard :: _____ : _____

_____

_____

_____

J-228   food : eat :: _____ : _____

_____

_____

_____

ANALOGIES—PRODUCE

DIRECTIONS: Now that you have practiced selecting and supplying the words to complete six different kinds of analogies, you are ready to create your own. See if you can produce eight or more analogies from the words in the choice box.

CHOICE BOX
bird, fins, fish, fly, horse, land, legs, sea, sky, swim, walk, wings

J-229 _____

J-230 _____

J-231 _____

J-232 _____

J-233 _____

J-234 _____

J-235 _____

J-236 _____